PENGUIN REFERENCE

The Penguin Writer's Manual

Martin H. Manser has been a professional reference-book editor since 1980. He received a BA Honours degree in linguistics at the conclusion of his studies at the universities of York, England, and Regensburg, Germany, and went on to gain an M.Phil. degree for research into the influence of English on modern German. A developing interest in lexicography led him to take up a post as a reference-book editor. Since 1980 he has worked on about one hundred reference books with a contemporary appeal. His English-language reference titles include the *Penguin Wordmaster Dictionary*, the Bloomsbury *Good Word Guide*, Chambers' *Dictionary of Synonyms and Antonyms*, the Macmillan *Student's Dictionary*, the Facts on File *Visual Dictionary*, the Oxford *Learner's Pocket Dictionary*, the Guinness *Book of Words*, the *New Penguin Thesaurus* and *The Wordsworth Crossword Companion* (with Stephen Curtis).

He has also compiled and edited many titles that encourage Bible reading, including the *NIV Thematic Study Bible* on which he was Managing Editor, (Hodder & Stoughton and Zondervan), the Hodder & Stoughton and Zondervan *Dictionary of Bible Themes*, *Bible Quotation Collection* (Lion), *The Christian Quotation Collection* (Westminster John Knox), the *Listening to God* Bible reading series, *Daily Guidance* (Cumberland House), the *Amazing Book of Bible Facts* (Marshall Pickering), *Crash Course in Christian Teaching* (Hodder & Stoughton), *Dictionary of the Bible* (co-author; Macmillan/Cumberland House), *Bible Stories* (Parragon), *Common Worship Lectionary* (Oxford University Press), *Handbook of Bible Promises* (co-author; Eagle) and *I Never Knew That was in the Bible* (Nelson).

He and his wife live in Aylesbury and have a son and a daughter.

Stephen Curtis was educated at The Queen's College, Oxford, where he took a first-class degree in Modern Languages, and at the University of York. He was an English lecturer for ten years and, after a brief spell as a Co-op milkman and call-centre interviewer, joined the publishing firm of Collier Macmillan as a lexicographer in 1984. Since 1988 he has worked as a freelance lexicographer, translator and writer. He has recently contributed to, among others, the Encarta *World English Dictionary*, *The New Penguin English Dictionary* and Chambers' *Dictionary of World History*. He is author of *Increase Your Word Power* and (also with Martin Manser) *The Wordsworth Crossword Companion*. He lives in Bath.

THE PENGUIN WRITER'S MANUAL

Martin Manser
Stephen Curtis

PENGUIN BOOKS

PENGUIN BOOKS

Published by the Penguin Group
Penguin Books Ltd, 80 Strand, London WC2R 0RL, England
Penguin Group (USA) Inc., 375 Hudson Street, New York, New York 10014, USA
Penguin Books Australia Ltd, 250 Camberwell Road, Camberwell, Victoria 3124, Australia
Penguin Books Canada Ltd, 10 Alcorn Avenue, Toronto, Ontario, Canada M4V 3B2
Penguin Books India (P) Ltd, 11 Community Centre, Panchsheel Park, New Delhi – 110 017, India
Penguin Group (NZ), cnr Airborne and Rosedale Roads, Albany, Auckland 1310, New Zealand
Penguin Books (South Africa) (Pty) Ltd, 24 Sturdee Avenue, Rosebank 2196, South Africa

Penguin Books Ltd, Registered Offices: 80 Strand, London WC2R 0RL, England

www.penguin.com

First published 2002

027

Set in 9.5/12 pt Minion
Typeset by Rowland Phototypesetting Ltd, Bury St Edmunds, Suffolk

Printed and bound in Great Britain by Clays Ltd, Elcograf S.p.A.

ISBN-13: 978–0–140–51489–6

www.greenpenguin.co.uk

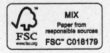

Penguin Books is committed to a sustainable future for our business, our readers and our planet. This book is made from Forest Stewardship Council™ certified paper.

Contents

Acknowledgments

The writers acknowledge with gratitude Nigel Wilcockson's comments on drafts of the text and Robert Allen's advice on points of usage in chapter 2.

Introduction

The Penguin Writer's Manual is intended as a guide and companion for anyone who wants to write or is faced with the task of writing.

Part One of this book helps you to learn how to write good and correct English by presenting in a clear and easily understandable way the rules, both written and unwritten, that underpin communication in English. It contains sections on grammar, usage, vocabulary, spelling, punctuation, and abbreviations.

Part Two is more directly concerned with the task of writing. It will show you, step by step, how to prepare and plan a piece of writing in order to give yourself the best chance of communicating effectively. It will help you to improve your writing style. It also discusses and illustrates how to tackle various everyday writing tasks, such as composing letters, essays, and reports.

There is no great secret to being a writer. There is no universal 'open sesame' that suddenly makes everything clear for everyone. That is, perhaps, bad news. The good news is that with care, common sense, and practice, everyone should be able to write plainly and well, or learn to write better and more confidently. Even if there is no universal key, it is still the authors' hope that every reader will find in this book guidance and encouragement to turn writing into a rewarding activity.

Martin Manser
Stephen Curtis

Part One

1 Grammar

Introduction

In Tom Stoppard's play *Travesties*, there is a scene in which the Dadaist poet Tristan Tzara takes a copy of Shakespeare's sonnet 'Shall I compare thee to a summer's day?', cuts it up into individual words with a pair of scissors, puts the words into a hat, and proceeds to draw them out again one at a time at random to create a new 'poem'.

If there were such a thing as a language without grammar, it would be rather like the words in that hat – a jumble, a meaningless collection – and the process of communicating in that language would be as haphazard as the Dadaist method of creating poetry. In fact, all languages have a grammar, and all users of language must know something of the grammar of the language they are using in order to be able to communicate in it at all. Children, unknowingly, learn grammar as they learn to speak and as they gradually increase the range and sophistication of the things they are able to say. They quickly learn the difference between a statement (*I want some*), a question (*Can I have some?*), and a command (*Give me some*) – three types of utterance to which grammar books might devote whole chapters. People frequently complain that they do not know any grammar or were never taught any grammar, but only the second of these complaints is likely to be strictly true.

The point is, of course, that knowledge exists at different levels. Most people nowadays know what a computer is. They can describe what a computer looks like from the outside and roughly what it can do. They can probably use one. Only an expert, though, can describe what a computer is like on the inside and precisely how it functions. The average user of language is perhaps like the average computer user – getting along quite happily until something goes wrong, at which point everything suddenly becomes technical and incomprehensible and someone with specialist knowledge is needed to put matters right.

The purpose of this section of the book is to give ordinary users of English some of the technical know-how they need to solve language difficulties if they should arise. It is also intended to help them acquire some inside knowledge of the way the English language actually works. Last but not least, it may also help them to become more able and confident communicators in a medium that is one of the most versatile and expressive methods of conveying thoughts and feelings that has ever existed.

Types of grammar

Languages are continually evolving. This is most obvious in the additions to vocabulary that are needed to cope with technological advances and other alterations to the landscape of everyday life. Words come into use and fall out of use again. Computers, for instance, have spawned an enormous number of new words, some of which have already fallen into disuse as the technical processes they refer to have become outmoded. The way existing words are used changes too – to take one obvious example, the word *gay* whose main meaning nowadays is 'homosexual' rather than the centuries-old meaning of 'cheerful' or 'bright'.

Grammar also evolves – but usually at a much slower pace because it is largely presented in the form of rules and for everyone who wants to change a rule there are usually others who want to preserve it. From time to time, however, attempts are made to overhaul the way in which we describe the grammatical structure of languages completely. One such attempt was made in the mid-twentieth century by the US linguist Noam Chomsky and his followers. While Chomsky's work has had a profound effect on the academic study of linguistics, most ordinary discussion of language is still conducted on the basis of more traditional concepts and rules. For the purposes of this book, therefore, grammar means traditional grammar.

Technical terms

There are a number of technical terms that the non-technical reader has to be familiar with in order to be able to understand fully what a grammar book or even an ordinary dictionary is trying to say. Most of the basic concepts of grammar are explained and illustrated as they are discussed in the following pages. There is also a brief glossary of terms at the end of the book. Someone who has no previous knowledge of language terminology may, however, find the following brief list useful for understanding its opening sections. A **noun** is a word that stands for a thing, a person, or quality (*book*, *reader*, and *readability* are all nouns). A **pronoun** is a short general word that can replace a noun. A **personal pronoun** is a word such as *I*, *you*, *her*, or *them*. A **verb** is a word that stands for an action (*be*, *have*, *kick*, and *spend* are all verbs). An **adjective** is a word that provides more specific information about a noun (*happy*, *hot*, *red*, and *terrible* are all adjectives). An **adverb** is a word that provides more specific information about a verb or an adjective (*happily*, *terribly*, and *very* are all adverbs). A word that is **singular** refers to one person or thing only, one that is **plural** refers to two or more. *Child* and *adult* are singular nouns; *children* and *adults* are plural nouns. *Is* is a singular form of the verb to be; *are* (as in *we are* or *they are*) is a plural form.

Sentences

As soon as words are taken and used to communicate meaning, they form **sentences**. It is usually assumed that any sentence must contain a verb, but it is better, perhaps, to start from the principle that a sentence is a unit of language that makes sense and is complete in itself. The normal convention for writing a sentence is that it should begin with a capital letter and end with a full stop, a question mark, or an exclamation mark. Under certain circumstances a single word could satisfy all these requirements:

> *No.*
> *Really?*
> *Impossible!*

Such single-word communications, along with slightly longer phrases such as:

For sale.

No parking.

Once bitten twice shy.

are known grammatically as **minor sentences** – *minor* because they contain no verb.

Major sentences are sentences that contain a verb. They too can be very short but still meaningful and complete in themselves:

Listen!

I see.

Is that so?

More often, however, major sentences contain other material – for example, a subject, a verb, an object, or words or phrases modifying any of these – and consist of more than one clause.

On the writing of sentences using 'good style', see pp. 222–9.

Clauses

A **clause** is, like a sentence, a meaningful series of words. Unlike a sentence, however, a clause is not always complete in itself as regards the meaning that it conveys or the action that it describes. Compare the two statements *I arrived late* and *Although I arrived late*. The first simply states a fact; there is not necessarily anything more to be said. The addition of *although* (or any similar word such as *when* or *because*) has the effect of implying that there must be more to say about the incident. In that sense, it is not complete in itself.

A clause that is complete in itself is known as a **main clause**. Every major sentence must have at least one main clause, and a main clause on its own can constitute a satisfactory sentence. A clause that is incomplete in itself is known as a **subordinate clause**.

A sentence may consist of a main clause on its own: *I ran all the way*. It may consist of two or more linked main clauses: *I ran all the way | and arrived completely out of breath*. It may consist of a main clause together with one or more subordinate clauses: *I ran all the way because I was afraid of being late.* (For more on these, see pp. 15–22.)

The parts of a clause or sentence

All clauses or sentences apart from the most simple ones are made up of different parts. These parts, which may consist of a single word or a group of words, are known as the subject, the verb, the object, the complement, and the adverbial. They are discussed individually in the sections below.

The subject

The **subject**, as its name suggests, is what the sentence is about, often the person or thing that carries out the action of the verb in the clause or sentence. In the sentences *Jane called a taxi* and *Money isn't everything*, the subjects are *Jane* and *Money*. To take a more complex example, in the sentence *Drinking wine with lunch makes me feel sleepy in the afternoon* the subject is *Drinking wine with lunch*. The subject can also be a subordinate clause (*How you do it doesn't really matter* in which the subject is *How you do it*) or consist of two or more nouns or pronouns (*Robert and I are very alike in that* in which the subject is *Robert and I*).

The usual position of the subject is at the beginning of the sentence in front of the verb, as in all the examples above. The subject, however, changes its position in certain types of sentence. In questions the subject normally follows the verb:

> *Are you there?*
>
> *How did the dog get out?*

It may also be placed after the verb following a piece of direct speech (*'There's going to be trouble,' said Anne*), for emphasis (*Out went the lights*), or in clauses introduced by words such as *hardly* or *no sooner* (*No sooner had I left than the guests arrived*).

Whatever its position in the sentence, the subject determines the form of the verb. If the subject is singular, the verb must be singular; if the subject is plural, the verb must be plural: *The rose is red* but *Roses are red.*

The same rule applies if the subject is replaced at the beginning of the sentence by *there*: *There is a fault in the software* (*is* because *fault* is singular); *There have been problems with the photocopier* (*have* because *problems* is plural).

The verb

The characteristics and functions of verbs will be discussed more fully in a later section (pp. 39–48) of this book. Suffice it to say at this point that the **verb** is often the focus of a sentence conveying the most important information in it, as in the following sentences:

He spat at me!

It really hurt.

The verb may simply act as a bridge between the subject and the other components of the sentence that relate to it. This is especially the case with so-called **linking verbs** such as *to be* and *to seem*. In sentences such as *The man in the brown overcoat smoking a cigar is a distant relative of the Duke of Loamshire*, the important pieces of information come before and after the verb (*is*): *The man in the brown overcoat smoking a cigar* and *a distant relative of the Duke of Loamshire*. The verb itself is little more than a convenient way of getting from the one to the other.

The object

The **object** of a sentence is a word denoting a person or thing affected by the action of the verb. There are two possible types of object in a sentence: a direct object and an indirect object. The **direct object** is the person or thing directly affected by the action of a verb. In the sentence *The car hit a tree*, the direct object is *a tree*. In the more complex sentence that was used to illustrate the subject *Drinking wine with lunch makes me feel sleepy in the afternoon* the direct object is *me*. It is usually possible to ascertain which word is the direct object of a sentence by asking a question about it beginning with *what?* or *whom* (*who?*): *What did the car hit?* – a tree. *Whom does drinking wine make sleepy?* – me. Like the subject, the object can also be a subordinate clause (*They explained why the television keeps breaking down*) or consist of two or more nouns or pronouns (*She took Celia, Jane, and me to the cinema*).

An **indirect object** is an additional object that occurs with some verbs, especially verbs that involve the action of giving. In the sentences *He gave me a kiss* and *They bought their daughter a flat in London*, the direct objects are *a kiss* and *a flat in London* respectively. The indirect objects are *me* and *their daughter*. The question that uncovers the indirect object is *to whom?* or *to what?* or *for whom?* or *for what?* For example, *What did they buy?* – a flat (direct object). *For whom did they buy it?* – their daughter (indirect object). Indirect objects are usually used together with direct objects, not on their own.

The usual position of both the direct and indirect object in the sentence is after the verb. If there are two objects the indirect object (highlighted here by underlining) is almost always placed before the direct object:

> *Give me the gun.*
>
> *She told the man what was happening.*

If both the direct and the indirect object are pronouns (*me*, *him*, *her*, *it*, etc.), the direct object (highlighted) is sometimes placed first, especially in informal speech:

> *Give it me.*
>
> *I sent it them weeks ago.*

The complement

In sentences where the verb is a linking verb of the type mentioned briefly above (*to be*, *to seem*, *to feel*, etc.), what follows the verb is not an object but a **complement**. In the sentence *James is a computer expert*, the complement is *a computer expert*. A complement, in simple terms, is a word or group of words that tells us more about the element of the sentence that it relates to. In the example just given, the phrase *a computer expert* is a subject complement because it contains a description of the subject of the sentence *James*. A subject complement usually follows the verb and takes the form of a noun or an adjective or a noun or adjective phrase, as in: *The task seemed utterly impossible* and *She became a fully paid-up member of the union.*

The adverbial

The **adverbial** is the part of the sentence that provides more information about the verb and the action it denotes. It may consist of a single word, an adverb, as in the sentence *They chose the site carefully* – where the adverbial is *carefully*. It may, however, consist of a phrase or a subordinate clause. In the following sentences:

> *I'm leaving first thing tomorrow.*
> *Put the book on the shelf.*
> *The picnic was cancelled because it was raining.*

the adverbials are, respectively, *first thing tomorrow*, *on the shelf*, and *because it was raining*. There may also be more than one adverbial in a sentence: *I'm leaving | first thing tomorrow | on a plane to Singapore.*

The adverbial is usually positioned after the verb at the end of the sentence, as in all the above examples. It may also, however, be placed at the beginning of the sentence or between the subject and the verb.

> *With trembling hands she opened the package.*
> *I immediately left the room.*

Agreement of verbs

As explained in the section on the subject (pp. 7–8), the form of the verb is decided by the nature of the subject. The correspondence that must exist between subject and verb is an example of what is known in grammar as **agreement** or **concord**. For a sentence to function as a satisfactory whole, there must be agreement between its component parts.

Since verbs in English generally have the same form in a particular tense whether the subject is singular or plural, agreement between verb and subject is not as great a problem in English as it is in some other languages. It does, however, sometimes cause difficulty in verbs such as *to be* or *to have* that change their form more frequently than other verbs. Rules of agreement make the phrases *you was* or *he do* incorrect – the form of the verb does not agree with the pronoun: the correct standard forms are *you were* and *he does.*

Agreement also dictates the form of subject and object complements. If a subject or object is plural, its complement must be plural as well: *Jan is an executor* but *She made Jan and Gordon executors of her will.* Agreement also determines which form of the **reflexive pronoun** (*myself, yourselves,* etc.) or the **possessive** (*my, your,* etc.) should be used. This usually involves little difficulty, but it is obviously important to distinguish between *You can please yourself* (addressed to one person) and *You can please yourselves* (addressed to more than one).

Troublesome grammatical point:
agreement of verbs 'Neither Jean nor her sister is coming' or 'Neither Jean nor her sister are coming'

Though keeping to the rules of agreement in English is usually a simple matter, there are occasions when it is difficult to determine whether the subject is singular or plural. When the subject consists of two nouns joined by *and* there is no problem, because the subject is obviously plural:

> *Jean and her sister are coming.*
>
> *Both Jean and her sister are members.*

But where the subject consists of two nouns linked together with *either . . . or* or *neither . . . nor,* the situation is less clear. If both or all of the nouns involved are singular, then the verb should be singular: *Neither Jean nor her sister (nor her mother) is coming.* If the nouns involved are all plural, the verb should be plural: *Either the Wilkinsons or the Petersons have the key.* Where one of the nouns is singular and the other plural, the usual rule is that the verb agrees with whichever stands nearest to it:

> *Neither Jean nor her brother and sister know* (rather than *knows*) *anything about this.*
>
> *Either those curtains or that carpet has* (rather than *have*) *to go!*

The same applies if two different personal pronouns figure in the sentence: *Neither he nor I have* (rather than *has*) *done anything we ought to be ashamed of.* (A little rewriting can often avoid any problems or awkwardness that might arise when trying to apply the rule of agreement in such cases.)

A similar difficulty may arise when the subject takes the form of a singular noun linked to a plural by *of*: *a number of things*; *a collection of paintings*; *a procession of visitors.* It often seems more natural to put the verb into the plural form. Although *a number* is strictly a singular form, few people would insist on replacing the plural *have* with the singular *has* in the sentence *A number of things have cropped up.* In other instances, however, standard English offers a choice, depending on whether the speaker wishes to emphasize the unity of the group or the multiplicity of the things or people that make it up: *His collection of paintings is going to be sold* (considered as a unity) in contrast to *A collection of miscellaneous objects were being sold off as a job lot* (considered as a multiplicity). (See also p. 25.)

Types of sentence

Sentences fall into four main categories: statements, questions, directives (i.e. commands, instructions, or requests), and exclamations.

Statements

The commonest type of sentence is a **statement.** It begins with a capital letter, ends with a full stop and presents the listener or reader with a piece of information without necessarily expecting any response from them. *My husband took the dog for a walk along the towpath* is a statement, and it has its components in the standard order – subject followed by verb, followed by object, followed by adverbial.

Questions

Questions – which end, of course, with a question mark instead of a full stop – ask for information instead of presenting it and usually expect a response from someone. The distinguishing mark of the majority of questions is a reversal of the normal word order of sentences and the placing of the verb before the subject. The statement *He is busy* is turned into a question by the reversal of the first two words: *Is he busy?* The order of subject and verb is similarly reversed following a question word such as *how, when, where, why*, etc.:

How did I know?

Why didn't you tell me?

It is not, however, always necessary to reverse the subject and verb. The way that a person speaks a sequence of words in the normal order can turn it into a question – the pitch of the speaker's voice usually rises towards the end of what he or she is saying. Instead of saying *Would you like some tea?*, it is possible to say *You'd like some tea?* with the pitch of the voice rising towards the end of the sentence with the same effect. The variation in the pitch of the speaker's voice is called **intonation.**

There are also questions known as **tag questions.** These are statements with a little tag such as *isn't it?, aren't you?*, or *won't they?* tacked on the end:

He's messed it up again, hasn't he?

It isn't time to go yet, is it?

Notice that the tag usually reuses the main verb or part of it (*He's* (he has) . . . *hasn't he*; *isn't . . . is it*). If the main verb is not, or does not contain, *be, do, have*, or *will*, etc., *do* is used to make a tag:

He smokes, doesn't he?

She drove here, didn't she?

Notice also that a positive main clause takes a negative tag and vice versa:

He's happy today, isn't he?

He's not happy, is he?

On the use of question marks, see pp. 155–6.

Directives

Directives are orders or requests to other people to do or to stop doing something. They usually have no subject because it is obvious from the situation who is being addressed. The verb is in what is known as the **imperative**, the command form, which is identical with its base form (see pp. 47–8):

Stop!

Listen!

Sit down, shut up, and eat your breakfast!

Orders such as these end with an exclamation mark.

Not all directives are so abrupt. Instructions, invitations, and requests also use the imperative form of the verb:

Bake in a moderate oven for 20 minutes.

Come to lunch with us next Sunday.

Please pass the butter.

The negative form of the imperative in ordinary English is made using *do*:

Don't say that!

Do not exceed the stated dose.

The straightforward negative form of the imperative is usually found only in older literary works: *Judge not that ye be not judged* (The Bible, Matthew 7:1, Authorized (King James) Version). *Do* can also be used to add emphasis to an instruction or request (*Oh, do stop talking and get on with it*) or warmth to an invitation (*Do come, we'd love to see you*). For the sake of politeness, directives are often rephrased as questions, especially using *would* or *could*:

Would you open the door for me, please?

Could you not smoke in here?

Exclamations

Exclamations – which always end with an exclamation mark – express a person's spontaneous reaction to a situation, usually one of surprise, approval, or annoyance. They often take the form of a minor sentence without a verb:

What fun!

More power to your elbow!

Longer exclamations sometimes follow the normal word order of statements *It's a girl!* Many exclamations, however, begin with *how* or *what* and in these the object or complement is placed before the subject and the verb:

How strange it seems!

What a wonderful time we all had!

On the use of exclamation marks, see pp. 156–7.

Interjections

Interjections are a group of words that have the exclamatory function of expressing an emotion such as surprise, approval, anger, or pain: *ah!*, *oh!*, *mmm!*, *ouch!*, *ugh!*, *psst!* They are more commonly used in spoken English; in written English they are rarely used except in direct speech.

Sentence structure

A simple sentence, that is a simple major sentence, consists of a single clause. As mentioned above (p. 6), a main clause on its own can constitute a satisfactory sentence: *The sun is shining today*. A sentence with more than one clause is known as a **multiple sentence**. Multiple sentences may consist of more than one main clause or a main clause together with a number of **subordinate clauses**. Again, as mentioned earlier (p. 6), a subordinate clause is one that is not complete in itself and cannot, on its own, form a satisfactory sentence. Subordinate clauses usually begin with words such as *that*, *which*, *if*, or *when*.

Compound sentences

A multiple sentence consisting of two or more main clauses is called a **compound sentence**. Compound sentences are linked together by *and*, *but*, or *or*:

Henry is a lorry driver and Jane works part-time in a supermarket.

We do stock those boots, but we haven't any in your size.

Generally speaking the order of the clauses can be reversed without affecting the sense of the sentence: *Jane works part-time in a supermarket and Henry is a lorry driver*. The process of linking clauses or other parts of a sentence together in this way is known as **coordination** (see p. 17). The above examples all illustrate simple coordination between two clauses, but multiple coordination is also possible: *The band was still playing and everyone was still dancing, but, for me, everything had suddenly changed.*

Troublesome grammatical point:
using 'and' or 'but' at the beginning of a sentence

The main function of *and* and *but*, which are known as **coordinating conjunctions**, is to link items within sentences. It is often suggested that it is either bad grammar or bad style to begin a sentence with either of them. Neither suggestion is correct. While it is inadvisable to use them to open a sentence too often, they can be used very effectively in the right circumstances: *But, soft! what light from yonder window breaks? It is the east, and Juliet is the sun . . .*

Complex sentences

A multiple sentence consisting of a main clause and one or more subordinate clauses is called a **complex sentence**. The subordinate clause usually follows the main clause:

They went for a walk, | while we tidied up the house.

I can't come | because I'll be in London on Tuesday.

The subordinate clause may also, however, begin the sentence: *Since you're busy, I'll call again later.*

Coordination

Coordination is the grammatical process of linking together elements of a sentence that have equal status. The section on 'Compound sentences' (pp. 15–16) considers how it operates with clauses in compound sentences. It also operates between individual words or phrases:

Do you take milk and sugar?
The day was fine but rather chilly.
You could drive over the bridge or through the tunnel.

These are all examples of **linked coordination** – i.e. a linking word *and*, *or*, or *but* is used in all of them. It is, however, possible to coordinate words, phrases, or clauses by using punctuation marks instead of the linking words, in which case the process is known as **unlinked coordination**. Instead of saying *It was a cold and frosty morning* it is perfectly possible to say *It was a cold, frosty morning*. Likewise, the *but* in the sentence *James likes coffee, but Henry prefers tea* could be replaced by a semicolon: *James likes coffee; Henry prefers tea*.

It should be noted that when two nouns or noun phrases are linked by *and*, two different combinations can be produced. Compare the sentences, *Jane and Joe kissed the bride* and *Jane and Joe kissed*. The former sentence could be split into two clauses: *Jane kissed the bride and Joe kissed the bride*. The technical name for combining two noun phrases in this way is **segregatory coordination**. The second sentence, *Jane and Joe kissed* cannot be split in the same way and still make sense. The two terms form a unit, as they do, for example, in the sentences *Management and unions met yesterday* and *Oil and water don't mix*. The technical term for this is **combinatory coordination**.

Subordinate clauses

The grammatical name for the relationship between parts of a sentence that do not have equal status is **subordination**. The parts of the sentence that show subordination are the incomplete or subordinate clauses (see pp. 6–7 and p. 15).

Subordinate clauses can perform many functions. They can substitute for any part of the sentence except the verb, appearing, for instance, as the subject: *How it got there is a mystery*, as the direct or indirect object:

> *She doesn't know what's going on.*
>
> *I'll give a prize to whoever comes up with a workable solution.*

or as the adverbial: *It broke while I was trying to clean it.* It is also possible to use a subordinate clause as a part of, or as an addition to, one of the main elements of the sentence, for example, after a noun as part of the subject or object:

> *The book that you lent me was very useful.*
>
> *I haven't finished reading the book that you lent me.*

All the examples of subordinate clauses shown so far have contained a **finite** verb (that is a verb in the present, past, or future tense; see p. 43). These are called **finite clauses.** It is also possible for subordinate clauses to be based on an **infinitive** (the root form of the verb, such as *(to) be* or *(to) carry* (see pp. 43–4), or a **participle** (a form of the verb ending in *-ing* (present participle) or *-ed*, etc. (past participle), see pp. 44–6). In the sentences *They were happy to see us again* and *I was just walking along, minding my own business*, the phrases *to see us again* and *minding my own business* are **non-finite clauses.**

Comparative clauses

A **comparative clause** is a special type of subordinate clause that expresses a comparison between two or more things. There are two kinds of comparisons: those in which the two things being compared are equivalents and those in which they are not.

Equivalence is shown by using the construction *as . . . as*:

> *She is as clever as you are.*
>
> *I waited as long as I could.*

Note that, for grammatical purposes, the relationship is one of equivalence even in a sentence such as: *She is nowhere near as clever as you are.*

Non-equivalence is shown by a combination of a **comparative element**, either an adjective ending in *-er* (*bigger*, *smaller*) or a phrase containing a word such as *more* or *less*, and a clause that begins with *than*:

She's a lot taller than I am.

He's doing less well now than he was a year ago.

In both types of sentence it is usual to drop any parts of the subordinate clause that repeat what is in the main clause:

She is as clever as you (are).

He's doing less well now than (he was) a year ago.

The job took far less time than (we) expected (it to take).

Comment clauses

Comment clauses are short clauses inserted into a sentence to show the speaker's attitude to what he or she is saying or to make clear what he or she is trying to do. Phrases such as *I'm glad to say*, *I'm sorry to say*, *to be frank*, or *to put it another way* are typical examples. Unlike other types of clause, they do not relate to a particular component of the sentence, but to the sentence as a whole, and, for that reason, can be inserted in it at almost any point:

To be honest, it doesn't make much difference.

It doesn't make much difference, to be honest.

It doesn't, to be honest, make much difference.

Comment clauses are more often used in spoken than in written English and are quite frequently used simply, as it were, to fill a gap. This is especially the case with phrases such as *you know*, *you see*, or *I mean*: *Well, I mean, it's a tricky situation.*

Reporting what someone has said

There are two ways of conveying what someone has said. It is, of course, possible to write down the exact words that the person used in inverted commas: *'I'm sorry, but I can't help you,' she said.* This is known as **direct speech.**

There are two parts to a sentence containing direct speech: the **reporting clause**, consisting of a subject and a verb of saying (in the above example *she said*), and the **reported clause**, the words spoken: *I'm sorry, but I can't help you.* The reported clause is the part in inverted commas.

The reporting clause can also be placed before, after, or in the middle of the reported clause. If it is placed after or in the middle, the normal order of subject and verb is often reversed: *'It looks very black outside,' said Jill* (or *Jill said*), *'I think it's going to rain.'* Note that subject and verb are not usually put in reverse order when the subject is a personal pronoun: *'Come on,' he said, 'let's go'* – not *said he* because it sounds old-fashioned and definitely not *shouted he, called he*, or *answered he.*

Reported or **indirect speech** is a method of conveying what someone said without using inverted commas. It integrates the speaker's words into the framework of a sentence. This is usually done with a clause beginning with *that*, although the actual word *that* is often omitted: *She said (that) she was sorry, but (that) she couldn't help us.* In some cases a *wh-* word (*what, where*, etc.) appears: *They asked us where we had been.*

There are a number of adjustments that have to be made when direct speech is changed into reported speech. The personal pronoun in the reported clause has to be changed: *She said, 'I'm sorry'* becomes *She said she was sorry.* Often changes need to be made to references to time or place: *They said, 'It'll be ready next week'* might, for instance, have to become *They said last week that it would be ready this week. If* or *whether* usually needs to be inserted when transferring a question: *'Can we come too?' they asked* becomes *They asked whether* (or *if*) *they could come too.* Notice also that the reporting clause always come before the reported clause in indirect speech, no matter where it is placed in direct speech.

The most significant change, however, is in the tense of the verb in the reported clause (see p. 40). The present tense in the reported clause of direct speech becomes the past tense in indirect speech: *'I'm coming,' he said* becomes *He said he was coming.* The future tense formed with *will* becomes the future-in-the-past formed with *would*: *'I will be there,' she said* becomes *She said she would be there.* The simple past tense or the past tense formed with *have* becomes the pluperfect tense formed with *had*: *'We've finished,' they announced* becomes *They announced that they had finished.*

Indirect speech is used in the compilation of minutes of meetings: see pp. 308–9.

Relative clauses

Relative clauses are clauses that begin with words such as *that*, *which*, *who*, *whose*, etc., which are known as **relative pronouns**, or the words *when* and *where*, which are known as **relative adverbs**. The main function of relative clauses is to give more specific information about the nouns they follow, as in *the boy who brought the message* or *the book that I lent you* or *a place where we can be alone.*

There are two types of relative clause and it is often important to be able to distinguish between them. The first type is called a **restrictive** or **defining clause** – the information that such a clause contains is intended to identify a particular person or thing specifically as the one that is being talked about. The second type is called a **non-restrictive** or **non-defining clause**. The information that it contains is incidental, an extra. The clause could be omitted from the sentence in which it appears without making it unclear who or what is being referred to.

The difference between these two kinds of relative clause can be seen in the two following examples:

> *The paragraph that mentions you by name comes about halfway down the page.*
>
> *The paragraph, which comes about halfway down the page, mentions you by name.*

In the first example the crucial piece of information (the fact that someone is mentioned by name) is put into the relative clause *that mentions you by name*. This clause defines which paragraph is being talked about. In the second example the crucial information is in the main clause and the fact that the paragraph is halfway down the page is put in as a useful but optional extra. That is the nature of a non-restrictive relative clause.

The same form of words can often be used or interpreted either restrictively or non-restrictively. For example, consider the sentence *My uncle who lives in Nottingham is a retired headmaster*. If someone were discussing all their uncles, then this might be read as a restrictive clause

My uncle who lives in Nottingham is a retired headmaster, and my uncle who lives in Derby is a grocer, and as for my uncle who lives in Leicester, he's a milkman. Uncle by uncle they are being specifically identified by the towns in which they live. On the other hand, perhaps the conversation is not about uncles but about teaching. In this case the fact that the speaker's uncle lives in Nottingham is really neither here nor there: *My uncle, who lives in Nottingham, is a retired headmaster, and what he thinks is . . .*

Non-restrictive clauses are usually enclosed in commas or dashes to indicate that they are dispensable from the sentence: *Paulton – which is where I grew up – is a small village in Somerset.* It is incorrect to put commas or dashes around a restrictive clause: *The paragraph that mentions you by name comes about halfway down the page.*

When a non-restrictive relative clause refers to a thing, it must begin with the relative pronoun *which*:

> *The car, which was at least forty years old, rattled alarmingly.*
> *Paulton – which is where I grew up – is a small village in Somerset.*

Restrictive clauses relating to things may begin with either *that* or *which*, although there is an increasing tendency for *that* to be preferred: *The card that/which I eventually chose was a humorous one.* If, as in the last example, the noun that the relative pronoun (*that, which*, or *whom*) relates to is the object of a restrictive clause, then the relative pronoun can be omitted: *The card I eventually chose was a humorous one.*

On the use of commas in non-restrictive clauses, see also pp. 150–52.

One further type of relative clause should be mentioned – it is called a **sentential relative clause** because it relates not to a specific word but to a whole clause or to the whole of the rest of the sentence. Such clauses are also introduced by *which*: *He was late for his appointment – which was not like him at all.*

Word classes: nouns

The following sections of this survey of grammar deal with individual types or classes of words, their nature and functions, and the changes that they undergo when they are used for different purposes. A **noun** stands for a person or thing. The word 'thing', in this instance, is being used in its widest sense, because nouns denote not only real-world objects or creatures (*table* is a noun, as are *bus*, *computer*, *lion*, and *virus*), but also events and actions and completely intangible things such as states, feelings, and concepts (*business* is a noun, as are *conversation*, *inertia*, *happiness*, and *unity*).

Types of noun

Nouns are usually classified by type – although many of them belong, or can belong, to more than one type – and these types are usually dealt with in contrasting pairs. There are proper nouns and common nouns, concrete nouns and abstract nouns, countable nouns and uncountable nouns, and collective nouns. These types will now be dealt with individually.

Proper nouns and common nouns

A **proper noun** is a noun that denotes a specific person or thing. It is, to all intents and purposes, a name. In fact **proper name** is an alternative term for proper noun.

Proper nouns include people's first names and surnames, the names of places, times, events, and institutions, and the titles of books, films, etc. They are spelt with an initial capital letter: *Sam*, *Shakespeare*, *New York*, *October*, *Christmas*, *Christianity*, *Marxism*, and *Coronation Street*.

All nouns that are not proper nouns are known as **common nouns.** The same word can be both a common noun and, in other contexts, a proper noun. An *enigma* (common noun) is a mystery, for example; *Enigma* (proper noun) is the name of a German encoding machine used in the Second World War, the title of a novel, and the name the British composer Edward Elgar gave to the theme on which he based his *Enigma Variations. Road* is a common noun when used in the sentence *I was walking down the road* and part of a proper noun in the name *London Road.*

Apart from being spelt with an initial capital letter, proper nouns have other characteristics that usually distinguish them from common nouns. They do not, generally, have a plural and they are not, usually, preceded by *a* or *an*. There is only one *Australia*; there was only one *Genghis Khan*.

Although this is the general rule, however, there are many exceptions to it. There are occasions when either a specific example or several examples of something denoted by a common noun must be referred to: *keeping up with the Joneses; buying a Picasso; one of the warmest Januaries on record.*

Proper nouns are quite often preceded by *the*: *the United Nations, the White House, the Olympic Games.* The *t* of *the* is spelt with a capital letter only when it forms an integral part of the name or title: *a copy of 'The Times'; a conference held at The Hague.*

Concrete nouns and abstract nouns

Concrete nouns stand for actual objects that can be seen, touched, tasted, etc. **Abstract nouns**, as the name implies, denote things that are abstract and cannot be seen or touched. *Table* and *lion* are concrete nouns; *happiness* and *unity* are abstract nouns. Many nouns have both concrete and abstract senses, the abstract sense often being a figurative or metaphorical version of the concrete one. Thus *key* is a concrete noun when it means an object that unlocks a door, an abstract one in a phrase such as *the key to the problem.*

Countable nouns and uncountable nouns

Countable nouns are nouns that can form a plural and can be preceded by *a* or *an*: *a table – tables; an equivalent – equivalents.* Countable nouns must in fact be preceded by a *determiner* (a word such as *a, the, this, that* or *my*; see p. oo) when they are singular. It is not possible, for example, to say *table stands.* Concrete nouns tend to be countable – though by no means all are.

Uncountable nouns are nouns that do not normally form a plural and cannot normally be preceded by *a* or *an*. They can, however, stand alone without a determiner (see p. 34) when they are singular. Concrete uncountable nouns include words such as *blood, mud,* and *foliage; concrete* in its normal everyday sense of a building material is an uncountable noun. Abstract nouns tend to be uncountable – words such as *happiness, gravity,* or *inspiration.*

There are many words that have both countable and uncountable senses. *Tea*, for example, is uncountable in phrases such as *a packet of tea*, *a cup of tea*, or *invite someone for tea*. Three different senses are involved and in each of them *tea* is uncountable. In the phrase *two teas please* (= cups of tea) it is, however, countable. *Feeling*, *emotion*, and many similar words are uncountable when they are used generally and abstractly (*Try to put more feeling into the way you say the line*) and countable when they refer to specific types or examples (*a feeling of joy*; *One can only guess at what their feelings were on that occasion*).

Collective nouns

Collective nouns are nouns that refer to a group of people or things. *Group* itself is a collective noun, as are *committee*, *crew*, *government*, *flock*, *herd*, *team*, etc.

Troublesome grammatical point:
using a singular or plural verb with a collective noun 'The government Is united' or 'The government are united'

Most collective nouns are countable; their peculiarity is that when they are used in the singular form they can take either a plural or a singular verb. It is possible to say that *the government is united* or *the government are united*. It is possible to say *the team has lost its last five matches* or *the team have lost their last five matches*. Choosing a singular verb treats the group as a unit; choosing a plural one emphasizes the fact that it is made up of many individuals. While it may be difficult sometimes to decide whether to opt for a singular or plural verb, it is very important that all the attendant words, such as possessive pronouns, match the form that has been chosen for the verb – so it would be incorrect to write either *the team has lost their last five matches* or *the team have lost its last five matches*.

The plural of nouns

Most English nouns form their plural by adding *-s*: *table* – *tables*; *team* – *teams*. Nouns whose singular form ends in *-ch*, *-s*, *-sh*, *-ss*, *-x*, or *-zz* add *-es* to make the plural: *bunch* – *bunches*; *cross* – *crosses*. Nouns that end in one or more consonants and *-y* (*lady*, *shanty*, *monarchy*, etc.) change the *y* to *ie* and add *s* in the plural (*ladies*, *shanties*, *monarchies*) (see p. 137).

All these plural forms are **regular** – that is to say that they follow the standard pattern for a particular feature or operation in a language.

Many common English words have **irregular** plurals – in other words they do not conform to the standard pattern. Obvious examples are words such as *man* and *woman* (plurals *men* and *women*) or *mouse*, *child*, and *foot* (plurals *mice*, *children*, and *feet* respectively). It is partly because these are very basic, common words with a long history in the English language that they have retained these unusual plurals, which were, in fact, regular in the forms of the language that were the ancestors of modern English.

Words that end in the letters *-f* (or *-fe*) and *-o* frequently cause difficulty because some of them have regular plurals and some have irregular ones. The plural of *thief* is *thieves*, but the plural of *chief* is *chiefs*. *Life* pluralizes as *lives*, but *fife* as *fifes*. Eminent people have been caught out by the fact that *potato* and *tomato* become *potatoes* and *tomatoes*, although large numbers of words ending *-o* simply add *-s* (*avocados*, *pianos*, *photos*, and *radios*). See also p. 138.

There are no easy rules, unfortunately, for irregular plurals in English. They simply have to be learnt and remembered.

Foreign plurals

There are a number of words that have been imported into English directly from foreign languages and have retained a foreign form as their only plural or, increasingly nowadays, as an alternative to a regular English one. The majority of these come from Latin or Greek. The more specialized and technical they are, the more likely it is that they will retain a Latin or Greek plural.

Latin nouns usually end in *-a*, *-ex* (or *-ix*), *-um*, or *-us*. The Latin plural of *-a* is *-ae*, while that of *-us* is *-i*, and words whose singular form ends in *-um* have a plural ending *-a*. *Larva* and *vertebra* become *larvae* and *vertebrae* in the plural, *nucleus* and *stimulus* become *nuclei* and *stimuli*, *bacterium* and *stratum* become *bacteria* and *strata*.

Words taken from Greek that have irregular plurals tend to end in *-is* or *-on*. Words whose singular form ends in *-is* usually end in *-es* in the plural (*basis* – *bases*; *crisis* – *crises*). Words such as *criterion* and *phenomenon* have plurals that end in *-a* (*criteria* and *phenomena*).

It should be noted that the fact that a word ends in one of the above combinations of letters does not automatically mean that its plural will be one of the irregular ones mentioned above. It is quite correct to speak of *arenas* or *eras, foetuses, sinuses, albums, museums, complexes, coupons,* and *electrons.* In fact to foist a Latin or Greek plural on any of these words would be incorrect. Additionally, there are quite a number of words where a more learned Latin or Greek plural exists side by side with an ordinary English one: *formulas* is as correct as *formulae, mediums* as correct as *media.* Sometimes one sense of a word usually has a Latin or Greek plural and another sense an English one. *Medium* is a case in point: communicators with the dead are *mediums,* means of mass communication are *media.*

Among the plural forms taken from modern foreign languages, perhaps the most noteworthy are words from French ending in *-eau,* which can form their plural as *-eaux* or *-eaus* (*bureaux* or *bureaus, tableaux* or *tableaus*), and words from Italian ending in *-o,* whose plurals can end in *-s* or *-i* (*tempos* or *tempi, virtuosos* or *virtuosi*).

This is an area of English usage where changes are currently taking place. On the whole, irregular forms from foreign languages are tending to be used less and ordinary English forms more. Though dictionaries do not always agree, a modern dictionary is the best place to look for guidance both for the spelling of tricky English plurals (*-os* or *-oes*) and to ascertain whether a foreign or an English form is more appropriate.

Zero plurals and invariable nouns

Nouns that change their form in the plural, whatever form that change may take, are known as **variable nouns.** Nouns that do not change their form are either zero plurals or invariable nouns.

A **zero plural** is a noun whose form does not change whether it is singular or plural. The word *sheep,* for example, remains the same whether a single animal or a flock is being referred to. A single *aircraft* in the sky or a dozen *aircraft* at an airfield may be described. There are a number of nouns, especially names of animals, which are sometimes treated as standard nouns and sometimes as zero plurals. The plural of *fish* is sometimes *fish* and sometimes *fishes.* There are *elephants* at the zoo or in a circus, but on the plains of Africa (that is to say, when using the word in a slightly more technical, zoological way) you are more likely to report seeing *elephant.*

Invariable nouns are nouns that are either always singular or always plural. The commonest type of invariable singular noun is the uncountable type (e.g. *mud* or *gravity*) discussed on p. 24. In addition, there are a number of nouns ending, rather confusingly, in *-s* which are strictly singular: *billiards, mumps, news*. None of these should be followed by a plural verb:

> *News has* (not *have*) *just come in . . .*
>
> *Mumps is* (not *are*) *a serious disease.*

Many of the words ending in *-ics* fall into this category, although many of them also have senses in which they can be used with a plural verb: *Politics is the art of the possible*, but *His politics* (= his political views) *are very right wing.*

Among the nouns that are invariably plural there are some that look plural because they end in *-s* (*dregs, glasses* (= spectacles), *scissors,* and *trousers*) and some that do not look as if they are plurals (*cattle* and *vermin*). They are always, however, followed by a plural verb:

> *My trousers are at the cleaners'.*
>
> *The cattle are grazing in the field.*

The gender of nouns

English does not divide nouns into masculine and feminine, or masculine, feminine, and neuter as ancient languages did and many foreign languages still do. English nouns show gender only in as much as they relate either to males or to females: *woman* is not a feminine word in the grammatical sense that *la femme* is in French or *die Frau* is in German, but it, obviously, refers to a female human being as *boy* refers to a male one. There are many similar pairs of words that describe animals of different sexes (*cock* and *hen, ram* and *ewe*, etc.), but these words too are not either masculine or feminine in the grammatical sense. Gender in this sense is most important, for grammatical purposes, in that it determines the form of the personal pronoun which is used in connection with a noun. Female creatures are referred to as *she, her*, males as *he, him*, and inanimate objects (and occasionally very young children) by the non-personal *it*.

There are a number of suffixes (word endings) that can be used to convert a noun that usually refers to a male into one that refers to a female. The commonest of these is *-ess*. A female lion is a *lioness*, the daughter of a king or queen is a *princess* and a woman actor may be referred to as an *actress*. Though it is not a grammatical issue as such, it is worth noting that the use in jobs and positions of gender-specific terms, especially women-only terms, is declining. This is an area where changes are currently taking place in the language in response to changes in society. It is usually inappropriate to employ a gender-specific term where a neutral one is available, and so *-ess* (and *-ette* and *-trix*) words should generally be avoided. See also pp. 131–2.

The possessive form of nouns

In many languages, nouns have different inflections depending on their role in the sentence, for example, whether they are the subject or object of a verb. An inflected form of a noun is known as a **case**. English nouns remain in their basic form – in what is known as the **common case** – except where it is necessary to show that one person or thing owns another. There is a **possessive** or **genitive case** for most English nouns. In the singular, it consists of adding apostrophe *s* to the base form: *Jill's car*; *a climber's equipment*; *the car's service history*. This rule applies also to singular nouns that end in *-s* (*Robert Burns' poetry*; *the dress's sleeves*). Plural nouns that end in *-s* add an apostrophe only: *members' voting rights*; *the animals' feeding time*. Plural nouns that end in a letter other than *s* add an apostrophe *s* as usual: *the children's toys*; *the media's obsession with smut*. (See also pp. 170–71.)

An alternative way of showing possession – the more frequent way for inanimate objects – is to use *of*: *the top of the hill*; *the history of the United States*.

Nouns as modifiers

A feature of modern English is its use of nouns as **modifiers** – words which provide more information about other words and describe the things or people that they stand for more specifically. Nouns are frequently used in front of other nouns in the way that adjectives are. In the phrases *car keys* and *house keys*, *car* and *house* are modifiers. Many everyday nouns are very frequently used in this way as a neater alternative to a longer phrase using, for example, the genitive with *of*, so that *the roof of the church* becomes *the church roof* and *the window of the kitchen* becomes *the kitchen window*.

Nouns used as modifiers may look like adjectives, but they do not share all their characteristics. They cannot be used in any position except in front of the noun they relate to and they do not have *comparative* or *superlative* forms (see p. 33).

Noun phrases

A **noun phrase** is a group of related words, one of which is a noun or pronoun. It may consist simply of a single noun or pronoun, a noun preceded by *a* or *the*, or a main noun accompanied by a phrase or clause. The following are all noun phrases based on the main noun *child*: *a child*; *a small child*; *a child with learning difficulties*; *a child who is of above average intelligence*.

Apposition

When a noun phrase is immediately followed by another noun phrase that refers to exactly the same person or thing and defines him, her, or it more closely, the two phrases are said to be in **apposition** to each other. For example, the following noun phrases are in apposition: *Paris, the capital of France*. Strictly speaking, the order in which the two phrases in apposition appear should make no difference to the meaning of the sentence:

Paris, the capital of France.

The capital of France, Paris.

Dr Brown, the head of the French department, is giving the lecture.

The head of the French department, Dr Brown, is giving the lecture.

Similarly, it should be possible to omit either of the two elements without making the sentence incomprehensible:

Dr Brown is giving the lecture.

The head of the French department is giving the lecture.

The term *apposition* is also, however, more loosely applied to cases where the two phrases cannot be transposed so freely (*my computer, a Gateway 2000* but not *a Gateway 2000, my computer*), where a word or phrase such as *namely* or *for example* comes between the two phrases in apposition (*her favourite poets, namely Keats and Shelley*), or where the second element cannot be dropped if the sense is to be preserved: *The play* Under Milk Wood *is on the radio tonight.* If the title of the play were omitted, the sense would be much less clear.

Appositive clauses

Appositive clauses are clauses beginning with *that* which are attached to abstract nouns such as *belief, fact, knowledge, suggestion*, and which indicate their content, that is, what is believed, known, suggested, or a fact: *the belief that God exists*; *the fact that she is away on holiday*. They are called appositive because their relationship to their main noun is the same as that between one noun phrase and another in apposition to it: Paris *is* the capital of France; the fact in question *is* that she is away on holiday.

It is important to distinguish between appositive clauses beginning with *that* and restrictive clauses beginning with *that* (see pp. 21–2) – for example between *the idea that was put forward at the meeting* and *the idea that the meeting should be postponed*. The first clause is a relative clause – *that* could be replaced by *which* and does not convey the content of the idea – the second is an appositive one.

Adjectives: types

Adjectives are words that describe particular qualities possessed by people or things. They are usually attached to or relate to nouns. Words such as *big, new, old, red*, and *small* are adjectives.

They are defined in two ways: according to their position in relation to the noun they relate to and according to whether or not they can form comparisons.

An **attributive adjective** is one that appears before the noun it relates to, as in *a red dress* or *bright colours*, where *red* and *bright* are adjectives used attributively. Some adjectives can be used only in this position, for example, *former*, *latter*, or *utter*.

A **predicative adjective** is one that is used after a verb such as *be*, *become*, or *seem* – in other words, it is the complement of its noun. In the sentences *The dress is red* and *The colours seem very bright*, *red* and *bright* are being used predicatively. Some adjectives can be used only in this position, for example, *afraid*, *asleep*, or *alike*.

Occasionally an adjective is placed immediately after the noun it relates to, in which case it is said to be **postpositive**. Postpositive adjectives are most often found together with pronouns, as in:

> *There's something fishy going on.*
>
> *Everything possible is being done.*

Here *fishy* and *possible* are being used postpositively. But there are a number of fixed noun phrases that contain a postpositive adjective (*body politic*, *court martial*, *princess royal*), and when the past participles of verbs (see p. 45) are used as adjectives, they often occur postpositively (*the money invested*, *the people involved*, *the time required*).

Gradable and non-gradable adjectives

Most adjectives are **gradable**, that is to say that they stand for a quality which can vary in degree. In other words, it is sensible to ask *how . . . is something?* and expect an answer *very*, *slightly*, *totally*, or *more . . . than something else*. Gradable adjectives can be used in comparisons or can be modified by adverbs such as *very*, *completely*, *fairly*, *slightly*. There are a number of adjectives, however, that, because of their sense, are **non-gradable**. To ask *how perfect*, *how impossible* or *how unique* something is does not make sense – or does not, strictly speaking, make sense. Those adjectives are therefore non-gradable.

Comparative and superlative

The **comparative** form of an adjective is, as its name suggests, the form used when making comparisons. Shorter and simpler adjectives in English form the comparative by adding *-er* (*lighter*, *sweeter*). Adjectives that end with a single vowel followed by a single consonant (*big*, *red*) double the consonant (*bigger*, *redder*): see p. 140. Adjectives that end in *-y* change to *i* (*angrier*, *warier*) (see p. 137), although single-syllable adjectives may sometimes keep the *-y* (*drier* or *dryer*). Adjectives that end in *-e* simply add *-r* (*bluer*, *later*). Longer adjectives – those with three syllables or more – form their comparatives with *more* (*more comfortable*; *more unusual*). Most adjectives with two syllables can form the comparative either way (*commoner/more common*; *shakier/more shaky*).

The comparative form should be used when comparing people or things in twos or when comparing one person or thing with another. This is the case even if an individual is being compared with a group or with a series of individuals:

> *This is the cheaper of the two options.*
>
> *John is taller than his brother or his father.*
>
> *Mary is more troublesome than all the rest of the children put together.*

The form used to indicate that a thing possesses a quality to a greater degree than two or more other things is the **superlative**. The superlative is formed in the same way as the comparative either by adding *-est* or by using *most* (*sweetest*; *biggest*; *driest*; *commonest/most common*; *most comfortable*). At least three things must be involved in a comparison for the superlative to be the appropriate form of the adjective to use – though it is also used when the number of things involved is unspecified:

> *John is the tallest of the three boys.*
>
> *It is the cheapest option currently on offer.*

The order of adjectives

Adjectives are often used in strings of two or more before nouns and are sometimes separated by commas. When they are used in this way, certain conventions usually dictate the order in which they appear. It is not idiomatic, for instance, to write *a red Italian fast car* or *a country remote village*. The usual order of adjectives (sometimes changed for emphasis or special effect) is first general adjectives (*big*, *fast*, *remote*), followed by parts of verbs used as adjectives (*excited*, *thrilling*), followed by adjectives of colour, followed by adjectives of nationality or region (*Chinese*, *Italian*, *Western*), followed by nouns used as adjectives or adjectives closely derived from nouns (*country*, *iron*, *wooden*). Reordered on these principles, the phrases shown above would reappear as *a fast red Italian car* and *a remote country village*.

Determiners

Determiners are a small but very important class of words that, like adjectives, appear in front of and relate to nouns. They include *a*, *the*, *this*, *that*, *all*, *each*, *every*, *few*, *more*, *much*, *many*, *some*, *which*, *whichever*, and *what*. Their function is to determine or specify the particular object or person, or the number of objects or persons, in a group that a noun refers to. Numerals (*one*, *two*, *three*, etc., and *first*, *second*, *third*, etc.) are also classed as determiners, as are also the possessive adjectives *my*, *his*, *her*, *your*, etc.

The position of determiners

Determiners, unlike most adjectives, must come before the noun they relate to – but they are also frequently used as pronouns (see p. 35). As is not uncommon in language, the same word can play different roles in different contexts. In the phrases *all the people* and *some green apples*, *all* and *some* are determiners; in the sentences *All is not lost* and *Save some for me*, *all* and *some* are pronouns. *All* and *some* also count as pronouns when followed by *of* in phrases such as *all of the time* or *some of the people*.

A noun may be preceded by more than one determiner (*each and every day*; *my one hope*; *all the many tributes*) or by a determiner and one or more adjectives (*a few happy days*; *more long sleepless nights*).

Determiners and nouns

Determiners are often limited as to the type of noun that they can accompany. The following determiners can be used only with singular countable nouns – *a, an, each, either, every, neither*, and *one* (*a book, each book*, etc.). The following are restricted to use with plural countable nouns *both, few* (and *a few*), *many, several, these, those*, together with *two* and all the other numerals (*both books, a few books*, etc.). Finally, *least, less, little* (and *a little*), and *much* are only used with uncountable nouns (*less applause, much applause*).

The articles

The commonest determiners are *a* and *the*, known respectively as the **indefinite article** and **definite article.** *A* is known as the indefinite article because, in a phrase such as *a book*, any book could be meant, whereas *the book* must refer to a book that has been referred to at least once before and is defined or definite to that extent.

Pronouns

Pronouns are words that can take the place of nouns and noun phrases, and sometimes of clauses. They are stand-in words, but vitally important for avoiding long-winded repetition. Consider for instance the unlikely passage:

> *James picked up the book. James carried the book over to James' sister Jenny and showed Jenny a passage. 'Isn't the passage in the book interesting?' James asked.*

If the pronouns *he, it, his, her*, and *this* are put in appropriate places instead of the names and nouns, it immediately becomes more readable:

James picked up the book. He carried it over to his sister Jenny and showed her a passage. 'Isn't this interesting?' he asked.

Personal pronouns

The most important class of pronouns contains the personal pronouns, words such as *I*, *you*, *he*, *she*, and *it* which stand for the names of the people and things that are the actual actors in sentences.

Personal pronouns are divided first of all according to **person.** For grammatical purposes, there are three persons. The **first person** is the speaker – if singular *I*, if plural *we*. The **second person** is the person spoken to – in both singular and plural *you*. The **third person** is the person (or object) spoken about by the first and second persons – in the singular, according to gender, *he*, *she*, or *it*, and in the plural always *they*.

The forms of the personal pronouns illustrated so far are those for the **subject case**, the forms used when the pronoun is the subject of the sentence. When a pronoun is the object of the sentence and when it follows a preposition, it goes into the **object case**: *I* becomes *me*; *we* becomes *us*; *he*, *she*, and *they* change to *him*, *her*, and *them* respectively; and *you* and *it* remain the same:

I ran.

He ran me over.

They shouted.

She shouted at them.

Troublesome grammatical point: the pronoun after a preposition 'Between you and I' or 'Between you and me'

In ordinary English grammar, prepositions are followed by the object form of the personal pronoun – that is to say the form that would be used as the object of a simple sentence (*me*, *you*, *him*, *her*, *it*, *us*, *them*). So *He hit me*, therefore *behind me* and *Give it to me* – not *behind I*, etc., *I* is a subject form). *Between* is a preposition just the same as *behind*, or *to*, and follows the same rule: *We divided the inheritance between us* (not *between we*). It makes no difference to this rule how many pronouns follow the preposition. Consequently, the correct form is *between you and me* (just as it would be *behind us* and *them* or *to both him and her*).

Possessive pronouns

The personal pronouns also each have their own distinctive possessive forms. We have already touched on the forms that are used as determiners: *my*, *your*, *his*, *her*, *its*, *our*, and *their*. The forms that are used as pronouns are: *mine*, *yours*, *his*, *hers*, *its*, *ours*, and *theirs*. These forms can be used as either the subject or complement of a verb:

That bag is mine.

Yours is over there.

It should be noted that although most of the forms of the possessive pronoun end in *s*, none of them ends in an apostrophe *-'s*.

Reflexive pronouns

The reflexive pronouns are a small group of words formed by adding *-self* (singular) or *-selves* (plural) to either the objective or the possessive forms of the personal pronoun: *myself*, *yourself*, *himself*, *herself*, *itself*, *ourselves*, *yourselves*, and *themselves*. They are used to show that the action of a verb affects the person or thing that is its subject – effectively that the same person or thing is both the subject and the object of the verb:

She fell down and hurt herself.

The machines switched themselves off.

Sometimes they follow a preposition rather than the actual verb, but still refer back to the subject: *He looks very pleased with himself.*

Emphatic pronouns

Emphatic pronouns are exactly the same in form as reflexive pronouns (*myself, himself*, etc.). They usually follow immediately after the noun or pronoun they relate to and, as their name suggests, their function is purely to give emphasis:

> *I myself have said as much on numerous occasions.*
>
> *It's not the fault of the machine itself, but of the person operating the machine.*

Sometimes the emphatic pronoun is moved to a position further away from the word it relates to, but its function remains the same: *He didn't actually say so himself, but his best friend told me that that's what he feels.*

Demonstrative pronouns

The **demonstrative pronouns** are *this, that, these*, and *those* when used as pronouns rather than determiners. They are called *demonstrative* because they point out or demonstrate which of a number of things are being referred to. *This* (singular) and *these* (plural) usually refer to things nearer to the speaker, *that* (singular) and *those* (plural) to things further away:

> *Whose book is this on my desk?*
>
> *Whose car is that parked on the other side of the road?*
>
> *Take these and put them over there with those.*

Interrogative pronouns

Interrogative pronouns begin questions. There are five of them: *who, whom, whose, what*, and *which*. (Other words that begin questions, such as *how, when*, and *where*, are called **interrogative adverbs.**) *What* and *which* can be used before any type of noun, singular or plural:

> *What size do you take?*
>
> *Which shoes are you taking?*

Who, whom, and *whose* are effectively three different forms of the same word. *Who* is a subject pronoun. *Who was at the meeting?* or in a reported question *I asked her who was at the meeting. Whom* is an object pronoun:

> *Whom should we ask?*
> *She told me whom she had spoken to.*

Note that in modern English, especially modern spoken and informal English, *whom*, though grammatically correct, would generally be replaced in both these examples by *who*.

Whose is the possessive form: *Whose are these trainers?*

On the use of question marks, see pp. 155–6.

Relative pronouns

A **relative pronoun** is the word *that, which, who, whom,* or *whose* when used to begin a relative clause (see pp. 21–2). *Which* is always used to refer to animals or things; *who* and *whom* are always used to refer to people. *That* usually refers to things, but sometimes to people; *whose* usually refers to people, but sometimes to things.

Indefinite pronouns

Indefinite pronouns are pronouns that refer to people or things without stating specifically who or what they are. Indefinite pronouns such as *anyone, everybody, nobody,* or *somebody* are used to refer to people only; the corresponding forms, such as *anything, everything, nothing,* and *something,* refer only to things. Other indefinite pronouns such as *all, both, some,* etc., may refer to either people or things.

Verbs: their forms

Verbs are a large, very important, and rather complex class of words. They denote action, in its broadest sense. Words such as *go, talk,* and *walk* are verbs. A verb is the one essential component of a major sentence.

Most English verbs have four or five forms. Regular English verbs, that is verbs that conform to the basic standard pattern for verbs, have four. The verb *cook*, for example, has a base form *cook*; a form ending in *-s*: *cooks*; a form ending *-ing*: *cooking*; and a form ending in *-ed*: *cooked*.

The base form is used to make the **infinitive** form (p. 43) *to cook*, the **imperative** form (see pp. 13–14; used for giving orders – *ready, steady, cook!*), and all the forms of the present tense except the third person singular (*I cook, they cook*, etc.).

The only function of the *-s* form is to make the third person singular of the present tense (*he cooks, she cooks, it cooks*). Note that just as nouns ending in *-ch*, *-ss*, etc., add *-es* to make their plural, verbs ending in the same combination of letters also add *-es* (*teaches, kisses, mixes*), verbs that end in *-y* change it to an *i* and add *-es* (*glorifies, tries*) (see p. 137), and that verbs ending in *-o* usually add *-es* (*echoes, embargoes*) (see p. 138).

The *-ing* form of the verb makes the present participle (see p. 44) (*cooking*) and the *-ed* form makes both the past tense (*we cooked*) and the past participle (see p. 45) (*cooked*).

Irregular verbs usually have one additional form – a past participle that is different from the past tense: *sing, sings, singing, sang* (past tense), and *sung* (past participle). Both the past tense and the past participle are completely different from the *-ed* forms of regular verbs. Nevertheless, the various parts of irregular verbs serve the same function as those of regular verbs.

The tenses of verbs

The **tenses** of verbs are the different time frames within which the action of the verb takes place. The *present tense* refers to action taking place now (*I cook; we are cooking*). The *past* and *future tenses*, obviously enough, refer to action in the past or future (*I cooked; she has cooked; they will cook*).

It will be noticed that the four or five forms of the verb discussed above provide only two of the tenses – the simple present (*you cook; he cooks*) and the simple past (*we cooked*). In order to make all the other tenses, another verb is used: *be, have*, or *will*. These are known as **auxiliary verbs** (see p. 42). Using auxiliary verbs it is possible to fill the time gaps left by the main forms of the verb.

Continuous tenses

Continuous tenses express actions that are going on, were going on, or will be going on at a particular time. They are constructed using *to be* together with the *-ing* form of the verb. The continuous present tense (*I am cooking*) is in fact commoner in everyday use than the simple present tense. *He cooks* often means *he is able to cook*, whereas to express the idea that he is at this time standing by the stove holding a frying pan, you would say *he is cooking* – he is doing it now. The same distinction holds for past time, where the past continuous tense is used especially to refer to an action that was going on when something else occurred: *She rang while I was cooking the lunch.*

The future tense

The **future tense** in English is usually formed using the auxiliaries *will* or *shall*. A distinction used to be drawn, especially in British English, between the first person *I* and *we*, which were strictly supposed to make their future tense with *shall* (*I shall cook tomorrow* or in the continuous form *we shall be cooking* tomorrow), and the second and third persons (*you* and *he, she, it,* and *they*), which made their future tense with *will*. To say *I will* (as in the marriage service) or *you shall* or *they shall* expressed a special determination to do something or to see something done (*Britons never, never, never shall be slaves!*). For the most part, however, this distinction is less strictly observed than it once was. The future tense is commonly formed nowadays with *will* (often informally shortened to *-'ll*) for all persons of the verb.

Perfect tenses

The **perfect tense** of a verb is a past tense formed with the auxiliary verb *have* together with the *-ed* form of a regular verb or the past participle of an irregular verb (*I have cooked; I had sung*).

When formed with the present tense of *have*, the perfect tense replaces the simple past tense in questions (*Have you told him?*), when emphasizing that a thing has been done (*Yes, I have told him*), or to indicate that an action that began in the past is still continuing in the present (*He has left the key at home and has gone back to get it*).

When formed with the past tense of *have*, the perfect (also called the *pluperfect* here) expresses an action that occurred at an earlier time than the past time of the main action:

I had been there before, so I knew what to expect.

After he had locked up the building, he went home.

Auxiliary verbs

Auxiliary verbs are verbs that are used with and in front of other verbs. Besides *be, have, will,* and *shall,* the auxiliaries that have already been mentioned while discussing tenses, there is the verb *do*, which is used to make variant and slightly more emphatic forms of both the present and the past tense:

I do sometimes make mistakes.

She did say she was coming.

They are also used to form questions in both those tenses:

Do you cook?

Did you see that?

The other auxiliaries express ability (*can, could*), obligation (*must, should*), wishes (*would*), or possibility (*may, might*). All the auxiliaries except *be* and *have* are always followed by the base form of the verb:

I can cook.

You must sing for us.

They might come.

Finite and non-finite verbs

A **finite** verb is any verb that has a specific tense, is in one of the three persons, and is either singular or plural. Generally speaking, a finite verb is a verb that has a subject (even if that subject is not expressed, as, for example, in the **imperative** or command form of the verb). A non-finite verb does not fit this description. The **non-finite** forms of the verb are the infinitive (the base form usually preceded by *to*: *to sing*), the present participle (*singing*) and the past participle (*sung*).

The infinitive

The infinitive with *to* is used after many verbs, nouns, and adjectives:

> *He learnt to sing in a church choir.*
>
> *I've no wish to sing.*
>
> *She's too nervous to sing for us.*

It can also form the subject of a verb (*To sing refreshes the soul*) or express a purpose like *in order to* (*To sing you don't have to be able to read music*).

The infinitive without *to* is only used after other verbs, especially auxiliaries:

> *She might sing, if you asked her.*
>
> *I heard Pavarotti sing once.*

Troublesome grammatical point:
splitting an infinitive 'to sweetly sing'

The infinitive of verbs in English is usually written as two words: *to* + the basic unchanged form of the verb: *to do*, *to go*, *to sing*, etc. In Latin and most modern European languages, however, the infinitive is represented by a single word, so that the equivalent of *to sing* in Latin is *canere*, in French *chanter*, in German *singen*, etc. On this basis, some teachers of English grammar argue that, though expressed in two words, the English infinitive is a single unified concept, and that it is bad grammar to insert any other word or phrase between, for example, *to* and *sing*. That is what is meant by 'splitting an infinitive', as in *to usually do, to not infrequently go*, or *to sweetly sing*. (Note that only a phrase of this sort counts as a split infinitive – in phrases such as *to be sweetly singing* or *to have usually done*, the adverbs (*sweetly, usually*) do not come between the two constituent parts of the infinitive, *to* and *be* and *have* respectively.)

The most famous example of the late twentieth century was '... to boldly go where no man has gone before', from the introduction to the television series *Star Trek*.

Some people say that you should never split an infinitive. Most guides to usage, however, advise a common-sense approach. If you can put the adverb before *to* or after the main part of the verb without making the sentence sound awkward or ambiguous, then do so:

> ... boldly to go where no man has gone before.
>
> ... to go boldly where no man has gone before.

However, moving the adverb sometimes makes the meaning unclear:

> *They planned to secretly exchange the prisoners.*
>
> *They planned secretly to exchange the prisoners.*

The first sentence contains a split infinitive, *to secretly exchange*. But if you move *secretly* before *to exchange*, as in the second sentence, it is not clear whether the adverb relates to the verb *planned* or *exchange*.

Sometimes a split infinitive simply sounds more natural, especially in informal spoken English:

> *You're supposed to partly cook the vegetables first.*
>
> *You need to really thump the keys.*

Participles

The **present participle** is used to make the continuous forms of verbs and in some clauses (*before/after/while cooking the dinner ...*). Present participles are also sometimes used as adjectives (*a singing waiter*) and sometimes as nouns (*Singing lifts the spirits*). When the present participle is used as a noun, it is sometimes preceded by a possessive form (*Does my singing disturb you?*).

Troublesome grammatical point:
pronoun + the '-ing' form 'Do you object to my bringing my sister?' or 'Do you object to me bringing my sister?'

From a grammatical point of view, the choice between *Do you object to my bringing my sister?* and *Do you object to me bringing my sister?* hinges on whether the phrase *bringing my sister* should be considered to be more like a noun or more like a verb. If it is more noun than verb, then the possessive *my* is more appropriate – as it would be in a more straightforward question, such as *Do you object to my comings and goings?*, where *comings* and *goings* are plural nouns. Constructing a different sentence in which the phrase is the subject of a sentence backs up the point – *My bringing my sister might cause problems* sounds far preferable to *Me bringing my sister might cause problems.* This is because it seems wrong for the object form *me* to play a part in the subject of a sentence. The form of the question with *my* is more correct and preferable in standard and formal writing. But in more informal English the form with *me* is common and generally acceptable.

The **past participle** is used to form the perfect tenses of verbs and the **passive** (see pp. 46–7). It is also used as an adjective (*a cooked dinner*; *a sung Mass*) and can form the basis of a clause: *Exhausted by his efforts, he collapsed on the sofa.*

Troublesome grammatical point:
dangling participle 'Blown to bits by the blast, workers were removing rubble from the buildings'

A so-called **dangling participle** is a phrase based on a present or past participle (an '-ing' form or, usually, an '-ed' form) – in this case *blown to bits by the blast* – that is wrongly or ambiguously placed so that it is not clear what or whom it refers to. The result is commonly a howler: *Blown to bits by the blast, workers were removing rubble from the buildings.* It was the buildings, not the workers, that were blown to bits. The safest place for a participle clause is next to the noun it describes (in this instance, the buildings): *Workers were removing rubble from the buildings blown to bits by the blast.* Consider this other example which is a less obvious mistake: *Through the window we saw, flying over the foothills of* *the Andes, a flock of scarlet parrots.* It could be that we are flying in an aircraft looking out, or that we are on the ground watching flying parrots. It would be clearer if the sentence were rearranged so that *flying over the foothills of the Andes* came next to *we* (*Flying over the foothills of the Andes, we saw through the window . . .*) or *parrots* (*. . . we saw a flock of scarlet parrots flying over the Andes*).

Transitive and intransitive verbs

A **transitive** verb is one that has a direct object (*bring a packed lunch*); an **intransitive** verb does not have a direct object (*winter came late that year*). Verbs that describe movement are often wholly or mainly intransitive:

Prices are rising.

Prices are falling.

The army advanced.

The army retreated.

Many verbs can be used both transitively and intransitively: *I can't sing* (intransitive); *She can't sing a note* (transitive). Verbs often come in pairs that have a similar form, one being transitive and the other intransitive. *Rise*, for example, which is always intransitive, has a transitive partner *raise*:

Prices are rising again.

They have raised their prices again.

Active and passive

The **active voice** is a form of a verb in which the subject performs the action denoted by the verb: *Hugh cooked the supper*. The **passive voice** is a form of a verb in which the subject is affected by the action of the verb: *The supper was cooked by Hugh*. Another way of expressing this is to say that the object of an active verb (in the above example *the supper*) becomes the subject of a passive verb in an equivalent sentence: *The supper was cooked by Hugh*. The subject of the active sentence (*Hugh*) becomes the passive **agent** in the passive one – usually preceded by the preposition *by*. It follows from this that only transitive verbs can be used in the passive, as an intransitive verb has, by definition, no object to form the subject of a passive sentence. The passive form is constructed using the auxiliary verb *be* together with a past participle: *The song is (being) sung/was sung/will be sung by . . .*

On the use of the active and passive in writing, see pp. 221–2.

Moods

There are three so-called **moods** of verbs. The **indicative** is the ordinary form of the verb used for making statements or asking questions. The **imperative** (that consists of the base form of the verb on its own without a subject: see pp. 13–14) is used for giving orders. The **subjunctive** is a special form of a verb that is sometimes used in clauses expressing a wish, demand, or recommendation. The present tense of the subjunctive for most verbs is the same as the ordinary present tense, except that the third person singular form drops its final *-s* or *-es*: *lest he forget*; *I suggest she give it more thought.* The present subjective of *to be* is *be* and of *to have*, *have*:

> *Lest I be thought remiss, I shall inform you immediately.*
>
> *They insisted he have another try.*

Using the subjunctive makes a sentence much more formal and the same result can be obtained with less formality by using *should*. *Should* could be inserted into all the above examples:

> *Lest he should forget . . .*
>
> *I suggest she should give it more thought.*
>
> *They insisted he should have another try.*

The present subjunctive is most often used in certain fixed phrases:

> *God bless you!*
>
> *If need be . . .*
>
> *Suffice it to say . . .*
>
> *Long live the Queen!*

Only the verb *to be* has a separate form for the past tense of the subjunctive, *were* as in *if I were you.* The past subjunctive is preferable to the ordinary past tense after *if* when something completely hypothetical is in question:

Even if that were the case . . .

What would you say if I were to tell you I'd won the lottery?

It is incorrect, however, to use *were* when the speaker is not putting forward a hypothesis but using an *if* clause to introduce a statement of fact or probability:

If she was upset, she certainly didn't show it.

If it was there this morning, it's probably still there now.

Phrasal verbs

Phrasal or **multi-word** verbs are verbs in which the base form is accompanied by an adverb or a preposition or both: *do down*; *do up*; *do away with.* These verbs usually have distinct meanings that are not always deducible from their component parts – *do down* means 'to criticize adversely', *do up* means 'to fasten', *do away with* means 'to get rid of'. Grammarians tend to distinguish between true phrasal verbs, which have their own, usually figurative, meaning and combinations of the verb in its literal sense together with a preposition or adverb: *run out of* is a phrasal verb in the sentence *We've run out of milk* but not in the sentence *He ran out of the room.* In most instances the object of such a verb follows the adverb or preposition, as in the examples above. But when a phrasal verb consists of a verb and an adverb the object can usually either follow the adverb or come between it and the verb: *She did up her coat* or *She did her coat up.*

Adverbs

Adverbs are a versatile class of words that can be used to modify words, phrases, or whole sentences. They are used especially often with verbs, adjectives, or other adverbs.

The majority of adverbs derive from adjectives and are formed by adding *-ly* or *-ally* to the base form of the adjective. The adjective *sad* becomes the adverb *sadly*, *original* becomes *originally*, and so on. The meaning of adverbs can often be rendered as 'in a (sad, original, etc.) way'.

Besides indicating the manner in which something was done, adverbs often indicate time (*always*, *now*, *often*, *then*, *today*, and *yesterday* are all adverbs, as well *currently*, *formerly*, *simultaneously*, etc.) and place (*here*, *there*, and *everywhere* are all adverbs, as are words like *around*, *down*, *in*, *out*, and *up*, which can also function as prepositions). Like adjectives, many adverbs also have a **comparative** and a **superlative** (see p. 33): *Jack ran fast, Jill ran faster, and the dog ran fastest of all. Fast* is, however, something of an exception. The majority of adverbs form the comparative and superlative with *more* and *most*:

The light was shining more brightly than before.

We are the most poorly paid workers in the whole industry.

The position of adverbs

Adverbs can usually be placed in almost any position within a clause without materially affecting its meaning:

Quickly I gathered my things.

I quickly gathered my things.

I gathered my things quickly.

The one place where it is normally impossible to put an adverb is between a verb and its direct object: *I gathered quickly my things* is not standard English.

Sometimes, however, changing the position of an adverb crucially affects the meaning. *Only this key fits that lock* and *This key fits that lock only* (or *only fits that lock*) do not mean the same. It is usually best to place the adverb next to the word it relates to. When adverbs modify adjectives or other adverbs, they are always placed before them, for example with *very*: *a very quick change*; *Things are changing very quickly*.

Troublesome grammatical point:
a double negative 'I don't know nothing'

See chapter 2, '**double negative**', p. 69.

Adverbial phrases and clauses

The role of an adverb is often performed by a phrase or clause. An **adverbial phrase** may be a group of words based on or around a main adverb (*as soon as possible*; *strangely enough*; *rather unusually*), but is also often a phrase based on a preposition (*in a minute*; *beside the lake*; *owing to circumstances beyond our control*). **Adverbial clauses** are introduced by words such as *because*, *if*, *when*, *where*, and *while*. All such clauses and phrases are also known simply as **adverbials:** see p. 10.

Prepositions

Prepositions are a group of words mainly consisting of small words, but they are some of the most frequently used words in the English language. They are words that are placed before other words, especially nouns, phrases, or clauses, to link them into the sentence. *After*, *at*, *before*, *behind*, *for*, *in*, *of*, and *out* are all prepositions. In the following examples the preposition *in* is followed first by a noun, then by a pronoun, then by an adverb, and finally by a clause:

> *There's nothing in the box.*
>
> *There's nothing in it.*
>
> *There's nothing in there.*
>
> *There's nothing in what she says.*

Not all prepositions are single words, however; phrases such as *because of*, *in spite of*, and *on account of* are prepositions too.

Many words that are prepositions also have other functions. *In*, for example, is both an adverb and a preposition. When it is functioning as a preposition, however, it must be followed by something else in order to complete the sense:

They are in the living room (*in* as preposition).

They are in (i.e. at home; *in* as adverb).

Before can function not only as a preposition and an adverb, but also as a conjunction:

I managed to do four hours' work before lunch (preposition).

I've never been here before (adverb).

Before you go, let me show you this photograph (conjunction).

Troublesome grammatical point: ending a sentence with a preposition

'This is the sort of English up with which I will not put' was Sir Winston Churchill's alleged response to the clumsy English produced by those who go out of their way to avoid ending a sentence with a preposition. Many great writers of the past have broken this 'rule':

And do such bitter business as the day/Would quake to look on. (William Shakespeare)

What a fine conformity would it starch us all into. (John Milton)

The present argument is the most abstracted that ever I engaged in. (Jonathan Swift)

. . . the less convincing on account of the party it came from. (Edmund Burke)

. . . too horrible to be trifled with. (Rudyard Kipling)

Supporters of the so-called 'rule' that a sentence should never end with a preposition insist that a *pre*position should always *pre*cede its complement. But this is sometimes undesirable or impossible:

He gave me some photographs to look at.

This seat is not very comfortable to sit in.

She had forgotten which page she was up to.

This pen is not easy to write with.

Was it worth waiting for?

You would not say *He gave me some photographs at which to look.* Nor would you say *She had forgotten up to which page she was.*

Similarly, the question *Was it worth waiting for?* cannot be expressed in any other way.

However, in formal written English, you can often keep the preposition before its complement without sounding stilted. You could write *one of the women with whom I work* in a formal letter, for example, though you would say *one of the women I work with* when talking to a friend.

You can also sometimes rephrase a sentence to move the preposition from the end:

> *This pen is easy to write with.* → *It is easy to write with this pen.*
>
> *This seat is not very comfortable to sit in.* → *Sitting in this seat is not very comfortable.*

Conjunctions

A **conjunction** is a word that links two clauses or two other parts of a sentence. There are two types of conjunction: coordinating conjunctions and subordinating conjunctions.

Coordinating conjunctions link words, phrases, or clauses that have equal status. Examples are *and*, *or*, and *but*, together with the paired joining phrases *both . . . and*, *either . . . or*, *neither . . . nor*, and *not only . . . but also*. See also p. 17.

Subordinating conjunctions link parts of a sentence that do not have equal status. Their main function is to introduce subordinate clauses used as adverbials:

> *I only found out after she had left the company.*
>
> *As you're not a member, you can't vote.*

See also pp. 17–18.

2 Usage

Usage is concerned with words whose use sometimes causes special difficulty or controversy. Although there is inevitably some degree of overlap between grammar and usage, usage is not primarily concerned with the general rules of grammar. Grammar lays down rules, but not everything that it is theoretically correct to say or write according to the rules of grammar is actually good English. Just as judgments handed down by actual courts modify the interpretation of statutes, the usage of language in practice sometimes differs from what its grammar might lead you to expect. So usage stands in a similar relation to grammar as case law does to statute law.

This chapter consists of a series of short entries dealing with words that are often a source of difficulty to users of English. The expressions are listed in alphabetical order.

a or an? The rule is that *an* should be used instead of *a* in front of all words beginning with a vowel sound. These include all words whose first letter is *a* or *i*, most words beginning with *e*, *o*, and *u*, and a few beginning with *h*: *an ace*; *an interesting evening*; *an obviously impossible task*. The exceptions among words spelt with an initial vowel are as follows. When *u* is pronounced *yoo*, it is preceded by *a*: *a unit*; *a useful tool*. Words beginning with *eu* (also pronounced *yoo*) take *a*: *a eucalyptus tree*; *a European*. *One* and words beginning with the same sound take *a*: *a one-off*; *a once mighty empire*. Words spelt with an initial *h* that is not pronounced take *an*: *an hour*; *an honour*. It is also not strictly incorrect to write *an hotel* or *an heroic achievement*, and in speaking it may seem less awkward to say *an (h)otel* than *a hotel*. Most modern authorities, however, recommend that words beginning with *h* should be preceded by *a*: *a hacker*, *a horse*, *a historian*, *a hotel*.

Letters of the alphabet and abbreviations made up of letters take *a* or *an* depending on their pronunciation. *B, C, D, G, J, K, P, Q, T, U,* V, W, *Y*, and *Z* are preceded by *a*: *a BA*; *a V-reg car. A, E, F, H, I, L, M, N, O, R, S*, and *X* follow *an*: *an MA*; You form the plural by adding an '*s*'.

Aboriginal or Aborigine? The indigenous people of Australia are referred to as *Aboriginals* or as *Aborigines* in many dictionaries. This has been replaced, in Aboriginal circles at least, by *Aboriginal* as both noun and adjective.

Aborigine or Aboriginal? See **Aboriginal** or **Aborigine?**

about, around, or round? See **around, round,** or **about?**

abrogate or arrogate? These two formal verbs are sometimes confused. To *abrogate* something such as a treaty or a right is to 'annul' or 'abolish' it. To *arrogate* is to 'claim or seize something without justification' – it is related to *arrogant* and usually occurs in the form *arrogate something to oneself*: *She has recently arrogated to herself the role of decision-maker for the whole group.*

abuse or misuse? There is a subtle distinction between these two words, which are generally similar in meaning both as nouns and as verbs. *Abuse* usually suggests morally improper treatment, often involving a breach of trust: *to abuse someone's hospitality*; *child abuse. Misuse*, on the other hand, may refer simply to incorrect use (*to misuse a word*), though often with suggestions of moral disapproval as well: *a misuse of taxpayers' money*. Somebody who, for instance, is said to be *abusing* the word 'integrity', may be using it hypocritically or in order to mislead. Somebody who is *misusing* it could be either using it in the wrong meaning or using it inappropriately. Note also that unlike *abuse*, *misuse* does not normally refer to the treatment of people.

accommodation *Accommodation* is often misspelt. It has two *c*'s, two *m*'s, and two *o*'s.

AD and BC *AD* is traditionally written before a number signifying a year: *AD 1625*. This is because the abbreviation *AD* means *anno domini* (in the year of our Lord), and if the phrase were written or spoken in full it would make better sense before the date than after it. This practice is by no means universally adhered to with year numbers, however, and when referring to centuries it is necessary to place *AD* at the end of the phrase: *in the third century AD*. *BC* always follows a date: *440 BC*; *the seventh century BC*. In printed text these abbreviations are often written in small capitals: AD and BC.

adverse or averse? These two words are sometimes confused. *Adverse* means 'acting against' or 'unfavourable' and is almost always used before a noun: *adverse criticism*; *adverse weather conditions*. *Averse* means 'strongly opposed to or disliking', usually comes after a verb, and is followed by the preposition *to*: *I wouldn't be averse to giving it another try.*

advice or advise? The noun *advice* is spelt with a *c*: *a piece of advice*; *Take my advice, don't do it*. *Advise*, the verb, is spelt with an *s*: *I'd strongly advise you not to do it.*

advise or advice? See advice or advise?

affect or effect? These two words, which are pronounced the same, are sometimes confused. *Affect* is a verb that means 'influence or change': *How will this affect my pension prospects? Effect* is most commonly used as a noun: *What effect will this have on my pension prospects?* The rule to remember is: the verb is spelt with an *a*; the noun is spelt with an *e*. *Effect* can also be used, slightly formally, as a verb. In this case its meaning is to 'bring about' or to 'carry out': *The police effected an entry into the premises*; *Frederick here! O joy, o rapture! Summon your men and effect their capture!* (W. S. Gilbert, *The Pirates of Penzance*).

agenda Although *agenda* was originally a plural noun, it is now always treated as a singular and has its own plural *agendas*: *draw up an agenda*; *Today's agenda includes a discussion of the financial subcommittee's report.* There is a singular form *agendum* ('an item to be dealt with'), but it is very rare and is best replaced with *item on the agenda.*

aggravate, aggravation *Aggravate* is related etymologically to the word *grave* ('serious'). Its oldest surviving meaning is 'to make worse or more serious': *We ought not to do anything that might aggravate the situation.* Some traditionalists contend that this is its only true meaning and disapprove of the use of *aggravate* to mean 'annoy'. This other meaning has, however, been well established for centuries. The use of the noun *aggravation* (often shortened to *aggro*) to mean 'trouble', however, is slang and to be avoided in serious writing.

ain't *Ain't* has never been fully accepted in standard English, though it was commonly used in place of *am not* in the eighteenth century. It is still unacceptable in speaking or writing standard English. See also **aren't**.

all right or alright? See alright or all right?

alright or all right? The spelling *alright*, although fairly common, is still considered by many users of English, especially the traditionalists, to be a wrong spelling of *all right*. There is no logical reason why the spelling *alright* should not catch on as the spellings *already* and *altogether* did some centuries ago, to distinguish in writing between *they're all right* (each one is correct) and *they're all right* (they're not bad, they're unharmed). But it has not caught on yet.

alternate or alternative? In British English there is a clear distinction between these two words: *alternate* is an adjective and a verb, *alternative* is an adjective and a noun. *Alternate* means 'every other' (*Meetings take place on alternate Wednesdays*) or 'occurring by turns' (*alternate layers of stone and brick*). To *alternate* is 'to do something by turns': *They alternated between urging us to go faster and telling us to slow down.* An *alternative* is 'another different thing that could act as a replacement': *an alternative venue*; *As an alternative to buying a new system, we could try to update the old one.*

In American English, however, *alternate* is widely used as an adjective in the sense of *alternative* (*an alternative venue*) and as a noun to mean 'a deputy or substitute'.

alternative or alternate? See **alternate or alternative?**

amend or emend? These two words are sometimes confused. To *amend* is a general word meaning to 'correct and improve': *She did her best to amend her behaviour.* It also has a specific meaning in relation to pieces of legislation, to 'alter or add to and improve' (*the Act of 1978 as amended in 1993*). *Emend* has a more limited use. It is used exclusively in relation to texts and means 'to remove errors or irregularities from' (*emended the text to bring it into line with modern spelling conventions*).

American Indian *American Indian* has been largely replaced by *Native American* as the preferred general name for a member of one of the indigenous peoples of, especially, North America. The terms *Indian* and *American Indian* are not considered intrinsically disrespectful, however, and are still quite frequently used by Native Americans themselves. See also **Native American**.

amiable or amicable? *Amiable*, meaning 'friendly and pleasant', is used mainly to describe people and their manner: *He seems a very amiable sort of fellow. Amicable*, meaning 'characterized by friendliness', refers chiefly to relationships and dealings between people: *reached an amicable settlement*; *Their relationship became more amicable once they had agreed the terms of the divorce.*

amicable or amiable? See **amiable or amicable?**

amoral or immoral? An *immoral* person is one who breaks accepted standards of right and wrong. To be *amoral* means that one rejects the whole concept of morality or does not know or cannot know right from wrong. Babies, animals, and robots could be said to be *amoral.*

an or a? See a or an?

ante- or anti-? These two prefixes are sometimes confused. *Ante-* means 'before' or 'in front of': *antechamber* ('a room leading into another room'); *antediluvian* ('before Noah's flood'; 'ridiculously outdated'); *antenatal* ('before birth'). The much commoner prefix *anti-* means 'in the opposite direction' or 'against' and can be, and is, attached to any number of words: *anticlockwise*; *antidepressant*; *anti-fox-hunting. Anti* (but not *ante*) can be used informally as a preposition (*I'm anti the whole idea*) or an adjective (*She's less anti now than when we first talked about the plan with her*).

anti- or ante-? See ante- or anti-?

antisocial, asocial, non-social, unsociable or unsocial? There are slight distinctions in meaning between these five related words that need to be observed. *Antisocial* means 'harmful to society': *antisocial behaviour*; *It's terribly antisocial to dump rubbish on the side of the road. Asocial* is a rarer word and implies total rejection, in this case of society or social contact – a recluse might be described as *asocial. Nonsocial* is used mainly as a technical term 'not socially oriented' – the life of many animal species could be described as *nonsocial.* To be *unsociable* usually means 'to be unfriendly and dislike company': *Our new neighbours are totally unsociable and have never even invited us in for a cup of tea.* In British English, *unsocial* is mainly found in the phrase *to work unsocial hours* meaning 'to work at times when most other people are at home'.

any *Any*, as a pronoun, may be used with a verb in either the singular or the plural: *I need some glue – is there any left?*; *We sold most of them, and any that were unsold we gave away to friends.* There is sometimes a subtle distinction in the choice of a singular or plural verb. *Is any of these seats free?* would mean, specifically, 'any one', whereas *Are any of these seats free?* could mean 'are some of them free?'

appraise or apprise? These two words are sometimes confused. To *appraise* is a fairly formal word meaning 'to assess' something or 'estimate its value': *appraise the damage caused by the fire.* To *apprise* is a very formal word meaning 'to inform' and is followed by the preposition *of*: *She had already apprised us of her intentions.*

apprise or appraise? See appraise or apprise?

apt, liable, and likely *Apt to*, *liable to*, and *likely to* are similar in meaning and use and need to be handled with care. *He is apt to exaggerate* means 'he often exaggerates (as we know from our experience of him)'; *he is likely to exaggerate* means 'he can be expected to exaggerate (in this instance)'. *He is liable to exaggerate* can mean either. When referring to a specific time in the future always use *likely*: *It is likely to rain tomorrow.* But *it is apt/liable/likely to rain in November* means in all three forms 'November is often a rainy month'. See also **likely**.

Arab, Arabian, or Arabic? *Arab* is the correct adjective to use in political contexts: *Arab nations*; *an Arab leader*. The adjective *Arabian* is mainly used to designate things geographically as belonging to Arabia (the Arabian peninsula; lying between the Red Sea and the Persian Gulf): *in the Arabian desert. Arabic* refers principally to the language of the Arab peoples: *to learn Arabic*; *Arabic grammar*; *Arabic poetry*. The numbers in general worldwide use are *Arabic numerals*.

Arabian See Arab, Arabian, or Arabic?

Arabic See Arab, Arabian, or Arabic?

aren't *Aren't I?* is the standard less formal alternative for *am I not?*: *Aren't I clever to have thought of that?*; *I am on the list, aren't I?* It is incorrect to use *aren't* with *I* except in questions.

around, round, or about? *Round* is in standard use in British English as a preposition (*came round the corner*) or an adverb (*show someone round*), where American English would more commonly have *around*. It is not incorrect in British English either to use *around* in such phrases. Americans also tend to say *around* where most British users would say *about* (*Don't mess around/about with my things*; *It must have taken around/about five hours*). Again, however, the use of *around* is quite common in British English and perfectly acceptable.

arrogate or abrogate? See **abrogate or arrogate?**

asocial See **antisocial, asocial, non-social, unsociable, or unsocial?**

assume or presume? *Assume* and *presume* are almost interchangeable in the meaning 'suppose'. *Presume* is rather more formal and tends to suggest that a supposition is made on the basis of a deduction or a reasonable likelihood, and has a slightly unfavourable tinge, possibly picked up from its other meaning ('to take liberties'): *Dr Livingstone, I presume?* (who else could it be?); *From what you said yesterday, I presumed that you'd already made up your mind. Assume* is, however, definitely the word to choose if something is being put forward as a basis for argument: *In drawing up your pension forecast, I assumed that interest rates would remain at about 5 per cent.*

assurance or insurance? British English uses the term *assurance* to refer to a form of insurance in which money is bound to be paid out at the end of a fixed period of time or on the death of the insured person: *life assurance. Insurance* is the general term covering all instances where money will only be paid in particular circumstances: *house contents insurance; travel insurance.*

assure, ensure, or insure? These three words are sometimes confused. The commonest meaning of the verb to *assure* is 'to inform (someone) positively': *I assured her that she had nothing to worry about. Assure* can also mean 'to make certain or safe' – but in this sense it is mainly found in the passive or adjectival form: *Their success is assured; Rest assured that we will do all we can to help you.* The verb generally used in the active form to mean 'make (something) certain' is *ensure* (often spelt *insure* in American English): *Our first duty is to ensure the safety of the passengers. Insure* refers simply to making arrangements to obtain financial compensation in the event of accident or loss: *The painting should be insured for at least a million pounds.*

aural or oral? These two words are pronounced the same and are easy to confuse. *Aural* relates to the ears and hearing and is connected with words such as *audible* and *audition*. An *aural* comprehension is one that tests a person's understanding of spoken language. *Oral* relates to the mouth and speaking. Students of foreign languages often have to take an *oral* examination, one that tests their ability to speak the language.

averse or adverse? See adverse or averse?

bacteria *Bacteria* is a plural noun and takes a plural verb. One single micro-organism is a *bacterium.*

BC and AD See AD and BC.

beg the question Strictly speaking, a statement that *begs the question* is one that is logically flawed because it is based on an unproven assumption, often taking for granted the very thing that it itself is seeking to establish. If someone argues: *The Loch Ness monster must exist because there have been so many sightings of it,* that statement *begs the question* because it assumes that the sightings were of the monster and not something else – which is the whole point at issue. This is the original meaning of the phrase and the only one allowed by traditionalists. It is, however, probably more frequently used nowadays to mean that a statement raises obvious questions which need to be answered: *Their claim that the scheme will benefit millions begs the question of precisely what benefit those millions will receive.* While this use can reasonably be argued to have a link with the original meaning in that unwarranted assumptions are usually involved, the use of *begging the question* to mean simply that someone is 'avoiding the issue' or 'not giving a straight answer' is not recommended. There could be confusion with the strict sense and there are plenty of other phrases that unambiguously suggest that somebody is being evasive.

between you and me Prepositions are followed by the object form of the personal pronoun, not the subject form: *from me to him*; *for us and against them*. *Between* is no exception: *We divided it between us* (not *between we*). Having been told repeatedly that it is incorrect to say, for example, *You and me are two of a kind*, people sometimes overcorrect themselves and say *between you and I* when the grammatically correct form is *between you and me.*

billion A *billion* is nowadays generally understood to be 'one thousand million'. Formerly, this was the American understanding of the term. In British English a *billion* was formerly 'one million million'. Modern dictionaries now mark that sense of the term as dated or obsolete.

black, Negro, and coloured The word *black* (without a capital letter) is currently the most widely accepted non-offensive word for people of African or African-American origin. The terms *Negro* and *coloured*, which both formerly had this function, are no longer felt to be acceptable by black people themselves, although *Coloured* has a specific use in South Africa where it refers to members of a population group of mixed-race origin. Dark-skinned people of Asian origin should not be referred to as *black*, in the context of British society, but as *Asian.*

blatant or flagrant? These two words are close together in meaning, both indicating that something is openly outrageous. There is a difference of emphasis, however. *Blatant* emphasizes the obviousness of an offence: *It was such a blatant attempt at emotional blackmail that not even his doting mother could fail to see it. Flagrant*, on the other hand, emphasizes the offence's brazenly shocking or outrageous nature: *If they fail to condemn such a flagrant breach of the regulations, will they ever condemn anything at all?* Both words are spelt with two *a*'s.

blond or blonde? The two spellings, which are both correct, derive from the masculine (*blond*) and feminine (*blonde*) forms of the word in French. English tends to retain the distinction, at least to the extent of preferring the form *blonde* for women, about whom the word is most often used: *She's gone blonde*; *Gentlemen Prefer Blondes* (novel by Anita Loos). On this basis, it would be logical to write *He* *is blond* and *She has blonde hair* and to use *blond* in neutral contexts such as *blond-coloured wood.*

blonde or blond? See blond or blonde?

borrow See lend, loan, and borrow.

can or may? *Can* is nowadays used far more frequently than *may* when asking permission to do something (*Can I go now, please? Can we come too?*), and the battle by traditionalists to preserve a clear distinction between *can* 'be able to' and *may* 'be allowed to' has been effectively lost. *May* is however used in polite requests in formal contexts (*Professor Duckworth, may I present Dr Lowther?*), when the distinction between 'being able' and 'being allowed' is all-important (*It's not a question of whether he can do it, but whether he may*), and when *may* is needed to avoid ambiguity (*She knows perfectly well what she may and may not do*).

It should also be noted that *may* itself can be ambiguous. In a sentence such as *If the minister is satisfied that it is reasonable to do so, he may award a higher pension* it is unclear whether the minister will make the award because the regulations allow him to, or whether it is simply possible that he might make one.

cannon or canon? These two words are easily confused. The noun *cannon* means 'a large gun' or 'a shot in billiards or snooker'. *Cannon* is also a verb: *The shot cannoned off the far post. Canon* is only used as a noun and means 'a senior member of the clergy', 'a piece of music', 'a body of principles or rules', 'an authoritative list of books or authors' works'. The verb *canonize* is derived from it.

canon or cannon? See cannon or canon?

canvas or canvass? The material that tents are traditionally made of is *canvas.* Before an election, political parties *canvass* the voters to try to obtain their support.

canvass or canvas? See canvas or canvass?

Celsius or centigrade? *Celsius* has been internationally adopted as the name of the temperature scale and is always used, for example, in giving weather forecasts. *Centigrade* is no longer in technical use.

centigrade or Celsius? See Celsius or centigrade?

centre *Centre* is the correct British English spelling for both the noun and the verb; *center* is the equivalent spelling in American English. As a verb, *centre* ought logically to be followed by the prepositions *at*, *in*, *on*, or *upon*: *The debate centres on the issue of funding.* Despite its illogicality with respect to physical mid-points that cannot go around anything, the phrase *centre around* or *round* is well established and has been used by many respected writers such as Conrad and Kipling. Some traditionalists may prefer, however, to use another verb such as *revolve* in its place: *The whole debate revolves around the issue of funding.*

cereal or serial? These two words, which are pronounced the same, are sometimes confused. *Cereal* refers to grain and food (*breakfast cereal*; *cereal crops*). The word derives from the name of the Roman goddess of corn and agriculture *Ceres*, which is why it is spelt with two *e*'s. *Serial* derives from the word *series* and refers to things that happen in a series: *a serial killer*; *a TV serial.*

ceremonial or ceremonious? These two adjectives, both derived from *ceremony*, are sometimes confused. *Ceremonial* describes the nature of an occasion or thing, the fact that it is a ceremony or is used in ceremonies: *a ceremonial wreath-laying*; *ceremonial robes. Ceremonious* describes the elaborate and formal manner in which something is done: *a ceremonious bow.* People may be described as *ceremonious*, but not usually as *ceremonial. Ceremonial* is also used as a noun, meaning the elaborate and formal activity that usually accompanies a ceremony.

ceremonious or ceremonial? See ceremonial or ceremonious?

challenged The word *challenged* was put forward in the 1980s as a solution to the problem of how to describe, sensitively and positively, the various disabilities from which some people suffer – thus, *physically challenged* (disabled) and *visually challenged* (blind or with deficient eyesight). The word quickly came to be seen as a clear example of euphemism and political correctness and to be ridiculed in such combinations as *cerebrally challenged* (stupid) and *vertically challenged* (short). The question of how physical disabilities can be referred to in a way that is not demeaning to the sufferer is an ongoing one, but *challenged* is no longer recommended for serious use.

classic or classical? These two adjectives are not usually interchangeable in modern English. If something is described as *classic* it usually either sets a standard of excellence (*a classic recording*) or perfectly illustrates a particular phenomenon (*a classic case of mistaken identity*). *Classical* generally refers to the world of ancient Greece and Rome (*classical antiquity*), to serious music (*classical composers such as Beethoven and Mozart*) and to long-standing or formerly authoritative forms when contrasted with modern ones (*classical mechanics as opposed to quantum mechanics*). The distinction was considerably less clear-cut, however, in former times.

classical or classic? See classic or classical?

climactic or climatic? These two words are easily confused, but can be just as easily distinguished if the nouns they come from are borne in mind. *Climactic* comes from *climax*: *the climactic moment of the play*. *Climatic* comes from *climate*: *the climatic conditions in northern Borneo.*

climatic or climactic? See climactic or climatic?

coloured See black, Negro, and coloured.

common, mutual, or reciprocal? See mutual, reciprocal, or common?

compare to and compare with Both prepositions, *to* and *with*, can be used following *compare*. Neither is more correct than the other, but a slight distinction can be made in meaning. *To* has traditionally been preferred when the similarity between two things is the point of the comparison and *compare* means 'liken': *I hesitate to compare my own works to those of someone like Dickens*. *With*, on the other hand, suggests that the differences between two things are as important as, if not more important than, the similarities: *We compared the facilities available to most city-dwellers with those available to people living in the country*; *to compare like with like*. When *compare* is used intransitively, it should be followed by *with*: *Our output simply cannot compare with theirs.*

complement or compliment? See compliment or complement?

complement or supplement? Both these words convey the idea of adding something. If one thing *complements* another, however, it goes well with it and enhances it when they are put together: *A hat should complement the rest of one's outfit, not draw attention to itself*. If one thing *supplements* another, it adds to it and reinforces it: *She supplements her income by giving private music lessons*. A good wine may be a *complement* to a meal, but a person might need a dietary *supplement* if some essential element is lacking from the food they normally eat. Note that neither of these words is spelt with an *i*. See also **compliment or complement?**

complementary or complimentary? See complimentary or complementary?

compliment or complement? These two words are easily confused. An expression of admiration is a *compliment*: *My compliments to the chef*; *The remark was intended as a compliment*. A *complement* is an accompaniment to something that sets off its good qualities (*Wine is the perfect complement to a good meal*), or the full number of something (*the ship's complement* (the entire crew, officers and ordinary sailors); *had the usual complement of arms and legs*). The verbs *compliment* and *complement* work in the same way: *May I compliment you on your cooking?*; *Their characters may be different, but they complement each other well.* See also **complement or supplement?**

complimentary or complementary? There is the same difference in meaning between *complimentary* and *complementary* as between their respective nouns. A *complimentary* remark is flattering and expresses admiration. A *complimentary* ticket or *complimentary* copy of a book is given free as a mark of respect. *Complementary*, on the other hand, refers to the relationship between things or people that go well together: *complementary colours.*

comprise *Comprise* is a difficult word to use, because it is close in meaning to, but should be treated differently from, such verbs as *consist (of)*, *compose*, and *make up*. There are two rules to remember. First, a whole *comprises* (consists of or is composed of) its parts; the parts *make up* or *constitute* the whole, but do not *comprise* it: *The collection comprises over 500 items*; *The meal comprised no fewer than fifteen courses.* Secondly, *comprise* should not be followed by *of*, even when it is used in the passive.

confidante(e) or confident? A *confidant* is a person to whom one entrusts one's secrets. It is spelt *confidante* when the person in question is a woman or girl. *Confident* is the adjective meaning 'assured, certain': *We know we're facing tough opposition, but we're confident we can win.*

confident or confidant(e)? See **confidant(e) or confident?**

consensus The only *c* in *consensus* is at the beginning of the word – it is spelt with three *s*'s.

contagious or infectious? A *contagious* disease is spread by direct physical contact with an affected person or by touching something previously touched by an affected person: athlete's foot is a contagious disease. An *infectious* disease is transmitted by airborne microorganisms: chickenpox and influenza are highly *infectious* diseases.

continual or continuous? The classic illustration of the difference between these two closely related adjectives compares a dripping tap (*continual* – occurring constantly, again and again and again with breaks in between) with a flowing tap (*continuous* – continuing in an unbroken stream). It follows from this that *continual* is generally the word to use with a plural noun: (*continual interruptions*;

continual requests for this record), whereas either word may accompany a singular noun: *a continual* (constantly renewed) or *continuous* (unceasing) *bombardment by the enemy.*

continuous or continual? See continual or continuous?

council or counsel? These two words, which are pronounced the same, are sometimes confused. A *council* is an administrative, advisory, or executive body of people: *stand for election to the local council; council workers.* A member of a *council* is a *councillor. Counsel* is a formal word for advice (*gave wise counsel*), and also means a lawyer or group of lawyers (*the counsel for the prosecution*). *Counsel* is also used as a verb meaning to 'advise', and a person who gives advice is a *counsellor.* Nowadays *counsel, counsellor,* and *counselling* are perhaps most frequently used in the context of professional help offered to people who have psychological, social, or personal problems or have had a traumatic experience: *Friends of the murdered teenager are being offered counselling.*

counsel or council? See council or counsel?

credible or credulous? These two words are sometimes confused. Something that is *credible* is believable: *His story seemed perfectly credible, if somewhat bizarre.* Someone who is *credulous,* on the other hand, is too ready to accept anything they are told as true: *Credulous punters were dazzled by promises of a 50 per cent return on their investments.*

credulous or credible? See credible or credulous?

crevasse or crevice? A *crevasse* is a large crack, for example in a mountain, glacier, or ice field. An unlucky mountaineer might fall down a *crevasse.* A *crevice* is a small or tiny crack, where dirt lodges or where one might lose a small coin.

crevice or crevasse? See crevasse or crevice?

criterion and criteria *Criteria* is the plural form of *criterion.* A phrase such as *this criteria* is incorrect. If a thing is judged by such and such *criteria,* then more than one standard of judgment is being applied to it: *Value for money is surely not the only relevant criterion in this case; The criteria by which schools will be judged to have succeeded or failed are set out in the report.*

currant or current? See current or currant?

current or currant? *Current* with an *e* has a wide range of meanings: *electric* *current; strong currents make swimming dangerous; current affairs; the current month. Currant* with an *a* is a fresh or dried berry: *redcurrants; currants and raisins.*

data *Data* is, strictly speaking, a plural noun with a comparatively rare singular form *datum.* With the advent of computers and data processing, *data* has come increasingly to be seen and used as a singular mass noun like *information* or *news: The data is currently being processed.* Traditionalists insist however that this should be: *The data are currently being processed.*

deceitful or deceptive? *Deceitful* implies an intention to deceive. Generally speaking, only people and their words and actions can be described as *deceitful. Deceptive* is applied to things that are able to mislead the unwary: *Appearances can be deceptive.*

deceptive or deceitful? See deceitful or deceptive?

decimate Historically, the word *decimate* refers to the practice in the Roman army of killing every tenth man in a mutinous unit in order to ensure loyalty of the surviving 90 per cent. Although the Latin word for 'tenth' is embedded in *decimate* (compare *decimal, decimetre,* etc.), the word is now accepted by all but the most historically minded as meaning 'kill or destroy a large number or part of something': *The famine decimated the population; The industry has been decimated.* It goes against the grain of the word, however, to link it with a specific quantity (*decimate by 50 per cent*), to apply it to an individual or indivisible thing, or to use it as a substitute for *annihilate* or *exterminate.*

defective or deficient? These two words are close together in meaning and can sometimes be used to describe the same thing, but there is a significant difference between them. *Defective* is applied to functioning things that fail to function properly: a *defective* component is faulty and does not work: *defective brakes. Deficient* primarily means 'lacking' or 'inadequate': a diet *deficient* in the vitamins necessary for healthy growth.

deficient or defective? See defective or deficient?

definite or definitive? These two words are sometimes confused. Both *definite* and *definitive* suggest that something is unlikely to be changed: a *definite* answer is clear, firm, and unambiguous; a *definite* date is one that has been decided on and fixed by the people involved. *Definitive* has connotations of being authoritative and conclusive: the *definitive* answer to a problem is one that solves it once and for all. If someone writes a *definitive* biography or gives us the *definitive* Hamlet, that person's book or performance becomes the standard by which all later ones are judged.

definitive or definite? See **definite or definitive?**

dependant or dependent? In British English *dependent* is an adjective (*dependent on her mother for support; too dependent on overseas imports*) and *dependant* is a noun meaning 'a dependent person' (*not earning enough to be able to provide adequately for her dependants*). In American English the form *dependent* is generally used both as an adjective and as a noun.

dependent or dependant? See **dependant or dependent?**

deprecate or depreciate? The difference in meaning of these two words is being eroded. To *deprecate* is a rather formal verb meaning to 'feel or express moral disapproval of (something)': *She deprecated their lack of courtesy towards the old lady.* To *depreciate* means both to 'fall in value' or 'lower the value of' (*The currency is depreciating*) and, more formally, to 'belittle (somebody or something)': *My efforts were depreciated and I was made to feel useless.* The distinction between expressing disapproval and belittling or disparaging is sometimes so fine that the words *deprecate* and *depreciate* are increasingly being used interchangeably.

depreciate or deprecate? See **deprecate or depreciate?**

derisive or derisory? See **derisory or derisive?**

derisory or derisive? These two words are sometimes confused. Both derive from the word *derision.* The main meaning of *derisory* in modern English is 'ridiculously small or inadequate' (and therefore deserving derision): *a derisory pay offer.* The only meaning of *derisive* is 'mocking' (expressing derision): *derisive jeers.*

desert or dessert? *Dessert* is a noun meaning 'the sweet course in a meal'. The stress in *dessert* is on the second syllable. A barren wilderness is a *desert* (a noun, with stress on the first syllable). The verb to *desert* (stress on the second syllable) means to 'abandon (somebody or something)' or to 'absent oneself from military duty without leave'. To *get one's just deserts* (plural noun, with stress on the second syllable) is to 'be treated as one deserves'.

despatch or dispatch? See **dispatch or despatch?**

dessert or desert? See **desert or dessert?**

dice and die Strictly and historically speaking, *dice* is the plural of *die*. The use of *dice* to mean a single small cube is, however, long established and perfectly acceptable. *Dice* therefore is both the singular and plural form: *to throw the dice* could refer to one or more cubes.

die and dice See **dice and die.**

different from/to/than The combination preferred by traditionalists is *different from*, which keeps *different* in line with to *differ* (*How does this version differ* (or *How is this version different*) *from the previous one?*). *Different to* has, however, been used for a very long time in British English, and most modern authorities on British English accept it as an alternative, at least in anything but very formal writing. *Different than* is in widespread use in American English and is cautiously accepted in British English when followed by a clause: *It's altogether different than I expected* (strictly: *different from what I expected*). *Different than* is not usually acceptable in either British or American English when followed by a noun.

dilemma Strictly, a *dilemma* refers to a situation in which one is faced by two, and only two, equally unpleasant alternatives – as in the slightly old-fashioned phrase *to be on the horns of a dilemma* or in the sentence *We are in a dilemma and can't decide whether to lower prices or risk losing sales.* A situation where there are more than two unpleasant alternatives is, strictly speaking, a *quandary*, though many dictionaries define a *dilemma* as involving 'two or more' unpleasant alternatives. *Dilemma* ought not to be used in careful writing if there is an open choice as to how to deal with a problem or if the alternatives faced are not unpleasant.

disc or disk? *Disc* is the correct spelling of the word in British English, except in the context of computers where the usual American English spelling *disk* is generally preferred: *a slipped disc* but *a disk drive.*

discomfit or discomfort? *Discomfit* originally meant to 'defeat' and from that came to mean to 'thwart': *His attempts at persuasion were of no avail and he retired discomfited.* Because it is usually pronounced the same, or virtually the same way as the commoner and weaker verb *discomfort*, it is now often treated as having the same meaning to 'make (someone) feel uneasy'. Careful users might feel that *discomfort* expresses this idea perfectly adequately and that it is worth keeping the older meaning of *discomfit* alive.

discomfort or discomfit? See **discomfit or discomfort?**

discreet or discrete? Though they are pronounced the same and look very similar, these two words have distinct and different meanings. When used of people, *discreet* means 'careful, reliable, and not likely to gossip' (*Can we rely on her to be discreet?*); when used about actions, it means 'unlikely to attract attention' (*We have made a few discreet enquiries*). *Discrete* is a more technical word meaning 'separate' or 'individually distinct': *The process can be broken down into a number of discrete stages.*

discrete or discreet? See discreet or discrete?

disinterested or uninterested? *Disinterested* is now so often used to mean 'unconcerned' or 'bored' (in other words *uninterested*), that it can easily be misinterpreted when used in its primary meaning in modern English of 'impartial' or 'not motivated by selfishness'. A *disinterested* observer is somebody who is not on anybody's side; an *uninterested* observer simply does not care about what is going on. Careful users of English should try to preserve this distinction.

disk or disc? See disc or disk?

disorient or disorientate? Both forms of the word are correct. *Disorient* is more often used in American English, *disorientate* in British English.

disorientate or disorient? See disorient or disorientate?

dispatch or despatch? Both spellings are equally acceptable; *dispatch* is the commoner of the two.

distinct or distinctive? These two words are sometimes confused. *Distinct* means 'clear', 'clearly noticeable' or 'separate and different': *a distinct air of unease*; *The word has two distinct meanings.* Something that is *distinctive* has its own special and unmistakable character: *a distinctive flavour.*

distinctive or distinct? See distinct or distinctive?

dived and dove *Dove* is an alternative past tense form of to *dive* in American English. It is not used in British English.

double negative The use of *not* together with another negative word as in *I don't know nothing* is not standard English. A less glaring error, but still an error, is the use of the second *not* in *It wouldn't surprise me if it didn't rain.* There the second *not* is simply superfluous: *It wouldn't surprise me if it rained* or, with a different emphasis, *It would surprise me if it didn't rain.*

Double negative forms may be used when the intention is to express a positive idea: *a not unusual* (quite common) *request*; *not unrelated* (there may be a link);

not infrequently (quite often); *One simply cannot not be impressed* (one cannot fail to be). The *not un-* construction is often used to express a slight reservation in the speaker's mind (*Let's say that it was not unimpressive*) and is useful for that purpose. The *cannot not* construction is usually best replaced by something less ungainly: *cannot but be impressed*; *cannot fail to be impressed*. Occasionally more than two negatives in a sequence are encountered: '*This does not imply that sexual relations that don't risk conception are unrelated to personal responsibility and morality*' (Margaret Drabble).

dove and dived See dived and dove.

due to or owing to? The traditional rule of thumb regarding the use of these two phrases is that *owing to* means and can be replaced in a sentence by 'because of', while *due to* means and is replaceable by 'caused by': *Owing to circumstances beyond our control, the departure of the train has had to be delayed*; *The delay is due to circumstances beyond our control*. The basis for this rule is said to be that *due* is an adjective and ought either to be attached to a noun (*a mistake due to ignorance*) or to follow a verb such as *to be* or *to seem*: *Her mistakes were mainly due to inexperience*. *Owing to*, on the other hand, is said to be a compound preposition that can introduce an adverbial phrase: *cancelled owing to rain*; *Owing to an earlier engagement, I reluctantly had to turn down the invitation*. Most modern authorities recommend that the rule should be remembered, while acknowledging that its grammatical basis is shaky (there is no reason why *due to* should not be seen as a compound preposition if *owing to* is one) and that *due to* is so frequently used in the sense of *because of* that many modern dictionaries show it with that sense.

dumb The use of *dumb* in the originally American and informal sense of 'stupid' has become so widespread that great care should be taken with the use of the word in its basic sense 'unable to speak'. If there is any risk of misunderstanding or offence, a word such as *mute* or *speech-impaired* should be used instead.

each other or one another? The traditional rule states that *each other* refers to a relationship between only two people or things (*We love each other and want to get married*), whereas *one another* refers to a relationship between more than two people (*Christ commanded his disciples to love one another*). Modern authorities point out, however, that there is no basis for this rule except tradition and there can be no objection in principle to sentences such as *Harris and Jones mistrusted their boss even more than they mistrusted one another* or *All members of this organization are expected to help each other*.

eatable or edible? Both *eatable* and *edible* mean 'reasonably pleasant to eat': *If you put plenty of sauce on it, it's just about eatable* or *edible*. The primary meaning of *edible*, however, is 'possible to eat', 'non-poisonous': *Are these berries edible?*

economic or economical? *Economic* means first 'relating to economics or an economy' (*an economic crisis; economic indicators*), secondly 'reasonably profitable' (*If the price of tin were to rise, it might become economic to reopen the mine*), and thirdly 'not wasteful'. This third meaning overlaps with that of *economical* (*an economical* or *economic use of resources*). *Economical* is, however, far more widely and commonly used in this sense. A person who is thrifty or a machine that uses resources frugally should be described by preference as *economical*: *a very economical little car*.

economical or economic? See economic or economical?

edible or eatable? See eatable or edible?

effect or affect? See affect or effect?

e.g. or i.e.? The abbreviation *e.g.* means 'for example' (Latin exempli gratia) and usually introduces a brief list of things or people to illustrate a concept: *a computer peripheral, e.g. a printer or a scanner*. The abbreviation *i.e.* means 'that is' (Latin id est). It usually introduces a brief amplification or explanation of a concept: *a computer peripheral, i.e. a device such as a printer or scanner that is connected up to a computer*.

egoism or egotism? The difference between these two words in ordinary use is slight, both being used as equivalents to self-centredness. The more technical uses of the two words give a clue to where the distinction should lie. *Egoism* is also a philosophical belief in selfishness as the only real (and only proper) motive for action: *egotism* is self-obsession, for example the excessive use of *I*, *me*, and *myself* when speaking. *Egoism* is, therefore, best used for *self-seeking* and *egotism* for *self-importance*.

egotism or egoism? See egoism or egotism?

either *Either*, when it is the subject of a sentence, should be followed by a verb in the singular: *Either of the plans is acceptable*. If both subjects are singular, a singular verb should be used (*Either Peter or Andrew is intending to come*) and if both subjects are plural, a plural verb should be used (*Either relatives or friends are welcome*). Where there is a combination of singular and plural subjects, it is best to let the form of the second one determine the form of the verb: *Either he or you have to go*. See also pp. 10–12.

elder or older? *Elder* is used only in comparing the ages of people, usually within a family group (*my elder brother/sister*), and cannot be followed by *than* (*My brother is two years older* – not *elder* – *than I am*). *Older* can be used in place of *elder* and is always used when describing things.

electric or electrical? *Electric* is the adjective generally used to describe specific things that carry or are powered by electricity: *an electric circuit*; *an electric motor*; *an electric toothbrush*. *Electrical* tends to be used with more general or abstract nouns: *an electrical appliance*; *electrical goods*; *electrical engineering*. There is, however, a good deal of overlap. *Electric* is the adjective usually used in figurative contexts: *The atmosphere was electric*.

electrical or electric? See electric or electrical?

elicit or illicit? These two words are sometimes confused. *Elicit* is a verb, usually followed by the preposition *from* meaning 'to call or draw forth (something)': *We managed to elicit from him how he obtained the information*. *Illicit* is an adjective meaning 'illegal' or 'not allowed': *an illicit love affair*.

embarrass *Embarrass* is spelt with two *r*'s and two *s*'s.

emend or amend? See amend or emend?

emotional or emotive? See emotive or emotional?

emotive or emotional? The main meaning of *emotive* is 'arousing strong feelings, appealing to the feelings (rather than reason)': an *emotive* issue is one which people get very worked up about, an *emotive* use of language chooses words specifically for their power to produce an *emotional* response. *Emotional* is the commoner word with a broader range of use; its core sense is 'feeling or expressing emotion'. An *emotional* person is one who is readily affected by and inclined to show emotion. *He made an emotional speech* would mean that the speaker showed in his speech how strongly he himself felt about something. *She made an emotive speech* would suggest that she was more interested in stirring up the crowd than expressing her own feeling.

enormity In modern English *enormity* means both 'huge size' (*the enormity of the task*) and 'outrageousness' or 'an outrageous crime' (*How could such an apparently innocuous person be guilty of these enormities?*). The second and third senses are the older-established ones (though probably less common now), and traditionalists think that the meaning 'huge size' should be rendered either by *enormousness* or another word such as *vastness* or *immensity*.

enquire or inquire? *Enquire* is the commoner British English spelling; *inquire* is generally used in American English. Some British users distinguish between *enquire* ('ask') and *inquire* (into) ('investigate'), but there are no strong grounds for making this distinction.

ensure, assure, or insure? See assure, ensure, or insure?

envelop or envelope? These two words are related and sometimes confused. *Envelop* (always pronounced with the stress on the second syllable *-vel-*) is a verb: *Fog envelops the city; enveloped in a huge black cloak. Envelope* (always pronounced with the stress on the first syllable *en-*) is the noun: *She opened the sealed envelope and drew out the winner's name.*

envelope or envelop? See envelop or envelope?

envisage or envision? These two words are similar in meaning, with the sense of to 'form a mental image of (something) in advance': *The group envisages a future in which all farming will be organic. Envisage* is more commonly used in British English; *envision* in American English. The meaning is quite close to that of *expect*, but the distinction should be preserved, and *expect* should be used in place of *envisage* in sentences such as *A further fall in interest rates is expected* – not *envisaged – next month.*

envision or envisage? See envisage or envision?

equable or equitable? These two words are sometimes confused. *Equable* means 'even-tempered' or 'free from extremes' and is frequently used to describe a person's character: *He has a very equable temperament. Equitable* means 'fair' or 'just': *an equitable system of taxation.*

equitable or equable? See equable or equitable?

erupt or irrupt? These two words are closely related and pronounced the same, but have distinct meanings. *Erupt* is much the commoner word and its basic meaning, taken from Latin, is 'break out' (volcanoes and skin rashes *erupt*), while the basic meaning of *irrupt* is 'break in': *He irrupted into the room demanding to know the whereabouts of his fiancée.* Generally speaking, *erupt* is the verb to use in figurative senses: *Violence erupted in the streets; When presented with the bill, she immediately erupted.*

Eskimo or Inuit? See Inuit or Eskimo?

especially or specially? There is some overlap in the meaning of these two words, but there are also areas in which their meanings should be distinguished. *Especially* means both 'very' (*an especially nice surprise*) and 'above all' (*I was impressed with all the performances, especially Nigel's*). *Specially* means 'in a special way' (*specially cooked using a totally new method*) and, more commonly, 'specifically, for a particular purpose' (*specially trained staff*; *I specially arranged it so that you would be in the same group as Jean*). In a sentence such as the following, however, either *especially* or *specially* could be used: *I made it especially* (or *specially*) *for you.*

-ess As part of the movement to eliminate sexism from language and from people's thinking, the use of the feminizing suffix *-ess* (and similar suffixes such as *-ette* and *-trix*) has, in the late twentieth century, come to be seen as inappropriate and patronizing. The 'male' term is treated as a neutral term with no sexual reference. A woman author should therefore be referred to as an *author*, not an *authoress*, a woman editor as an *editor*, not an *editress* or *editrix*, etc. However, a few forms are retained. Female titles of nobility such as *countess* or *baroness* are still correct. *Manageress* is acceptable when referring to a woman who runs a shop, but not when referring to a woman company executive. A *priestess* is a woman priest of a pre-Christian religion, not an ordained Christian minister. See also pp. 131–4.

etc. The full form of *etc.* is traditionally written as two words *et cetera*, though the one-word variant is now equally acceptable. The first word or syllable of *et cetera* should be pronounced *et* (as in *pet*), not *ek*.

-ever, ever *Whoever, however, whatever*, etc. are written as one word when they mean 'any person who', 'in whichever way', or 'no matter what': *However you decide to do it, make sure you get it done quickly.* But when *ever* is used with a word like *who, how*, or *what* in the intensifying sense of 'on earth', the two words are written separately: *Who ever can it be?*; *What ever did he mean by that?*

exceptionable or exceptional? See **exceptional or exceptionable?**

exceptional or exceptionable? These two words are sometimes confused. *Exceptional* means 'outstanding' (*an exceptional student*) or 'extremely unusual' (*only under exceptional circumstances*). *Exceptionable* is a formal word meaning 'objectionable', 'offensive': *I was not the only one who found her remarks exceptionable.* See also **unexceptional or unexceptionable?**

expedient or expeditious? *Expedient* means 'useful or convenient in the circumstances (often disregarding moral considerations')*: It might be expedient to deny* *any knowledge of the plan.* It is also a noun meaning 'a useful or convenient action or plan': *a short-term expedient to get us out of difficulty.* It is sometimes confused with *expeditious,* which is a formal word meaning 'quick and efficient': *the most expeditious method of sending supplies.*

expeditious or expedient? See expedient or expeditious?

extant or extinct? Though rather similar in spelling, these two words have opposite meanings. *Extant* is a rather formal word meaning 'still in existence': *the only extant copy of the document.* Something that is *extinct* is no longer in existence: *The species is in danger of becoming extinct.*

extinct or extant? See extant or extinct?

factious or fractious? These two words are sometimes confused. *Factious* means 'caused by or producing dissension within a larger body such as a political party; divisive': *factious infighting. Fractious* means 'unruly' or 'quarrelsome': *a fractious three-year-old.*

faint or feint? In the sense of paper with pale horizontal rulings, either spelling may be used, but *feint* is the preferred form: *A4 narrow feint margin paper.*

farther or further? These two spellings are sometimes confused. When referring to physical distance, *farther* and *further* are equally correct: *Penzance lies farther* (or *further*) *west than Truro.* In abstract and figurative senses, *further* is the preferred form: *of no further use; closed until further notice.* As a verb, only *further* is used: *to further God's purposes.*

fatal or fateful? These two words are sometimes confused. *Fatal* means 'causing or resulting in death': *a fatal accident* or 'causing ruin; ending in disaster': *a fatal mistake. Fateful* means 'momentously important': *their fateful meeting.* In the sense of 'having significant, often unpleasant consequences' either word may be used, although *fateful* is more usual: *that fateful day.* Care should be taken to avoid misinterpretation: a *fateful* experiment may change lives; a *fatal* experiment may lead to death.

fateful or fatal? See fatal or fateful?

feasible *Feasible* means 'able to be done or capable of being dealt with': *a feasible project.* Its use to mean 'likely' or 'probable' (*a feasible explanation of the events*) is best avoided.

feint or faint? See faint or feint?

female or feminine? *Female* is used to describe the sex that bears offspring or produces eggs, and plants or flowers that produce seeds: *a female deer is called a doe. Feminine* is used only of human beings, not plants or animals, and describes qualities and behaviour that are traditionally ascribed to women rather than men: *feminine charm. Feminine* is also used in some languages to describe nouns, adjectives, and pronouns in contrast to those that are masculine or neuter.

feminine or female? See female or feminine?

ferment or foment? Either of these two verbs may be used in the sense 'to rouse or incite a state of agitation': *to ferment/foment rebellion*. In their literal senses, the verbs differ: *foment* means 'to apply a hot moist substance to the body' and *ferment* 'to (cause to) undergo a chemical change with the release of bubbles of gas'.

fewer or less? The general rule is to use *fewer* with plural nouns (*fewer people, fewer books*) and *less* with singular nouns (*less time, less work, less sugar*). More precisely, *fewer* is used with people or things that can be counted (*fewer than 100 people came to the meeting*) and *less* is used with quantities and numbers that give a quantity or size: *less than two years ago*. The use of *less* with plural nouns should be avoided: *fewer opportunities*, not *less opportunities*. This incorrect usage is, however, frequently found in informal contexts.

fictional or fictitious? These two words are sometimes confused. *Fictional* means 'of fiction': *fictional heroes*; *fictitious* means 'not real or genuine; false': *He gave a fictitious name to the police.*

fictitious or fictional? See fictional or fictitious?

fish Traditionally, the plural form of *fish* is *fish*: *He caught several fish between 3lb and 7lb in weight; Two rounds of fish and chips.* The plural *fishes* is mainly used when describing different species and in technical contexts: *marine fishes such as the mullet and sea moth.*

flagrant or blatant? See blatant or flagrant?

flair or flare? These two words, which are pronounced the same, are sometimes confused. A *flair* is a natural aptitude or talent, especially one in which intuitive discernment is shown: *a flair for speaking foreign languages.* A *flare* is a device that produces a sudden blaze of light (*fired a flare so that the rescue party could find them*) or a part that spreads outwards (*trousers with wide flares*).

flammable or inflammable? Although *flammable* and *inflammable* may appear to be opposites, in fact they have the same meaning. Since *inflammable* may seem to mean 'not flammable' (from the prefix *in-* meaning 'not' + *flammable*) and because of the risk of fire and danger to life, use of the word *flammable* is increasingly preferred, especially in technical contexts: *highly flammable solvents.* The preferred negative is *non-flammable*: *non-flammable clothing.*

flare or flair? See **flair or flare?**

flaunt or flout? These two words are sometimes confused. To *flaunt* means 'to display ostentatiously': *to flaunt one's superiority*; *to flaunt one's wealth*; *flout* means 'to treat with contemptuous disregard': *flout one's parents' wishes*; *The present laws are widely flouted.* The verb *flaunt* is sometimes incorrectly used for *flout*: *to flaunt the rules* and *to flaunt convention* are wrong.

flounder or founder? *Flounder* means to struggle to move (*floundering in the mud*); *founder* when referring to a ship means 'to sink' and when referring to an animal means 'to go lame'. In their extended senses these two words are sometimes confused, but it is helpful to maintain the following distinctions: *founder* implies complete failure: *The plans foundered after attempts to raise money failed*; while someone who *flounders* is struggling awkwardly: *flounder through a speech.*

flout or flaunt? See **flaunt or flout?**

foment or ferment? See **ferment or foment?**

for- or fore-? These two prefixes are sometimes confused. The prefix *for-* denotes prohibition (*forbid*) or omission (*forsake*). The prefix *fore-* means 'before' (*foresee*). See also **forbear or forebear?**; **forego or forgo?**

forbear or forebear? The verb that means 'refrain from' is spelt *forbear*, with *bear* stressed (*forbore to reply to the accusation*); the noun that means 'ancestor' is spelt either *forebear* or *forbear*, with *for(e)* stressed.

fore- or for-? See **for- or fore?**

forebear or forbear? See **forbear or forebear?**

forego or forgo? The spelling *forego*, meaning 'to go before', is usually only found in the forms *foregoing* (*The foregoing remarks apply in all instances*) and *foregone* (*The victory was a foregone conclusion*). *Forgo*, more rarely spelt *forego*, is a different verb that means 'to refrain from': *The country decided to forgo its right to intervene.*

for ever or forever? When the meaning is 'for all future time' the spelling as two words is preferred: *I will love you for ever*. When the meaning is 'constantly; with persistence' the spelling as one word is more common: *The children are forever asking me for money*.

forever or for ever? See for ever or forever?

forgo or forego? See forego or forgo?

former and latter The *former* refers back to first of two previously mentioned things or people, the *latter* to the second. They are used to avoid tedious or awkward repetition: *Given the choice of being vilified by a newspaper or being ignored by it, I would instinctively opt for the former*. They should never be used when more than two things are listed. In that case use *first*, *first-named*, *second*, *last* etc. They should also be avoided when it is not absolutely and immediately clear what they refer to.

fortuitous or fortunate? Primarily, and from its origins, *fortuitous* means 'occurring by chance': *I had no idea she was going to be there; our meeting was entirely fortuitous*. In modern writing and speech *fortuitous* has also come to refer to things that happen by good fortune, not simply by chance (*The event could not have happened at a more fortuitous time*), but this is a usage that traditionalists seek to avoid. *Fortunate*, by contrast, means 'lucky' or 'auspicious'.

fortunate or fortuitous? See fortuitous or fortunate?

founder or flounder? See flounder or founder?

fractious or factious? See factious or fractious?

-ful The standard modern way of forming the plural of nouns ending in *-ful* is simply to add *-s* to the end of the word: *handfuls*, *pocketfuls*, *cupfuls*, *spoonfuls*. It is generally preferable to the alternative way, where *-s* is added to the end of the first element (*handsful*, *pocketsful*), which may seem quaint or pedantic.

fulsome In its standard modern meaning, *fulsome* is a strongly uncomplimentary word. *Fulsome praise* is embarrassingly excessive or insincerely flattering. Though *fulsome* derives originally from a word meaning 'abundant', its use in a positive sense to mean 'copious', 'very full', or 'lavish' should be avoided for fear of misunderstanding.

further or farther? See farther or further?

gay The primary meaning of *gay* in contemporary English is 'homosexual'. As an adjective or a noun, it is the standard term used by homosexuals to describe themselves and as such has become part of the standard vocabulary of world English. This development has only occurred since the 1960s. Before then, in standard usage, *gay* was an adjective meaning 'cheerful' or 'bright'. These senses are still sometimes used, but care should be taken when using the word with these meanings to avoid misunderstanding.

gender and sex Efforts have been made in recent years to enforce a distinction between *gender* and *sex*, using *gender* to refer to femaleness or maleness in cultural, social, and linguistic contexts and *sex* in biological ones. This distinction is far from being universally applied or accepted, and it is still perfectly in order to speak of 'sex roles' or 'sexual stereotypes'. *Gender* should, however, be used where there is a risk of *sex* being misunderstood to mean 'sexual activity' rather than maleness or femaleness. *Gender* is the correct term to use in language contexts when classifying nouns as masculine, feminine, or neuter.

gibe, gybe, or jibe? *Gibe* means 'a taunting comment' or 'to jeer'. *Gybe* is a technical term in sailing meaning 'to change tack' or (of a sail) 'to swing sideways across the boat'. In British and American English *jibe* is an alternative spelling for *gibe*. In American English *jibe* is also an alternative spelling for *gybe*, besides having a separate meaning 'to accord with'.

gotten The form *gotten* as a past participle of *get* is not used in British English but is common in American English, although often considered to be non-standard. In American English *gotten* is generally used when the sense is 'obtained or acquired': *She's gotten herself a new apartment*, and the past participle *got* may be used when the sense is 'possessed', though Americans usually use *have*: *We already have one. We've already got one.*

-gotten is standard in British English in *ill-gotten*: *ill-gotten gains.*

gourmand or gourmet? These two words are often confused. A *gourmand* is somebody who eats large or excessive amounts of food. It is not a complimentary word. A *gourmet*, on the other hand, is a complimentary word that refers to somebody with a refined taste in food, whose interest is in quality not quantity.

gourmet or gourmand? See **gourmand or gourmet?**

graceful or gracious? These two words are sometimes confused. Both derive from the noun *grace*, but pick up different senses of that word. *Graceful* usually refers to physical movement or shape (*a graceful dancer; the slim, graceful curves of the yacht*). When applied to moral actions (*a graceful apology*), it implies kindness or generosity as well as social deftness. *Gracious* is only used of people's characters or moral acts and usually implies that a person of superior standing is showing kindness, generosity or mercy to someone of lower status (*by gracious permission of Her Royal Highness*).

gracious or graceful? See graceful or gracious?

graffiti *Graffiti* is a plural noun and should, theoretically, always be followed by a plural verb. It comes from Italian and has a regular Italian singular form, *graffito*. In English, however, the singular form is rare and its use is apt to seem pedantic. The form *graffiti* is therefore commonly used with a singular verb to refer to a single drawing (*a graffiti*) or to drawings collectively: *Graffiti is a good way of telling people your message.*

gray or grey? See grey or gray?

grey or gray? *Grey* is the correct spelling in British English; *gray* is the correct spelling for the same word in American English.

grill or grille? A set of metal bars on which food is cooked is a *grill*. A restaurant serving grilled food is a *grill*, and the upper heating element in a cooker is also a *grill*. Either spelling, however, can be used when the word means a mesh or grating, for example, on the front of a car (*a radiator grille* or, less commonly, *grill*).

grille or grill? See grill or grille?

gybe, gibe, or jibe? See gibe, gybe, or jibe?

hail or hale? These two words, which are pronounced the same, are sometimes confused. To *hail* someone or something is to call out to them or summon them (*hail a taxi*), or to acclaim them (*hailed as the new Fred Astaire*; *hail, Caesar!*). To *hail* from a place is to come or originate from it. Icy raindrops fall as *hail*, and someone can *hail* missiles or abuse down on someone else. To *hale* is a rather literary or old-fashioned verb meaning to haul or to compel to come (*haled him before the magistrate*). As an adjective, *hale* means 'in good health' (*hale and hearty*).

hale or hail? See hail or hale?

hanged or hung? *Hung* is the correct form of the past tense and past participle of *to hang*, except in the sense 'to execute by hanging'. In this sense the form *hanged* (*was hanged at Tyburn*) is preferable, although *hung* is often found (*hung, drawn, and quartered*). *Hanged* is always used for a mild rather dated oath: *(I'll be) hanged if I know!*

hardly *Hardly* should not be used as the adverbial form of *hard*; *hard* itself performs this function (*hit someone hard*; *be hard pressed*). *Hardly* means the same as *barely* or *scarcely* and, like them, has an in-built negative effect, so that *I can hardly see* and *hardly anything* are correct, and *I can't hardly see* and *nothing hardly* are incorrect. When *hardly* begins a sentence, the usual order of auxiliary verb and subject is reversed: *Hardly had the meeting begun, when trouble erupted.* Note that the clause following this construction should begin with *when* or *before*, not *than*.

Hindi or Hindu? These two words are sometimes confused. *Hindi* is a language spoken in northern India and is one of India's two official languages. A *Hindu* is a follower of Hinduism, the main religion of India.

Hindu or Hindi? See Hindi or Hindu?

historic or historical? These two words are sometimes confused. A *historic* event is one that is very important or memorable and thought likely to be recorded as such in history. A *historical* event is any event that took place in the past.

historical or historic? See historic or historical?

hoard or horde? These two words are pronounced the same but have different meanings. A *hoard* is a store or collection, often of valuable things (*a pirate's hoard*). A *horde* is a large and sometimes unruly group of people (*resorts overrun by hordes of tourists*).

homely or homy? In British English, *homely* means 'reminiscent of home and the simple life' – familiar, unpretentious, or sympathetic and kind. In American English, however, its main meaning is 'not good-looking' (*She didn't look like a film star, in fact she was downright homely*). The word *homy* (usually *homey* in American English) means 'comfortable and relaxed, like a home' (*a homy atmosphere*).

homy or homely? See homely or homy?

hopefully Though the use of *hopefully* as a sentence adverb in the sense, 'it is to be hoped (that); let us hope' in sentences such as *Hopefully, they'll be home before it gets dark* is still decried by traditionalists in Britain and America, it has generally established itself as part of normal usage. It is interesting to note, however, that opposition to such words as *thankfully* and *regrettably* with a similar function has not been expressed. So while it may appear unnecessarily restrictive to reserve the use of the word to such constructions as *She eyed the plate of jam tarts hopefully* it is probably better to limit the sentence adverb use of *hopefully* to informal or spoken contexts.

Care should be taken over the position of *hopefully*. When *hopefully* is placed immediately in front of the verb, ambiguity may result: *They will hopefully wait for an answer* may mean either 'I hope they will wait for an answer' or 'they will wait for an answer with hope'. *Hopefully they will wait for an answer* and *They will wait for an answer hopefully* are less ambiguous.

horde or hoard? See **hoard or horde?**

human or humane? *Human* means 'belonging or relating to human beings as a race' (*human nature, human society*). *Humane* has a more limited use. It means 'showing compassion or kindness' (*humane treatment of animals*) or, more rarely, 'culturally broad and liberal' (*a humane education*).

humane or human? See **human or humane?**

hung or hanged? See **hanged or hung?**

hyper- or hypo-? These two prefixes are easily confused. *Hyper-* means 'excessively' or 'higher than normal': *hypercritical, hypersensitive, hyperinflation*; *hypertension* is abnormally high blood pressure. *Hypo-* means 'below' or 'less than normal': a *hypodermic* needle pierces beneath the skin, *hypotension* is abnormally low blood pressure. Note that someone who is exposed to extreme cold suffers from *hypothermia*. The word *hyperthermia* also exists, but refers to a condition in which the body temperature is abnormally high.

hypo- or hyper-? See **hyper- or hypo-?**

i.e. or e.g.? See **e.g. or i.e.?**

if and whether *If* and *whether* can often be used interchangeably: *He asked if* (or *whether*) *he could come too*; *I doubt whether* (or *if*) *we'll have time*. *Whether* should be preferred in more formal writing, however, and where there is a danger that using *if* could be ambiguous. *Let me know if he calls* could mean 'tell me that he's calling, when and if he calls' or 'tell me (afterwards) whether he called or not'.

illicit or elicit? See **elicit or illicit?**

immoral or amoral? See amoral or immoral?

immunity or impunity? *Immunity* and *impunity* have similar meanings and should not be confused. *Immunity* means a state of being protected against or exempt from something that could affect others: *immunity from a disease, immunity from prosecution*. *Impunity* has a more restricted use and is almost always found in the phrase *with impunity*, meaning 'without suffering punishment or bad consequences': *Are we going to let them break all the rules with impunity?*

impact Many traditionalists dislike the use of the verb *impact on* in figurative contexts – *Higher interest rates have impacted on consumer spending* – preferring the use of such verbs as *affect* or *influence* instead. *Impact* is pronounced differently depending on whether it is used as a noun or a verb. The stress in *impact* the noun (*braced themselves for the impact*) is on the first syllable *im-*. The stress in verbal use (*How will this impact on our plans for expansion?*) is on the second syllable.

imperial or imperious? *Imperial* means 'relating to an empire or emperor' (*an imperial edict; imperial robes*). *Imperious* refers to a person's character or behaviour and is usually uncomplimentary; it means 'haughty' or 'overbearing' (*demanding in an imperious tone to be served immediately*).

imperious or imperial? See imperial or imperious?

impinge or infringe? *Impinge* is a formal word meaning 'to affect' (often adversely) and is always followed by the preposition *on* or *upon*: *impinge upon someone's private life*. *Infringe* is often used in the same way and with the same meaning: *infringe on the rights of others*. *Infringe* is also and, according to some traditionalists, more properly used with a direct object meaning 'to violate': *to infringe the regulations/a patent/someone's rights*.

imply or infer? These two words are sometimes confused, though they in fact are opposite in meaning. To *imply* something is to suggest it by what you say without stating it explicitly: *She implied that I was untrustworthy*. To *infer* something is to deduce it from what someone says, even though they have not explicitly said as much: *I inferred from her remark that she thought me untrustworthy*. That said, the use of *infer* to mean the same as *imply* has become increasingly common.

impracticable or impractical? See impractical or impracticable?

impractical or impracticable? These two words are very close in meaning, but it is useful to distinguish between them. A plan that is *impractical* may be fine in theory but is difficult to carry out or of little use in practice. An *impracticable* plan is, quite simply, impossible to carry out. A person can be described as *impractical* ('not good at ordinary tasks' or 'not down-to-earth'), but not as *impracticable*.

impunity or immunity? See immunity or impunity?

inapt or inept? These two words are close together in meaning and sometimes confused. *Inapt* means 'inappropriate' (*an inapt quotation*); *inept* means 'clumsy' or 'incompetent'. A person can be described as *inept* but not, usually, as *inapt*.

incredible or incredulous? These two words are sometimes confused. Something that is *incredible* is impossible or difficult to believe (*a frankly incredible story*), whereas someone who is *incredulous* does not or cannot believe what they are told or witnessed (*received my explanation with an incredulous stare*). *Incredible* is also used informally to mean 'amazing' or 'wonderful': *an incredible piece of good luck*.

incredulous or incredible? See incredible or incredulous?

indexes or indices? The plural of *index* in its common sense of an alphabetical guide or catalogue is *indexes* (*a book with two indexes; card indexes*). In technical uses, especially in mathematics and economics, the plural is more commonly *indices*: *indices of economic progress*.

indices or indexes? See indexes or indices?

inept or inapt? See inapt or inept?

infectious or contagious? See contagious or infectious?

infer or imply? See imply or infer?

inflammable or flammable? See flammable or inflammable?

infringe or impinge? See impinge or infringe?

ingenious or ingenuous? These two words are easy to confuse. *Ingenious* means 'clever' or 'effective', especially in an original or surprising way: *an ingenious method of recycling household waste*. *Ingenuous* means 'innocent', 'artless', or 'guileless': *too ingenuous to imagine that they might not mean what they said*.

ingenuous or ingenious? See ingenious or ingenuous?

inhuman or inhumane? These are both words of condemnation: *inhuman* is, however, a considerably stronger one than *inhumane. Inhumane* means 'lacking compassion or kindness' (*inhumane treatment of animals*). To describe someone's treatment of animals or other people as *inhuman*, however, suggests that it is deliberately cruel or shockingly neglectful and shows none of the qualities that are desirable in a human being: *inhuman torture of prisoners.*

inhumane or inhuman? See inhuman or inhumane?

inquire or enquire? See enquire or inquire?

insurance or assurance? See assurance or insurance?

insure, ensure, or assure? See assure, ensure, or insure?

intense or intensive? These two words, though similar in form and meaning, have different areas of use. *Intense* usually means 'extreme': *intense heat; under intense pressure to find a solution.* It can also be used to describe people who are serious and feel emotion deeply (*a very intense young man*) and, when used in connection with people and their activities, usually suggests a high degree of personal commitment or emotional involvement: *an intense effort to stave off bankruptcy. Intensive*, on the other hand, is used more objectively and means 'highly concentrated', suggesting organized effort more than personal involvement: *intensive farming; conducted an intensive search of the area.*

intensive or intense? See intense or intensive?

inter-, intra-, or intro-? These three prefixes are easily confused. *Inter-* means 'between': *international; intermarriage. Intra-* means 'within': *an intrauterine device. Intergalactic* travel would go from one galaxy to another; *intragalactic* travel would take place within a single galaxy. *Intro-* means 'inwards': *introspection; an introvert.* The *Internet* is the system of (or between) computer networks throughout the world; an *intranet* is an internal network of computer communications within an organization.

interment or internment? These two words are sometimes confused. *Interment* is a formal word for 'burial'; *interment* is the confinement of people who have not committed a crime but are thought to constitute a possible danger to the state, especially in wartime.

internment or interment? See interment or internment?

intra-, inter-, or intro-? See inter-, intra-, or intro-?

intro-, intra-, or inter-? See inter-, intra-, or intro-?

Inuit or Eskimo? The indigenous peoples of the Arctic prefer to be known as the *Inuit* rather than *Eskimos*. The term *Eskimo* is still sometimes used, but *Inuit* should be preferred.

inveigh or inveigle? These two words are sometimes confused. *Inveigh* is always followed by the preposition *against*. To *inveigh against* someone or something is to speak or write about them in a very bitter, hostile and condemnatory way: *inveighed against the enemies of the working class*. *Inveigle* is followed by a direct object and means 'to use cunning or deceitful methods in order to get someone to do something': *inveigled her into parting with most of her savings*.

inveigle or inveigh? See inveigh or inveigle?

irregardless *Irregardless* is a non-standard word that means 'regardless'. It was probably formed from joining *irrespective* and *regardless*.

irrupt or erupt? See erupt or irrupt?

-ise or -ize? Either spelling is correct, in British English, for most of the many verbs, old and new, that end with this suffix: *criticise* or *criticize*; *privatize* or *privatise*. The *-ize* form reflects the original Greek spelling *-ize*, whereas the *-ise* form reflects an intermediate spelling in French, from which many of these words are derived. Many British people, British newspapers, and British English spellcheckers prefer the *-ise* form. The *-ize* form is, however, standard in American English and totally acceptable in British English, so that it has come to be regarded as the world English norm and, as such, has been adopted by most modern dictionaries and many British publishers. There are, however, a number of verbs which in their standard world English form must end in *-ise*, either because they are related to other words with an *-ise* spelling (such as *advertisement*) or because the ending is not the active suffix *-ize/ise* at all but a longer element such as *-cise* (typically meaning 'cut') or *-vise* (typically meaning 'see'): for example, *advertise, advise, chastise, comprise, compromise, despise, devise, enfranchise, excise, exercise, franchise, improvise, merchandise, revise, supervise, surmise, surprise*, and *televise*.

its or it's? Note the difference between these two forms. *Its* is the possessive form of *it* (*The bottle has lost its top*; *my car is in for its MOT*): it has no apostrophe *s*, but neither has *his* or *ours*. *It's* is a shortened form of *it is* or *it has*: *it's raining*; *it's been an awful day*. See also pp. 170–71.

-ize or -ise? See -ise or -ize?

jibe, gibe, or gybe? See gibe, gybe, or jibe?

judgement or judgment? Either spelling is acceptable in all varieties of English. In British English, however, *judgement* is often used (with *judgment* in legal contexts), whereas in American English *judgment* is employed in all contexts.

judgment or judgement? See judgement or judgment?

judicial or judicious? These two words are sometimes confused. A *judicial* decision is one made by a court of law or by a judge; a *judicious* decision is one that shows wisdom and good judgment. A person can be described as *judicious* but not as *judicial. Judicial* is typically used in phrases such as *a judicial enquiry, judicial proceedings*, and *the British judicial system.*

judicious or judicial? See judicial or judicious?

junction or juncture? A *junction* is a place at which two or more things join (*a road junction; a junction box*). *Juncture* is a fairly formal word meaning 'a point in time' especially one at which important developments are taking place: *at this critical juncture the USA decided to intervene. At this juncture* is sometimes used to mean simply 'at this moment' or 'now'. This is a cliché and should be avoided.

juncture or junction? See junction or juncture?

kind, sort, and type Though quite common in casual speech, constructions such as *these kind of things, those type of people* are ungrammatical and should be avoided in careful speech or writing. *This sort of thing* is a perfectly acceptable phrase; problems arise when a plural form is required because the singular form does not seem inclusive enough. *These sorts of thing* or *those types of books* are grammatically correct. Understood strictly, however, these phrases imply that there are several different categories of thing or book involved. Probably the best and most elegant way of overcoming the difficulty is to reverse the construction: *books of that kind* (many books, all of the same type) or *books of those kinds* (many books of several different types).

latter and former See former and latter.

lay or lie? These two words are sometimes confused, especially since the past tense of *lie* is *lay*. To *lay* (past tense *laid*, past participle *laid*) usually takes a direct object and describes the action of putting something down: *to lay a carpet; to lay an egg; she laid herself down on the bed.* To *lie* (past tense *lay*, past participle *lain*) never takes a direct object and describes the state of resting on something: *I think* *better lying down; he lay groaning on the sofa; the stones had lain undisturbed for centuries.* To *lie* meaning 'to tell untruths' is a completely separate verb – its past tense and past participle is *lied.*

learn *Learn* should never be used to mean 'teach'. *Learn* never takes a personal pronoun or a person's name as a direct object: *I learnt my acting skills from her; she taught me to act.*

leave or let? There are one or two phrases in which *leave* is often used as a substitute for *let* with the meaning 'allow (someone) to do something', especially *leave alone, leave go,* and *leave be.* These are acceptable in conversational English, but *leave go* and *leave be* should not be used in formal writing. *Leave someone alone* needs special care since it can mean both *let someone alone* (not interfere with them) and, literally, to leave someone on their own. Compare: *If you'd left your little brother alone, he wouldn't have hit you* and *How could you just go off and leave your little brother alone?*

lend, loan, and borrow These words are sometimes confused. To *lend* means 'to allow someone to take and use something that is yours'. It can be followed by a personal pronoun or a person's name as indirect object: *They lent me their lawn mower.* To *borrow* means the opposite: 'to take and use something that belongs to someone else': *I borrowed their lawn mower.* To show who lent you the thing you borrowed, use *from*: *I borrowed ten pounds from Bob.* To *borrow* something *off* someone is only acceptable in very informal English. To *loan* means the same as to *lend* and is mainly used with reference to money: *The bank loaned them £100,000. Loan* is also a noun: *a loan of £10,000; requested the loan of our lawn mower.*

less or fewer? See fewer or less?

lest *Lest* should be followed by a verb in the subjunctive form (pp. 47–8) or by a verb formed with *should*: *lest it rain before we are finished; lest there should be any doubt about the seriousness of the situation.*

let or leave? See leave or let?

liable, apt, and likely See apt, liable, and likely.

liaison This word is often misspelt. It has two *i*'s and one *a.*

licence or license? In British English *licence* is the only spelling for the noun meaning 'freedom of action' or 'a document authorizing the holder to do or possess something': *a licence to kill; May I see your licence, please?* The spelling for the equivalent verb in British and American English is *license*: *You are only licensed to drive vehicles in categories C, D, and E.* Thus also *licensed premises* and a *licensed restaurant* – one that has been granted a licence to serve alcoholic drink. In American English, the spelling *license* is used for both the verb and the noun.

license or licence? See licence or license?

lie or lay? See lay or lie?

lightening or lightning? See lightning or lightening?

lightning or lightening? The flash in a thunderstorm is *lightning* without an *e*. *Lightening* comes from the verb lighten: if you see a *lightening* in the sky, dawn is about to break or the clouds are about to part.

like and such as Sometimes the use of *like* can be ambiguous: *a boy like you* could mean either 'a boy, for example, you' or 'a boy who resembles you'. The ambiguity can be avoided if *like* is used to introduce a comparison and *such as* is used to introduce an example. However, in the latter case, the use of *such as* is normally restricted to more formal contexts.

-like Adjectives ending in *-like* may be written with or without a hyphen (*catlike, hair-like*) although common compound adjectives ending in *-like* are usually written without a hyphen (*childlike, lifelike*). When *-like* is attached to a word ending in *-ll* a hyphen is added (*bell-like*). When the root word ends in a single *l*, the spelling with or without a hyphen is permissible: *owllike* or *owl-like*.

likely *Likely* is not used on its own as an adverb meaning 'probably' in British English. A sentence such as *They will likely try again* is acceptable in American but not in British English. However, phrases such as *quite likely, more than likely* and *very likely* present no problems: *They have very likely been delayed*; *She will more than likely call again*. See also **apt, liable, and likely**.

likely, liable, and apt See apt, liable, and **likely**.

liqueur or liquor? These two words are sometimes confused. A *liqueur* is a particular type of alcoholic drink that is strong, sweet and usually drunk in small quantities at the end of a meal: *Cointreau and Tia Maria are popular liqueurs. Liquor* is alcoholic drink in general: *He took the pledge in 1995 and hasn't touched a drop of liquor since.*

liquor or liqueur? See liqueur or liquor?

literally *Literally* is commonly used to show that a familiar phrase or idiom is especially relevant or should be understood in a real or physical sense: *He was literally red with anger.* It is also used informally as a kind of intensifier in a metaphor, in which the literal meaning is apparently absurd: *He was literally beside himself with anger.* This last use is justifiable in linguistic terms, but is controversial.

loan See lend, loan, and borrow.

loath, loth, or loathe? *Loath* and *loth* are alternative spellings of the same word, an adjective meaning 'reluctant': *She was very loath to part with the money. Loath* is the preferred spelling in modern English. *Loathe* is a verb meaning 'to dislike intensely': *I absolutely loathe greasy food.*

loathe, loath, or loth? See loath, loth, or loathe?

loose or lose? The spelling of these two words can cause problems. *Loose*, spelt with *-oo-* and pronounced with a soft *s* to rhyme with *goose*, is mainly used as an adjective meaning 'not tight': *a loose-fitting dress; the knot has worked loose. Lose*, with one *o* and pronounced to rhyme with *whose*, is a verb meaning 'to be unable to find': *I'm always losing my spectacles.*

lose or loose? See loose or lose?

loth, loath, or loathe? See loath, loth, or loathe?

lour or lower? See lower or lour?

lower or lour? Either spelling is possible for this verb which means 'to look threatening' or 'to frown': *a lowering* or *louring sky full of black clouds.* In this sense they are pronounced to rhyme with 'tower'.

luxuriant or luxurious? These two words are sometimes confused. *Luxuriant* means 'growing thickly and abundantly': *luxuriant vegetation.* It can also, less commonly, mean 'highly ornamented': *luxuriant prose. Luxurious* is the adjective connected with the ordinary sense of *luxury*: *the sort of luxurious accommodation you would expect from a five-star hotel.*

luxurious or luxuriant? See luxuriant or luxurious?

male or masculine? *Male* is used to describe the sex that does not bear offspring, and plants or flowers that do not produce fruit or seeds: *a male deer is called a stag. Masculine* is used only of human beings, not plants or animals, and describes qualities and behaviour that are characteristic of or traditionally ascribed to men rather than women. *He doesn't think pink sheets are very masculine. Masculine* is also used in some languages to describe nouns, adjectives, and pronouns, in contrast to those that are feminine or neuter.

man *Man* can be used without an indefinite or definite article to mean the human species or the whole human race: *Man is a political animal.* This usage is, however, felt by many people to be inappropriate in the modern age since it suggests that the male defines or embodies the species, ignoring the female. *Man* should not be used unthinkingly in any context to mean 'men and women' or 'the human race'. Substitutes are *humanity, human beings, the human race, humans, humankind, people*, or, occasionally, *individual* or *person*: *one person, one vote.* Many compounds with 'man' (and 'woman') can be altered to gender-inclusive forms: *man-hours* to *working hours*; *man-made* to *artificial* or *synthetic*; *cameraman* and *camerawoman* to *camera operator*; *fireman* and *firewoman* to *firefighter*; *policeman* and *policewoman* to *police officer*. See also pp. 131–4.

mankind The same objection is often raised to the use of *mankind* to mean 'human beings as a race or species' as to the use of *man* in the same sense: it seems sexist. The expressions *humanity, humankind, human beings*, and *the human race* will generally fit neatly into any context where *mankind* might be employed and should be preferred. See also man and pp. 131–4.

masculine or male? See male or masculine?

masterful or masterly? Both these words can be used to mean 'having or showing the skill of a master', but *masterly* should be preferred in this sense: *a masterly performance*; *a quite masterly exposition of a very difficult topic.* The main sense of *masterful* is 'showing strength or dominance': *a masterful type who took charge in any situation.* In modern usage *masterly* cannot be used in this sense.

masterly or masterful? See masterful or masterly?

may or can? See can or may?

media *Media* is a plural form, the plural of *medium*: *Television is a medium*; *Television and radio are media.* The form *a media* is grammatically incorrect. The form *the media* meaning 'all the various institutions that spread news and information' should be followed by a plural verb: *The media have shown little interest in this event.* '*He looks forward to an age where the media is redundant*' (*The Guardian*) is incorrect. It is perfectly acceptable usage to use *media* in front of another noun: *a media event.*

meter or metre? In British English a *metre* is a measurement of length equal to 100 centimetres, while a measuring instrument is a *meter*: *to read the meter.* Likewise, in British English, the rhythmic pattern of a line of poetry is its *metre*, though the words for specific types of *metre* end in *-er*: *hexameter*; *iambic pentameter*. In American English the spelling *meter* is used for all these senses.

metre or meter? See meter or metre?

militate or mitigate? These two words are sometimes confused. *Militate* is related in form and meaning to *militant* and *military*, and its earliest meaning is 'to serve as a soldier' or 'to fight'. It is usually followed by *against* and in modern English means 'to exert a powerful influence against' or 'to make very difficult or unlikely': *Present circumstances militate against an early resumption of peace talks. Mitigate* is followed by a direct object and means 'to make less severe': *measures intended to mitigate the harshness of prison life.*

millennium *Millennium* is spelt with two *l*'s and two *n*'s, separated by an *e*.

minuscule *Minuscule* meaning 'tiny' or 'a small letter' is spelt with one *i* and two *u*'s. It can never be spelt *miniscule.*

Miss, Mrs, or Ms? See Ms, Mrs, or Miss?

misuse or abuse? See abuse or misuse?

mitigate or militate? See militate or mitigate?

momentary or momentous? *Momentary* means 'lasting only a moment or a very short space of time': *a momentary hesitation*; *a momentary lapse of concentration.* It should not be confused with *momentous,* which means 'very important' or 'having far-reaching consequences': *a momentous decision*; *a momentous event.*

momentous or momentary? See momentary or momentous?

moral or morale? These two words are sometimes confused. *Moral*, the adjective, with a stress on the first syllable, means 'relating to principles of right and wrong' (*moral judgments*) or 'showing a proper sense of right and wrong' (*a moral person*). As a noun, *moral* usually means 'the moral lesson to be drawn from a story'. *Morale*, with a stress on the second syllable, means 'the general mood of a group of people': *The general decided to lay on a concert party to boost the troops' morale.*

morale or morale? See moral or morale?

Mrs, Ms, or Miss? See Ms, Mrs, or Miss?

Ms, Mrs, or Miss? Traditionally, the title *Miss* was used by a woman before marriage together with her maiden name, while *Mrs* was used after marriage together with her husband's surname: *Miss Jones became Mrs Smith when she married.* From the 1950s onwards, the title *Ms* began to be used by women who did not wish to disclose their marital status, thought it irrelevant, or felt that an all-purpose title for women equivalent to *Mr* was needed. This title was also used by some people when writing to or addressing women whose marital status was unknown: it is very useful for this purpose. *Ms* is gradually acquiring wider acceptance, especially among younger people. Some people, however, dislike its associations with feminism and insist on using or being addressed by the traditional titles.

mutual, reciprocal, or common? These three words are sometimes confused. *Mutual* and *reciprocal* can both mean 'directed towards each other'. Two people can be said to share *a mutual* or *reciprocal hatred*, if they hate each other. They can also, however, be said to share *a common hatred* if they both independently hate the same other thing or other person. Because *common* has several other meanings apart from 'shared', *mutual* is sometimes used where the strictly correct word would be *common*. The best-known example is *our mutual friend*, meaning 'your friend as well as mine', a phrase that is now generally acceptable and reinforced by the title of Dickens' novel, whereas *our common friend* might be thought to mean 'our vulgar friend'.

native There are few problems with *native* used as an adjective: *native land*, *native language*, and *native Liverpudlian* are all unexceptionable. It is with the noun that the trouble starts. The word *native* is extremely offensive if used to mean simply 'a non-white person', and scarcely less so now if used to mean 'an original (and by implication usually uncivilized) inhabitant of a country'. The only currently safe use of the noun *native* is in the meaning 'a person who was born in a particular place': *I am a native of Hertfordshire.* See also Native American.

Native American This is now generally accepted as the correct term to use for a person whose ancestors lived in America before the arrival of Europeans. The term *Red Indian* for a Native (North) American should be avoided. See also American Indian.

naught or nought? In British English *nought* is the usual spelling for the word meaning '0' or 'zero': *a one followed by six noughts.* This word is usually spelt *naught* in American English. In both British English and American English *naught* is a rather literary term meaning 'nothing': *naught for your comfort*; *come to naught*.

Negro See **black, Negro,** and **coloured.**

neither *Neither*, like *either*, should be followed by a verb in the singular when it is the subject of a sentence: *Neither of them was caught*. If two or more particular things or people are being mentioned, *neither* is followed by *nor*, not by *or*: *Neither Janet nor her sister is coming*. If both subjects are singular, a singular verb should be used (*Neither Peter nor Andrew is intending to come*), and if both subjects are plural, a plural verb should be used (*Neither relatives nor friends were made to feel welcome*). Where there is a combination of singular and plural subjects, it is best to let the form of the second one determine the form of the verb: *Neither he nor you are entirely blameless*. See also p. 11.

non or non-? *Non* as a prefix is generally used with a hyphen in British English to preserve the identity of the word elements, especially in forms such as *non-event* and *non-native*, and in longer words such as *non-productive* and *non-professional*. In American English, and increasingly in British English, *non-* words are spelt as single words: *nonstandard*; *nonviolence*. Some words have become familiar as single words, for example *nonconformist* and *nonentity*.

non- and un- See **un- and non-.**

none *None* can be used with a singular or a plural verb, depending on the meaning. To emphasize the individuals in a group, the singular is used, and *none* is equivalent to 'not one': *None of them is a professional actor*. To emphasize a group or collection of people or things, the plural is more usual and *none* is equivalent to the plural meaning of 'not any': *None of them are professional actors*. A singular construction can often sound formal or pedantic: *None of them is over eighteen*. When *none* is used of non-countable things, it is treated as singular and is equivalent to the singular meaning of 'not any': *None of the cheese is left*.

non-social See **antisocial, asocial, non-social, unsociable or unsocial?**

notable or noticeable? These two words are close in meaning but there is nevertheless a clear distinction between them. *Notable* means 'worthy of notice' and thus, often, 'important' or 'remarkable': *a notable achievement*. *Noticeable*, on the other hand, means 'visible' or 'perceptible': *a noticeable improvement in quality*. A *notable difference* between two things would generally be a large as well as a significant one, whereas a *noticeable* difference might only be very small.

noticeable or notable? See notable or noticeable?

nought or naught? See naught or nought?

number of The phrase *a number of* meaning 'some' or 'several' should be used with a verb in the plural: *There are a number of things to discuss; A number of you, I know, disagree.* When *number* means 'the overall quantity in' *the number of* is used with a singular verb: *The number of meningitis cases is increasing.*

of *Of* should never be spoken, let alone written, following *could, should, would,* or *must.* For example, *I should have told you* can become *I should've told you* in colloquial speech or writing, but *I should of told you* is always wrong.

official or officious? A letter, a document, or an announcement can be *official* ('written or made by someone in authority'). Only a person or their words or behaviour can be *officious* in its ordinary meaning. It is an uncomplimentary word meaning 'bossy and interfering'.

officious or official? See official or officious?

older or elder? See elder or older?

one *One* is a useful word for making statements that apply to everyone in general and no one in particular: *One seldom makes that particular mistake twice. You* can serve the same purpose (*You can't make an omelette without breaking eggs*) and sounds less formal and impersonal. It must be clear, however, that *you* is intended to have a general meaning and does not refer to a particular person or particular people. *One* does sound rather formal, but it does not sound too affected unless it is being used in place of *I.*

one another or each other? See each other or one another?

only The notion that the adverb *only* should always be placed next to the word in the sentence that it refers to is a superstition that runs counter to the natural position of such modifying words in English (compare *often* and *usually*). The typical position is between the subject and the verb in sentences such as *I only drink wine at weekends* and after an auxiliary verb in sentences such as *I can only lend you a pound.* (Compare *I often drink wine at weekends* and *I can usually lend you a pound.*) In ordinary conversation, the tone of voice makes it clear that *only* refers forward to the phrase *at weekends* and not more immediately to the words *drink* or *wine*, and that the sense is not (for example) *I drink wine at weekends but I don't cook with it* or *I drink wine at weekends but not beer.* In more formal written English, especially in legal documents, the position of *only* becomes more important, because in these contexts the language needs to be precise. So a contract, for example, might include the words *This penalty will be applied only if the contractor has been warned in writing at least three weeks in advance of the due date.* But in ordinary English *only* would go after the verb *will.*

onto There is no objection to spelling *onto* as a single word when it means 'into a position on': *The book fell onto the floor.* Some people have reservations about using *onto* after a verb that is often followed by the preposition *on.* In a sentence such as *We walked on to the end of the lane* ('until we reached'), *onto* would be incorrect. Compare *We walked onto the end of the red carpet* ('we walked forward and stood on'), in which *onto* is correct. Sentences such as *She latched on to the idea at once* and *I want to move on to another topic* are, however, a grey area. *Onto* is increasingly being used in them, but the safer option is to use *on to.*

or When *or* connects two nouns that are both singular a verb following them must be singular: . . . *if your money or your luggage is stolen.* If it connects two plural nouns, the verb is plural: . . . *when your relatives or your friends come to visit.* If *or* separates a singular and a plural noun or two different personal pronouns, the rule is that the verb should agree with whichever comes second: *What if my money or my valuables go missing?*; *Either you or he has made a mistake.*

oral or aural? See aural or oral?

orient or orientate? Both forms of the word are correct. *Orient* is more often used in American English, *orientate* in British English.

orientate or orient? See orient or orientate?

-orous See -our, -orous.

ought The negative form of *ought* is *ought not* which can be shortened to *oughtn't*: *Oughtn't we to let them know in advance?* The form *didn't ought* is not standard English. *Ought* should always be connected to a following verb by *to*, even in a sentence such as: *They ought to and could have explained things better.*

-our, -orous Words in British English whose final syllable is spelt *-our*, drop the *u* before the *r* to form adjectives ending in *-ous*: *glamour* but *glamorous*; *humour* but *humorous.* See also p. 139.

out The use of *out* to mean *out of* is standard in American English but seems rather casual in British English and is better avoided in formal writing or speech: *She simply turned and walked out of* (American also *walked out*) *the door.*

overlay or overlie? *Overlay*, like *lay*, takes a direct object and refers to an action, the action of putting something on top of something else: *They overlaid the wood with gold leaf. Overlie*, like *lie*, refers to a state, that of being on top of something else: *A thick covering of snow overlies the lawn and flowerbeds. Overlie* has the past tense *overlay*. Note that, unlike *lie*, *overlie* takes a direct object. See also **lay or lie?**

overlie or overlay? See **overlay or overlie?**

owing to or due to? See **due to or owing to?**

partially or partly? These two words are often interchangeable, but there is a subtle distinction between them that is worth noting. *Partly* is the preferable choice with the meaning 'as regards one part': *The building is constructed partly of brick and partly of stone. Partially* is the preferable choice with the meaning 'to a limited extent; incompletely': *partially sighted. Partly* is more common than *partially* to introduce an explanatory clause or phrase, sometimes in the expression *partly . . . partly*: *Partly because of the weather and partly because of the weak economy, profits were down last year.*

partly or partially? See **partially or partly?**

passed or past? These two words, which are pronounced the same, are sometimes confused. *Passed* is the only standard form of the past tense and past participle of *to pass*: *We passed the house on our way to the bus stop*; *That danger has now passed. Past* is used for all other forms: noun, adjective, preposition and adverb: *That's all in the past*; *Past mistakes should be forgotten*; *half past three*; *The car drove past.* The possibility of confusion is perhaps greatest in sentences such as: *Time passed very slowly* (because the phrase *time past* is possible: *remembrances of time past*) or *What's past is past* (because *what's past* sounds like a shortened form of *what has passed*). As a rule of thumb, *passed* rarely follows *is* and *past* rarely follows *has.*

past or passed? See **passed or past?**

people or persons? *People* is generally used as the plural of *person*: *one person*; *two people.* The form *persons* is reserved for formal or legal contexts: *committed by a person or persons unknown.*

perceptible or perceptive? *Perceptible* refers to things perceived, *perceptive* to the people perceiving them. *Perceptible* means 'that can be seen, heard or sensed': *a perceptible change in their attitude*; *The difference is barely perceptible*. *Perceptive* means 'showing a sharp awareness': *a very perceptive comment*; *perceptive enough to see that there was something strange going on*.

perceptive or perceptible? See perceptible or perceptive?

perquisite or prerequisite? *Perquisite* is the full and formal form of the common word *perk*: the *perquisites of an office* are the additional or fringe benefits someone acquires by being in office over and above the position and the salary. *Prerequisite* is usually followed by the preposition *for* and means 'a necessary condition or attribute': *The presentation of a passport or a birth certificate is a prerequisite for the issuing of a marriage licence*.

persons or people? See people or persons?

phenomena or phenomenon? See phenomenon or phenomena?

phenomenon or phenomena *Phenomenon* is a singular noun. *Phenomena* is its plural and should never be used as if it were singular: *a strange phenomenon that occurs during an eclipse*; *the strange phenomena that occur during eclipses*.

plain or plane? These two words, which are pronounced the same, are sometimes confused. *Plain* is usually an adjective and has many adjectival meanings – 'clear', 'ordinary', 'undecorated', 'unattractive', etc.: *That makes everything plain*; *plain water*; *a plain Jane*. It has only one common noun sense – 'an area of flat country': *the rolling plains of the American West*. *Plane*, on the other hand, has many noun senses – 'an aircraft', 'a levelling tool', 'a level': *He's on a different plane to the rest of us*. It has only two adjectival senses: 'completely flat' (*a plane surface*) or 'two-dimensional' (*a plane figure*).

plane or plain? See plain or plane?

politic or political? See political or politic?

political or politic? These two words are not interchangeable. *Political* is much the commoner word and means, broadly, 'having to do with politics'. *Politic* means 'sensible or advantageous under the circumstances' and can be used in contexts which have nothing at all to do with politics: *It might be politic to postpone your visit*.

practicable or practical? See practical or practicable?

practical or practicable? These two words are close together in meaning and sometimes confused. A *practical* plan or suggestion is one that is useful, realistic, and effective: the *practical* applications of a theory. A *practicable* plan is, simply, one that it is possible to carry out. It might, for instance, be *practicable* to carry a grand piano on the roof of a car, but this is not a very *practical* method of transporting it. A person can be described as *practical* ('good at ordinary tasks' or 'down-to-earth'), but not as *practicable*.

practice or practise? In British English *practice* is the correct spelling for the noun in all its senses: *do some piano practice*; *in theory and in practice*; *a veterinary practice*. The spelling for the equivalent verb is *practise*: *to practise the piano*; *to practise one's religion*; *a practising dental surgeon*. In American English, the spelling *practice* is used for both the noun and the verb.

practise or practice? See **practice or practise?**

precede or proceed? These two words are sometimes confused. To *precede* is to 'go before': *She preceded me into the room*; *The meeting had been held on the Tuesday preceding the Easter weekend*. To *proceed* means to 'go forward': *I was proceeding along the High Street*; *The work is proceeding well*. Only *proceed* can be followed by *to* and another verb: *She then proceeded to read the paragraph in question*.

prerequisite or perquisite? See **perquisite or prerequisite?**

prescribe or proscribe? To *prescribe* is what doctors do – they specify a particular medicine for a patient. It means 'to lay down or order' positively that something should be done: *in the form prescribed by law*. To *proscribe* is a much rarer word and it has the opposite meaning – 'to forbid' or 'to ban': *Such practices were considered immoral and were proscribed by law*.

presently The standard British English meaning of *presently* used to be 'soon', 'in a minute': *I'll be with you presently*. What used to be thought of as an American or Scottish meaning 'now', 'at present' or 'currently' (*He's presently engaged with a client*) is becoming increasingly widely used in British English as well. The tense of the verb is usually an indicator of which sense is intended: used with the future tense the meaning is 'soon'; with the present tense the meaning is 'now'. Care should be taken to avoid the ambiguity in a sentence such as: *He's presently starting a new job*.

presume or assume? See **assume or presume?**

principal or principle? These two words, which are pronounced the same, are often confused. *Principle* is only ever a noun and has the basic sense of 'a fundamental truth or standard': *It's the principle of the thing; I object to that on principle. Principal* is most often used as an adjective meaning 'main': *their principal aim in life.* As a noun, *principal* means the 'head of an educational establishment' (it is the American English word for a 'headteacher') or 'a leading actor or performer'.

principle or principal? See principal or principle?

proceed or precede? See precede or proceed?

program or programme? British English has adopted the spelling *program* as standard in computer contexts: *a computer program; to program a computer.* In all other contexts the correct British English spelling is *programme*, while the correct American English spelling is *program.*

programme or program? See program or programme?

proscribe or prescribe? See prescribe or proscribe?

protagonist Strictly speaking, only dramas have *protagonists.* The word, which comes from Greek, originally meant 'first or main actor' and became extended to mean 'the main or a main character' in a drama, an artistic work, or a dramatic real-life situation: *By chapter three the protagonist is in conflict with all the other members of her family. Protagonist* is also frequently used to mean a 'supporter' (*a protagonist of the campaign/movement*). This use is based, it is suggested, on the mistaken assumption that the *pro-* at the beginning of the word is the common prefix meaning 'in favour of', whereas in fact the prefix involved is *prot(o)-* 'first', as in *prototype.* Given that it is based on a mistake and that it often represents an attempt to find a fancy substitute for 'supporter' or 'advocate', this use is best avoided.

questionnaire *Questionnaire* is spelt with two *n*'s and one *r*.

raise or raise? *Raise* is a verb with *raised* as the regular past tense and past participle and it takes a direct object: *All those in favour please raise your hands. Rise* is a verb with an irregular past tense (*rose*) and past participle (*risen*) and it never takes a direct object: *Leave the dough to rise for at least an hour.* In British English an increase in salary is also called *a rise*, while American English calls it *a raise.*

re- Most verbs that begin with the prefix *re-* meaning 'again' are spelt without a hyphen: *reboot the computer*; *recycle domestic waste*. Some people prefer to use a hyphen when the verb to which *re-* is attached begins with a vowel, especially *e*. However, spellings such as *reinsure* and *reuse* are shown in all modern British English dictionaries and forms such as *reentry* and *reexamine* in some. The hyphen is crucial, however, where two different meanings are involved, for example in distinguishing between *re-cover* ('cover again') and *recover* ('recuperate'), *re-creation* ('creating anew') and *recreation* ('leisure'), or *re-form* ('form again') and *reform* ('change for the better').

reason It is argued by some traditionalists that when *reason* means 'cause' it already contains the idea expressed by causal words such as *because* and *why*, which means that it is unnecessary and incorrect to use them together with it. Strictly then, the sentence *The reason that the plan failed was that it overlooked two simple facts* is correct, and the sentence *The reason why the plan failed was because it overlooked two simple facts* is incorrect. Any problems in sentences involving *reason* can often be regarded by recasting and leaving out the word *reason* altogether: *The plan failed because it overlooked two simple facts.*

reciprocal, mutual, or common? See mutual, reciprocal, or common?

regretful or regrettable? *Regretful* refers to the state of somebody's feelings: *Do you feel at all regretful about missing the opportunity? Regrettable*, on the other hand, comments on an event, an action, or a state of affairs: *It is most regrettable that she didn't see fit to come and answer these questions in person.*

regrettable or regretful? See regretful or regrettable?

replace or substitute? These two words are close in meaning but differ somewhat in use. One *replaces* an old thing *with* a new thing, or one *substitutes* a new thing *for* an old thing. The meaning is essentially the same in both cases, but the prepositions are different (*replace . . . with* (or *by*); *substitute . . . for*) and the order in which 'old thing' and 'new thing' follow the verb is also different: *replace the House of Lords with an elected second chamber*; *substitute an elected second chamber for the House of Lords.*

restive or restless? Because they are similar not only in form but also in meaning, these two words are difficult to keep apart. *Restive* means 'difficult to control or keep still': children and horses are commonly described as *restive* and the word is also applied to people who get impatient with restrictions placed on them: *The military were growing restive and kept urging the government to act. Restless* ('fidgety', 'unable to rest' or 'constantly moving') is applied much more widely than *restive*

– not only to people, but also to movements and things: *restless pacing to and fro*; *a restless night.*

restless or restive? See restive or restless?

reverend or reverent? *Reverend* is a title used for a member of the clergy: *the Reverend Val Hughes. Reverent* is an adjective meaning 'deeply respectful': *A reverent hush descended on the congregation.*

reverent or reverend? See reverend or reverent?

rise or raise? See raise or rise?

round, around, or about? See around, round, or about?

salubrious or salutary? These two words are sometimes confused. *Salubrious* is a fairly formal word, though often used humorously, meaning 'health-promoting' and thus 'hygienic' or 'decent': *There was a toilet, but it wasn't what you'd call salubrious.* A *salutary* experience or reminder, on the other hand, is one that teaches a necessary and beneficial lesson: *not a pleasant experience, but a very salutary one.*

salutary or salubrious? See salubrious or salutary?

same The use of *same* as a pronoun (*To installing one electric shower and connecting and testing same: £170*) is a commercial or legal use. It should not be used in formal speech or writing.

Scotch, Scots, or Scottish? *Scotch* is, for general purposes, an outdated adjective and disliked by many Scots. It should only be used in the specific combinations where it is familiar and established: *a Scotch egg*; *Scotch whisky. Scottish* is an all-purpose adjective that can be used for people, places, and things in or relating to Scotland: *a Scottish soldier*; *a Scottish tourist resort*; *the Scottish education system. Scots* may be used to describe people (*a Scots politician, the Scots Guards*), but its use seems to be becoming less common.

Scots, Scotch, or Scottish? See Scotch, Scots, or Scottish?

Scottish, Scots, or Scotch? See Scotch, Scots, or Scottish?

seasonable or seasonal? See seasonal or seasonable?

seasonal or seasonable? These two words are sometimes confused. *Seasonal* means 'connected with or dependent on the season': fruit is naturally *seasonal*, employment in a seaside resort is often *seasonal* and there may be *seasonal* fluctuations in the prices of goods. *Seasonable* is the word that means 'appropriate to the season'. Weather, particularly, can be *seasonable* or *unseasonable. Seasonable advice*, therefore, is advice that is given at an appropriate time.

seeing It is permissible in modern English to use *seeing* as a conjunction meaning 'since' or 'in view of the fact that': *Seeing we're late anyway, another five minutes probably won't make any difference.* The correct way to use it, however, is on its own or followed by *that.* The form *seeing as how* is considered non-standard by most modern authorities. Care should also be taken to ensure that the conjunction *seeing* cannot be confused with the present participle of *to see. Seeing that he was in trouble, she decided to help him* is ambiguous to the extent that it is not entirely clear whether or not she was an eyewitness to the fact that he was in trouble.

sensual or sensuous? *Sensual* is the more common word and the one that frequently carries overtones of sexual desire or pleasure: *pouting sensual lips; sensual pleasures. Sensuous* is the more neutral word: it also means 'appealing to the senses' but without the feeling of self-indulgence or sexiness associated with *sensual: the artist's sensuous use of colour and texture.*

sensuous or sensual? See sensual or sensuous?

separate *Separate* is spelt with two *a*'s and only two *e*'s. It may help to remember that it is related etymologically to the words *pare* and *prepare.*

serial or cereal? See cereal or serial?

sex and gender See gender and sex.

shall or will? Traditionally *shall* was used to form the future tense for the first person singular and plural (*I/we shall go tomorrow*) and to state a firm intention if used with any other personal pronoun (*You shall go to the ball; Britons never, never, never shall be slaves*). Conversely *will* formed the future tense for the second and third person (*You/they will know soon enough*) and expressed a firm intention if used with *I* or *we* (*I will not put up with this*). This distinction has largely died out, with *I will* or *we will* being used in informal usage and the general use of the contraction *'ll*, e.g. *I'll, we'll. Shall*, however, is needed when asking questions that relate to the immediate situation: *Shall we dance?* is an invitation to someone to dance now; *Will we dance?* only makes sense if the speaker is looking ahead to the possibility of dancing at some future event, as in *Will there be dancing?*

shear or sheer? To *shear* is a verb meaning 'to cut' or 'to be cut': *to shear a sheep; The end of the bolt sheared off.* It has two possible past participles. In the context of cutting hair or wool, or in the figurative meaning 'deprived', the past participle is *shorn: a shorn lamb; shorn of his authority.* In the context of cutting metal, the past participle is *sheared: It had sheared right through the cable.* A pair of *shears* is a cutting implement for garden use. *Sheer* is an adjective, an adverb, and a verb. As an adjective it means 'vertical' (*a sheer cliff*), 'see-through' (*sheer tights*) or 'pure' (*sheer nonsense; sheer determination*). As an adverb it means 'straight up or down without a break' (*the cliffs fell sheer*). As a verb, to *sheer* 'to swerve' or 'to turn abruptly': *The yacht sheered off at the last moment, narrowly missing the end of the jetty.*

sheer or shear? See **shear or sheer?**

should or would? Traditionally, *should* and *would* were used in reported speech in the same way as *shall* and *will* were used in direct speech – *should* for the first person singular and plural, *would* for the second and third persons: *I said I should be there; She told me she would be there.* This distinction is now made more rarely, and *would* is generally used instead of *should.* In spoken and informal contexts any distinction between *should* and *would* is hidden by the use of the contraction *'d: I'd; we'd,* etc. Note however that only *should* is used with the meaning 'ought to' as in: *I should go, but I don't particularly want to.* See also **shall or will?**

sic *Sic* is used when quoting someone else's words exactly to show that a mistake or oddity in them comes from the person quoted, not from the person quoting: *According to the chairman, 'These figures apply only to the months of Febuary (sic) and March.'*

sociable or social? See **social or sociable?**

social or sociable? *Social*, as an adjective, is an all-purpose neutral word meaning 'connected with society': *social conditions; social work. Sociable* is a complimentary term used mainly to describe people meaning 'fond of company' or 'friendly': *She's not feeling very sociable this evening.*

soon When the phrase *no sooner* starts a sentence, the normal order of the verb and subject following it should be reversed: *No sooner had she said this, than the telephone rang.* Note that the correct word to use after *no sooner* is *than*, not *when*: *I had no sooner sat down than Mary started calling for me from the garden.*

sort See **kind, sort, and type.**

speciality or specialty? The subject that a person specializes in is their *speciality* in British English, but *specialty* in American English.

specially or especially? See especially or specially?

specialty or speciality? See speciality or specialty?

stationary or stationery? These two words, which are pronounced the same, are often confused. *Stationary* is the adjective meaning 'standing still': *a stationary vehicle. Stationery* refers to the type of goods sold by a *stationer* (which is perhaps the easiest way of remembering the difference in spelling): paper, envelopes and the like.

stationery or stationary? See stationary or stationery?

stimulant or stimulus? A *stimulus* (plural *stimuli*) is anything that stimulates a reaction from someone or something: a prod with a stick, a promise of more pay or the threat of dismissal might act as a *stimulus* to somebody, making them work harder. A *stimulant*, on the other hand, is specifically a substance, especially a drink or drug, that temporarily makes someone more energetic or alert.

stimulus or stimulant? See stimulant or stimulus?

substitute or replace? See replace or substitute?

such as and like See like and such as.

suit or suite? Both these words mean a 'set' of things, but different things are involved. A *suit* is a set of clothes or armour, or one of the four sets of playing cards making up a pack (hearts, clubs, spades, or diamonds): *follow suit. Suit* can also mean 'a court action' or 'a request or appeal to someone': *grant somebody's suit.* A *suite* is a set of matching furniture, of rooms, of related pieces of music (*Holst's Planets Suite*), or computer software. It can also mean the retinue of servants or staff attending a grandee or high-ranking official.

suite or suit? See suit or suite?

supersede *Supersede* has no *c* in it and no double *e*. It comes from a Latin verb *supersedēre*, which literally means 'to sit above someone'.

than *My sister can run faster than I.* This is the grammatically correct form – *than I*, as traditionalists frequently point out, is short for *than I can*. However, the form that is considered correct by traditionalists sometimes sounds rather pedantic in speech: *My sister can run faster than I can* is correct, but *My sister can run faster than me* is more frequently used. Filling in the missing verb is often a good way of preserving grammar and avoiding awkwardness: *She spent far less time on it than he did.* It is also important to be aware of the possibility of confusion in a sentence such as: *You know her better than me.* Grammatically, this means 'you know her better than you know me'. It is often used, however, to mean 'you know her better than I do'. This last form of words is the one to adopt to make that particular meaning crystal clear.

thankfully *Thankfully* has now, like *hopefully*, been widely accepted as an adverb that can relate to a whole sentence as well as to a single verb: *Thankfully, no damage was done.* It is usually easy to distinguish in speech between this sense, meaning 'fortunately', and the other sense 'in a thankful way': *He sank down thankfully into the soft warm bed.* In writing, care should be taken to make sure that it is clear which sense is intended.

that, which, and who The general rule is that either *that* or *which* can be used to introduce clauses attached to nouns that add crucial identifying pieces of information: *The briefcase that* (or *which*) *I left on the train contained important papers* (my other briefcase didn't); *This is the book that* (or *which*) *you need.* There is an increasing tendency for *that* to be preferred to *which* in such sentences, and whichever is used the clause is not separated from the noun by commas. *Which*, on the other hand, must be used in clauses that give purely incidental information: *The weather, which was sunny that day, contributed greatly to the success of the event.* Such clauses must be enclosed by commas and – the crucial test for distinguishing between the two kinds – can be wholly removed from the sentence without making it unclear what is being referred to.

Although *who* is the usual pronoun used for people, it is perfectly acceptable to use *that* in place of it: *I've been sent a letter by someone that I met on holiday*; *You are the only person that knows the whole truth.* See also pp. 21–2.

their, there, or they're? These three words, which are pronounced the same, are sometimes confused. *Their* is the possessive form of *they* (*It's their fault*; *They'll bring their own tools*). *There* is an adverb of place (*You'll find it over there*) and is used with the verb *to be* (*There is nothing I can do about it*; *Are there any more questions?*). *They're* is the shortened form of *they are*: *They're not quite ready yet.*

themselves and themself *Themselves* is the standard reflexive form of *they*: *I hope the children enjoyed themselves. Themself* is a fourteenth to sixteenth century form that has recently been revived for use as an equivalent to *they* meaning 'a person of either sex': *No one should blame themself for this tragedy.* There is a certain logic to this if *they* is given a singular meaning, but the form *themselves* is also used in this context: *Everyone ought to try it for themselves.* '*We are looking for a Producer/Director who, when necessary, can use a camera themselves, and who has . . .*' (BBC advertisement). This is a very controversial area of English usage where, in formal writing, it is often best to abide by what is universally approved or to take avoiding action: *Everyone ought to try it for himself or herself* or *Everyone ought to try it personally.* See also **they**.

there, their, or they're? See their, there, or they're?

they The use of *they* as a singular pronoun meaning 'a person of either sex' has a very long history. It is no less controversial for all that. It is no longer appropriate to use *he, him, his* or *himself* after words like *everyone* or *no one.* A sentence such as *Everyone should do his best* would rightly be seen as sexist except where all the people referred to were male. The forms *he or she, his or her*, etc. are undoubtedly often awkward to use. The use of *they, them* and *their* presents itself as an obvious and convenient solution – except that, traditionally, *they* is plural. A blanket objection to a singular *they* seems unreasonable. It is best perhaps to avoid it in formal writing and where the clash between singular and plural is very marked. *Everyone should do their best* is acceptable inasmuch as *everyone* is a plural concept if not a plural word. *A lawyer must respect their clients' confidence* is far less acceptable and could so easily be recast in unexceptionable form: *Lawyers must respect their clients' confidence.* See also pp. 131–4.

they're, their, or there? See their, there, or they're?

till or until? *Till* and *until* can be used interchangeably. *Until* is slightly more formal than *till* and in writing *until* is more commonly found than *till.*

titillate or titivate? These two words are sometimes confused. To *titillate* someone means to 'arouse or stimulate someone, especially sexually': *The pictures were mildly titillating, but scarcely obscene.* To *titivate* something is to 'smarten it up': *She couldn't afford a new hat, so she titivated the old one with a new band and a few feathers.*

titivate or titillate? See titillate or titivate?

to, too, or two? Being pronounced the same, these three words are sometimes confused. *To* is mainly used as a preposition (*to London*; *to the top of the hill*; *to the utmost*) and in forming the infinitive of a verb (*to make*). *Too* is the adverb that means 'overmuch' and usually precedes an adjective (*too difficult for me*; *too hot to handle*). It also means 'as well', in which case it often comes at the end of a sentence (*Can Jenny come too?*). *Two* is the number between one and three (*Two and two make four*).

too, to, or two? See to, too, or two?

transpire *Transpire* has two common non-technical meanings – 'to become known' (*It eventually transpired that the documents had been lost*) and 'to happen' (*A most unfortunate incident transpired as the guests were leaving the hotel*). The use of the word in the second meaning is objected to by some traditionalists. There are no historical grounds for this, but it is argued, first, that *transpire* is simply a pompous alternative for *happen* or *occur* and, second, that in phrases such as *what transpired at the meeting* it is impossible to know which sense is intended. On these grounds, *transpire* is better avoided in the second sense.

troop or troupe? These two words are sometimes confused. A *troop* is a group of soldiers or Scouts, and the word is sometimes extended to mean simply any 'large group': *The visitors were beginning to arrive in troops. Troop* can also be used as a verb meaning 'to move in a group': *After the picnic, we trooped back down the hill.* A *troupe* is a group of actors or circus performers.

troupe or troop? See troop or troupe?

turbid or turgid? *Turbid* is a comparatively rare, literary word meaning 'muddy' – like a river that is clouded with sediment – or 'confused and obscure'. *Turgid* literally means 'swollen'. It is used most commonly in its extended sense of 'pompous and boring' as an uncomplimentary description of someone's writing style.

turgid or turbid? See turbid or turgid?

two, too, or to? See to, too, or two?

type See kind, sort, and type.

un- and non- Both these prefixes are used to produce negative forms of words. In cases where they can both be attached to the same root, the resulting *un-* word is generally stronger than the *non-* word. A *non-professional* tutor is one who is not qualified; *unprofessional* behaviour contravenes professional ethics. If someone's methods are described as *unscientific*, a criticism is usually implied (the methods do not come up to the standards required by science); if they are described as *non-scientific*, the effect is usually more neutral (the methods come from some field other than science).

underlay or underlie? *Underlay* is most commonly a noun meaning a layer of material placed beneath a carpet. When used as a verb *underlay*, like *lay*, takes a direct object and refers to an action, the action of laying something beneath something else: *We underlaid the carpet with felt. Underlie*, like *lie*, refers to a state, that of being underneath something else; but unlike *lie*, *underlie* takes a direct object. It is most commonly used figuratively to mean 'form the basis for': *the underlying causes of the revolution. Underlie* has the past tense *underlay*. See also lay or lie?

underlie or underlay? See underlay or underlie?

unexceptionable or unexceptional? See unexceptional or unexceptionable?

unexceptional or unexceptionable? These two words are quite close together in meaning and could be confused. *Unexceptional* means 'not outstanding', therefore 'ordinary' or 'rather dull' (*an unexceptional year for wine*). If a thing is *unexceptionable* it causes no offence or controversy: *It was just that one remark – the rest of the speech was totally unexceptionable.* See also exceptional or exceptionable?

uninterested or disinterested? See disinterested or uninterested?

unique If something is *unique* it is the only one of its kind. It is consequently illogical to speak of one thing being *more* or *less unique* than another or of something as being *rather, very, comparatively* or *somewhat unique*. It is correct to talk of, for example, *a unique opportunity* or to describe something as *almost unique* or *nearly unique*, but, where any kind of comparison is implied, it is better to choose another adjective such as *unusual* or *rare*.

unsociable See antisocial, asocial, non-social, unsociable, or unsocial?

unsocial See antisocial, asocial, non-social, unsociable, or unsocial?

until or till? See till or until?

used to The strictly correct negative form of *used to* is *used not to*, which can be shortened to *usedn't to*: *You used not to* (or *usedn't to*) *mind if we came in a little late.* This often sounds rather formal, so that *did not use to* or *didn't use to* (but not *didn't used to*) are generally acceptable in informal speech or writing. Likewise, the traditionally correct negative question form *used you not to . . . ?* or *usedn't you to . . . ?* is often replaced, more informally, by *didn't you use to . . . ?* If neither of these options seems acceptable, *you used to . . . , didn't you?* can be used.

venal or venial? See venial or venal?

venial or venal? These two words are sometimes confused. *Venial* is usually applied to sins, faults, or errors and means that they are minor and can be forgiven. *Venal* is usually applied to people and means that they can be corrupted or bribed.

waiver or waver? See waver or waiver?

waver or waiver? These two words are easily confused. To *waver* is a verb meaning 'to be unable to decide', 'to show signs of indecision' or 'to totter': *A week ago she was firmly on our side, but now she's starting to waver. Waiver* is a noun from the verb to *waive* and means 'a statement or document renouncing a right or claim': *We had to sign a waiver giving up our right to compensation in case of injury.*

well- Adjectives such as *well-mannered* and *well-known* should always be spelt with a hyphen when used before a noun: *a well-mannered young man; a well-known story.* The hyphen is not usually necessary when the adjective is used after a verb: *She seemed so well mannered; As is probably well known to most of you . . .* The correct way of forming the comparative and superlative of most such adjectives is with *better* and *best*: *the best-equipped research department; You would be better advised to wait.*

whether and if See if and whether.

which See that, which, and who.

white When describing people of a particular skin colour, *white*, like black, should generally be used without an initial capital letter. Although *white* is an acceptable term in most contexts, American usage often prefers to refer to race in terms of geographical origin, thus preferring *European* or *Caucasian* to *white*. Neither of these terms, however, is particularly common British English.

who or whom? Grammatically, *who* and *whom* are the subject and object forms respectively of the same word. *Who* corresponds to *I, he, she* or *they*; *whom* corresponds to *me, him, her* or *them*: *They saw whom? – They saw him. Whom*, however, is being increasingly relegated to very formal use in modern English, especially in questions: *Whom have I the honour of addressing?*, but *Who were you speaking to just then?* or *Who did you see at the meeting?* The same is largely true for the use of *whom* as a relative pronoun. Many people would argue that if *the man who I saw yesterday* is grammatically incorrect, *the man whom I saw yesterday* sounds pedantic, and it is better to say *the man that I saw yesterday* or, simply, *the* *man I saw yesterday*. It is most difficult to avoid *whom* immediately after a preposition: *To whom* (never *to who*) *were you speaking?*; *Nobody told me from whom* (never *from who*) *the message had come*. If the preposition is sent to the end of such sentences, however, the use of *who* seems more acceptable: *Nobody told me who the message had come from* (better still: *who had sent the message*). See also that, which, and who.

whom or who? See who or whom?

who's or whose? These two words are pronounced the same, but it is important to distinguish between them in writing, especially in questions. *Who's* is the shortened form of *who is* or *who has*: *Who's that? – It's only me*; *Who's done the washing-up? Whose* is the possessive form of *who*: *Whose is that?* ('Who owns that?'); *Whose turn is it to do the washing-up?* See also pp. 170–71.

whose or who's? See who's or whose?

will or shall? See shall or will?

-wise Sentences such as *How are things going workwise?* and *Careerwise, it seems like a good move* are very commonly used. The use of *-wise* added to the end of a noun, disliked by some traditionalists, is often a neat way of conveying the idea 'as far as something is concerned'. It is not, however, recommended in formal writing, and if *-wise* words are overused, or if *-wise* is attached to a long word or phrase (*research-and-development-wise*; *cost-effectivenesswise*) the results sound like jargon or are unintentionally comic.

worthwhile In front of a noun, *worthwhile* is usually as written one word: (*a worthwhile effort*). After a verb it may be written as either one or two words: *The effort was not worthwhile* (or *worth while*). The two parts of the word are separated in the phrase *to be worth one's while*: *It wouldn't be worth your while to spend too much time on the job.*

would or should? See should or would?

you or you're? *Your* is the possessive form of *you* (*It's your turn now*; *May I borrow your pen?*) and should not be confused with *you're*, which is pronounced the same, but is the shortened form of *you are*: *You're not as young as you were*; *I hope you're not getting bored.*

you're or your? See your or you're?

3 Vocabulary

Introduction

The aims of this section are: to give some basic advice on how to improve and enlarge your vocabulary; to show how a lot of the words that make up the vocabulary of English are formed; to look at the origins of English words from foreign languages and discuss the ways in which meaning has changed over time; and, finally, to deal with a specific problem in modern language use – sexism and discrimination in language – and investigate ways in which the social changes of the last few decades can be reflected in the language we use.

But what is meant by the term 'vocabulary'? The vocabulary of a language is the stock of individual words that it contains. A person's vocabulary consists of those words of their native language, or of a foreign language, that they understand and can use. If grammar and usage could be said to belong to the service sector of language, vocabulary is its primary resource, the raw material of the language. The English language has a vast array of words at its disposal – more than any individual person is likely to know, let alone need, in the course of a lifetime, more than are contained in the *Oxford English Dictionary*, however comprehensive its many volumes may appear.

Vocabulary building

It is usual to distinguish between a person's **active vocabulary** and their **passive vocabulary**. A person's **active vocabulary** consists of the words that they use frequently and confidently. If someone asks them to make up a sentence containing such and such a word – and they can do it – then that word is part of their active vocabulary. A person's **passive vocabulary** consists of the words whose meanings they know – so that they do not have to look the words up in a dictionary – but which they would not necessarily use in ordinary conversation or writing. Anyone who is interested in words or whose business involves using words will naturally want to build up and strengthen both their active and passive vocabularies, particularly the former.

Unfortunately, nobody has yet invented an effortless way of assimilating new vocabulary. There is no substitute for looking up words that you do not know in the dictionary and remembering their meaning and, if possible, their correct spelling. Dictionaries are fascinating books to browse through – more than that, they are essential storehouses of knowledge. Arthur Scargill, the miners' leader and socialist, once told *The Sunday Times*, 'My father still reads the dictionary every day. He says your life depends on your power to master words.'

If the word you know already is not quite the right word to express precisely what you want to say, then a thesaurus may help. A thesaurus is a dictionary of synonyms. Instead of providing a definition of the meaning of a word, it offers its users a list of words with the same or a similar meaning. Starting from the word you know but which is not quite right, it can help you to find the word which most clearly and accurately encapsulates your thought.

Once a word has been obtained from the dictionary or thesaurus, it still has to be put to use before it can be claimed as part of your active vocabulary. Members of previous generations – like Mr Scargill senior – were perhaps less diffident about the process of educating themselves than people are today. One way of doing this is that whenever a new word is learnt, it should be included in the next piece of writing, e.g. a letter that you write. Vocabulary is there to be used, to enliven and to enrich discourse in whatever medium of communication. 'Try it on your friends,' as the advertisements say.

Some people are – or seem to be – lucky enough to be born with a feeling for language. But people who take language seriously and regard mastering words as a worthwhile aim can develop a feeling for language or refine the language consciousness that they already possess. The more words you know and learn, the more you become aware of the relationships between words and the elements they have in common. Knowledge of these will frequently help in making a reasonable guess at the meaning of an unknown word and the way in which it might be used, even if there is no reference book to hand to look it up in. The next sections provide some pointers to this.

Word formation

Very few words actually spring into existence out of nothing. When people need new words, they are more likely to put them together from existing words or word components, or to borrow them from foreign languages, than to invent brand-new combinations of letters or sounds. There are exceptions. Words such as *clobber*, *gizmo*, and *zilch* have no known origin as far as language scholars are concerned. They were perhaps created simply because someone liked the sound of them. But these are a minority. Most words have a history and were formed, or formed themselves, over the years in accordance with a set of fairly logical principles.

Etymology

The branch of language study that deals specifically with the origin and development of words is called **etymology**. The word *etymology* is also used to mean an account of the origin and development of an individual word. Most dictionaries provide an etymology at the end of their entries for the more important words. The etymology of the word *etymology* itself is that it existed in Middle English (the form of English that was used from about 1150 to about 1500, by, among others, the poet Geoffrey Chaucer) in the form *ethimologie*, that it came from a Latin word *etymologia*, and that this Latin word itself goes back to a Greek word formed from two elements *etymon* (the literal and original meaning of a word) and *-logia* (a suffix with the same meaning as English *-(o)logy*, the theory or study of a subject). The Greeks and Romans, in other words, were used to making what Lewis Carroll called *portmanteau words* – words in which two or more elements are combined or blended.

The process of making portmanteau words has continued throughout the ages and still continues now. It is common for the dictionary entry for a simple word such as *boat* or *home* or *ring* to be followed by a string of entries beginning with the same four letters. In *The New Penguin English Dictionary*, for instance, *boat* is followed by *boatbill* (a small heron), *boat deck*, *boatel*, *boater*, *boathook*, *boathouse*, *boatie*, *boating*, *boatman*, *boat people*, etc. All of them have been constructed by adding an additional element to the root word *boat*. In fact, in order to pronounce *boathook* or *boathouse* correctly, you have to be able to recognize it for what it is – a word constructed simply by putting two simple English words together – and not be misled into thinking that it is some complicated word with a *th-* sound in the middle.

It is comparatively easy to form new words in English by joining two existing words together end to end, more or less irrespective of the word class of the components. New nouns, for example, can be formed from two nouns (*boat|man*, *ring|bolt*), an adjective and a noun (*mad|house*, *red|neck*) or a verb and a noun (*hover|craft*, *sling|shot*). Three of the words on the original list above, however, are compounds of a different kind. In *boatel*, *boatie*, and *boater* what has been added to the stem word *boat* is not a complete other word but a little particle, a word component that could be added to many other words to change their meanings as well. By far the commonest and most useful of the three *suffixes* in question (a *suffix* being specifically a component added to the end of a word to change its meaning) is *-er*. It has several uses, one of them being to be attached to the ends of verbs (and sometimes other nouns) to create nouns meaning 'a person who does such and such'. A *farmer* farms, a *player* plays, and a *boater* boats. This is true even though the main meaning of the word *boater* is no longer 'a person who goes boating' but a type of hat formerly worn mainly by people who went boating.

The suffix *-ie* is a less widespread and more informal one. It is also quite modern in this particular sense, meaning 'a person who is enthusiastic about such and such'. A *foodie* is a person who has a particular interest in food, a *boatie* is someone who is always in and out of boats.

Boatel is a slightly different kind of word. No dictionary records *-el* as a suffix forming nouns meaning 'a type of hotel'. It is more a case that the last syllable of *hotel* has been removed and tacked onto *boat* – a process made easier by the fact that *boat* rhymes with the first syllable of *hotel*. The same process made the earlier word *motel*.

Finally, it should perhaps be pointed out that, although the list of words with *boat* contains both two- and one-word compounds, none of the compounds is hyphenated. Whereas fifty years ago a word such as *boathouse* might well have been spelt with a hyphen, the general tendency nowadays is to show a compound either as two separate words or as a single word.

Suffixes

A **suffix** is a component that is added to the end of a word to change that word's meaning. Suffixes have a double function. Besides creating new meanings from an existing root word, as shown in the examples in the previous section, they are also used to form words in a word class that is different from the one to which the root belongs. To take a very simple example, the suffix *-ly* is chiefly used to form adverbs from adjectives – the adjective *brief* becomes the adverb *briefly*, *light* becomes *lightly*, *universal* becomes *universally*, etc.

There are many word-building suffixes whose function is specifically to create words of a particular class from words of another class. To take *light* (in the sense 'not heavy') as an example once again: the addition of the verb-building suffix *-en* creates the verb *lighten* (compare *redden*, *whiten*, *shorten*, *lengthen*, etc.); the addition of the noun-building suffix *-ness* creates the noun *lightness* (compare *redness*, *whiteness*, *shortness*, etc.). The process does not necessarily stop there, of course. Once one suffix has been added and a new word formed, further suffixes can be added as well, for example, to create the different forms of the verb, so that *lighten*, like any other regular English verb, takes the suffixes *-s*, *-ed*, and *-ing* to form its principal parts. To take another example, the adjective *civil* was made into a verb by the addition of the very common verb-building suffix *-ize* or *-ise* (see chapter 2, p. 86), and the verb *civilize* in turn was made into the noun *civilization* by adding *-ation*, an equally common noun-building suffix.

From the point of view of word recognition, therefore, suffixes, though often short and seemingly inconspicuous combinations of letters, are very important to know about. Recognizing a particular suffix usually enables you to tell whether the word that it is attached to is a noun, adjective, adverb, or verb, and this is obviously an important stage in uncovering its meaning. In most larger dictionaries the major suffixes are treated equally with ordinary words.

There follow selective lists of suffixes that create words belonging to particular word classes. Some, especially among the noun suffixes, have specific senses and are consequently very useful guides to the meaning of the word of which they form a part. Others are mainly functional, that is they basically convert one class of word into another without adding much meaning. Little is added to the basic meaning of the verb *illuminate* when it is transformed by a suffix into the noun *illumination*. If you knew the meaning of the word *appendix*, however, you would not be able to guess the meaning of the words *appendicitis* and *appendectomy* unless you knew the independent meanings of the suffixes *-itis* and *-(o)tomy*.

Noun suffixes

Suffix	Function and/or meaning	Examples
-age	makes nouns from verbs	*dotage, spillage*
	makes nouns from other nouns	*acreage, orphanage*
-al	makes nouns from verbs	*betrothal, refusal*
-ance	makes nouns from verbs	*appearance, clearance*
-ant	makes nouns from verbs	*applicant, defendant*
-arium	(artificial living space)	*aquarium*
-ation	makes nouns from verbs	*application, devastation*
-cide	(killing)	*homicide, suicide*
-cy	makes nouns from adjectives	*dependency, literacy*
	makes nouns from other nouns	*captaincy, infancy*
-dom	makes nouns from other nouns	*kingdom, martyrdom*
-ee	makes nouns from verbs	
	(person to whom something has been done)	*appointee, divorcee*
-eer	makes nouns from other nouns	
	(person who performs an action)	*auctioneer, profiteer*
-ence	makes nouns from verbs	*dependence, existence*
-er	makes nouns from verbs	
	(person or thing that performs an action)	*farmer, player*

-ery	makes nouns from verbs	*carvery, mockery*
-ese	makes nouns from other nouns	
	(inhabitant or language of country)	*Japanese, Portuguese*
	(type of language, jargon)	*journalese, officialese*
-ess	makes nouns from other nouns	
	(female equivalent of male job, etc.)	*manageress, tigress*
	(see also chapter 2, p. 74)	
-ette	makes nouns from other nouns	
	(female equivalent of male job, etc.)	*usherette*
	(smaller version)	*cigarette, diskette*
-ful	makes nouns from other nouns	
	(amount contained in something)	*bucketful, spoonful*
	(see also chapter 2, p. 78)	
-gram	(written or representational thing)	*diagram, hologram*
-graph	(written or representational thing)	*autograph, photograph*
-graphy	(writing or representation)	*biography, cryptography*
-hood	makes nouns from other nouns	
	(state or period of being something)	*childhood, widowhood*
-ian	makes nouns from other nouns	
	(person engaged or skilled in an activity)	*musician, politician*
-ion	makes nouns from verbs	*action, dilution*
-ism	makes nouns from other nouns	
	(system of belief)	*Marxism, Protestantism*
-ist	makes nouns from other nouns	
	(practitioner of something)	*Darwinist, theorist*
-ity	makes nouns from adjectives	*ability, ductility*
-let	makes nouns from other nouns	
	(smaller version)	*booklet, droplet*
-ling	makes nouns from other nouns	
	(young creature)	*duckling*
-mania	(deranged or obsessive behaviour)	*kleptomania, pyromania*
-ment	makes nouns from verbs	*bereavement, encouragement*
-(o)logist	(person who studies something)	*geologist, musicologist*
-(o)logy	(study of something)	*biology, sociology*
-or	makes nouns from verbs	

	(person or thing that performs an action)	*actor*, *investigator*
-phile	(lover or devotee of something)	*Anglophile*, *paedophile*
-philia	(love of or devotion to something)	*Francophilia*, *necrophilia*
-phobe	(hater of something)	*Europhobe*, *hydrophobe*
-phobia	(fear of or aversion to something)	*agoraphobia*, *claustrophobia*
-ship	makes nouns from other nouns	
	(state or period of being something)	*chairmanship*, *headship*
-ure	makes nouns from verbs	*departure*, *investiture*

People who take a keen interest in their own health would be well advised to bone up on suffixes. Below is a brief list of specialized suffixes frequently encountered in medical terminology.

Suffix	Function and/or meaning	Examples
-algia	(pain in some part of the body)	*arthralgia*, *neuralgia*
-itis	(inflammation)	*appendicitis*, *bronchitis*
-oma	(tumour)	*carcinoma*, *haematoma*
-(o)pathy	(treatment of disease)	*homeopathy*, *osteopathy*
	(disease)	*psychopathy*, *retinopathy*
-scopy	(examination or observation)	*endoscopy*, *microscopy*
-(o)tomy	(cutting or incision)	*appendectomy*, *lobotomy*

Two things are worth noting about the above list. The first is that many of the suffixes listed have further suffixes dependent on them, allowing further word formation: *-graph* and *-graphy* produce *-graphic*; *-ology* produces *-ological*; *-mania* gives *-maniac*, etc. The second is that several of them also exist, without a hyphen, as words in their own right – a *graph*, *mania*, *phobia*. This provides another way of checking up on their meaning.

Adjective suffixes

Suffixes are no less commonly used to form adjectives. The following are usually attached to verbs: *-able*, *-ant*, *-atory*, *-ible*, *-ive*, and *-some* (*admirable*, *resistant*, *exploratory*, *irresistible*, *active*, and *tiresome*). To make adjectives from nouns, suffixes such as *-al*, *-an*, *-ary*, *-esque*, *-ful*, *-ic*, *-ish*, *-less*, *-ly*, *-ous*, and *-y* are available (*magical*, *Italian*, *legendary*, *picturesque*, *beautiful*, *heroic*, *foolish*, *faithless*, *friendly*, *iniquitous*, and *buttery*). It is also possible to make a new adjective from an existing one by adding a suffix; *-ish* and *-most* are the two suffixes most commonly used in this way (*greenish*, *topmost*). They are closely related in function to *-er* and *-est*, the suffixes that form the comparative and superlative forms respectively (*high – higher – highest*).

On the spelling change, e.g. from *humour* to *humorous*, see chapter 2, p. 96 (entry '**-our, -orous**') and p. 139.

Verb suffixes

There are fewer suffixes that form verbs. The suffixes *-en* and *-ize* (*-ise*) have already been mentioned. Like them, *-ate* and *-ify* can be added to both adjectives and nouns to form verbs: *activate* and *hyphenate*, *loosen* and *lengthen*, *justify* and *speechify*, *legalize* and *hospitalize*.

Prefixes

A **prefix** is a component that can be attached to the beginning of an existing word to change that word's meaning. Prefixes play a less important role than suffixes in changing words from one class to another, although they do sometimes have this function. If the common prefix *un-* is added to a noun, adjective, adverb, or verb it remains a noun, adjective, etc. (*happiness – unhappiness*, *happy – unhappy*, *happily – unhappily*, *tie – untie*). If, however, a prefix such as *pro-* (in favour of) or *anti-* (opposed to) is attached to a noun, it frequently changes into an adjective: *a pro-democracy movement*, *antiaircraft fire*.

Standing as they do at the very beginnings of words, prefixes are a crucial guide to meaning. Most modern dictionaries, again, treat all the major prefixes as having equal status with other words. In fact, it sometimes appears that words consist simply of a prefix and a suffix tacked together – it is possible to look up the prefixes *bio-* and *geo-* in the dictionary together with the suffix *-(o)logy* and come away with most of the information required to understand the meanings of the words *biology* and *geology*. This is not a very accurate way of describing how these words were actually formed, but for the purpose of understanding their meaning it is quite helpful.

The New Penguin English Dictionary has a lengthy list of words beginning with the letters *bio*, from *bio-* itself through to *biotin*. Almost all of them derive ultimately from the Greek word *bios* meaning 'life'. While it may be helpful to know a little Latin or Greek, because a great many English words and word components come from those languages, it is not necessary to do so because the dictionary treats *bio-* as an English prefix, meaning 'to do with life or living organisms'. A *biography* is so called because it is an account of a person's life – the suffix *-graphy*, listed in the previous section and also with its own dictionary entry, forms nouns with the meaning 'a form of writing or representation' (*calligraphy*, *photography*, etc.). *Biodiversity* means the existence of a wide variety of living creatures within a particular area; *bioluminescence* is a process by which living creatures such as glowworms give off light.

To take another example, *auto-* comes from the Greek word *autos* meaning 'self' and words beginning with *auto-* often refer to processes that happen by themselves or things that relate to the self. Something that is *automatic* happens by itself without deliberate intervention by human beings or another machine, etc.; an *automobile* moves itself without the need of a horse; an *autobiography* is an account of the writer's own life; an *autocrat* rules alone.

The meanings of prefixes

Once again, space does not allow an exhaustive list of prefixes of Greek and Latin origin of the same type as *auto-* and *bio-*, but here are some of the most important:

Prefix	Meaning	Examples
ab-	(away from)	*abduct, abstract*
ad-	(towards, to)	*adhere, advance*
aero-	(air)	*aerodynamics, aeroplane*
ante-	(before, in front of)	*antecedent, anteroom*
	(see also chapter 2, p. 57)	
anti-	(contrary or opposite to)	*anticlockwise, antihero*
	(against, not in favour of)	*anti-Semitic, anti-war*
	(see also chapter 2, p. 57)	

aqua-	(water)	*aqualung, aquarium*
auto-	(self)	*autograph, autonomy*
bi-	(two, twice)	*bicycle, bifocal*
bio-	(life)	*biochemistry, biosphere*
cent-	(hundred)	*centennial, centenarian*
crypto-	(obscure, secret)	*crypto-Communist, cryptography*
dec(i)-	(ten)	*decimal, decimate*
di-	(two, twice)	*dichotomy, diphthong*
dia-	(through)	*diameter, diarrhoea*
eco-	(environment)	*ecology, ecosystem*
endo-	(inside)	*endogenous, endosperm*
epi-	(above)	*epicentre, epigraph*
	(additional)	*epilogue*
	(outer)	*epidermis*
equi-	(equal, equally)	*equidistant, equipoise*
ex-	(out of)	*exhume, extract*
extra-	(outside)	*extramural, extraordinary*
geo-	(earth)	*geocentric, geology*
giga-	(one thousand million)	*gigabyte, gigahertz*
hetero-	(other)	*heterogeneous, heterosexual*
homo-	(same)	*homogeneous, homosexual*
hyper-	(above, in excess of, excessively) (see also chapter 2, p. 82)	*hyperactive, hypersensitive*
hypo-	(below, lower than normal) (see also chapter 2, p. 82)	*hypodermic, hypothermia*
intra-	(within, inside) (see also chapter 2, p. 85)	*intramural, intrauterine*
intro-	(into, inward) (see also chapter 2, p. 85)	*introspection, introversion*
iso-	(equal)	*isobar, isosceles*
kilo-	(thousand)	*kilobyte, kilometre*
mega-	(million)	*megabyte, megaton*
	(very large or great)	*megalomania, megalopolis*
micro-	(very small)	*microchip, micrometer*
milli-	(one thousandth)	*millimetre, millisecond*

mon(o)-	(one, single)	*monocle, monotony*
multi-	(having or consisting of many)	*multinational, multi-purpose*
oct-	(eight)	*octagon, octet*
pan-	(universal, all)	*pan-African, pantheism*
pent(a)-	(five)	*pentagon, pentathlon*
phil-	(loving, devoted to)	*philanthropic, philharmonic*
photo-	(light)	*photograph, photosensitive*
poly-	(having many)	*polychrome, polygon*
post-	(after)	*postwar*
pre-	(before, in front of)	*prelude, preposition*
pro-	(for, in favour of)	*pro-British, pro-Conservative*
	(forward, onward)	*proceed, protract*
	(in place of)	*proconsul*
proto-	(first)	*protoplasm, prototype*
psycho-	(mind)	*psychology, psychopath*
pyro-	(fire)	*pyromania, pyrotechnics*
quad-	(four)	*quadruped, quadruplet*
quin(t)-	(five)	*quintet, quintuplet*
sub-	(below)	*submarine, subterranean*
	(less than)	*subhuman, subsonic*
super-	(above)	*superscript, superstructure*
	(greater than)	*superhuman, supersonic*
tele-	(at a distance)	*telepathy, television*
tri-	(three)	*triangle, tripartite*
ultra-	(beyond, beyond the range of)	*ultrasound, ultraviolet*
	(exceedingly)	*ultracautious, ultramodern*

As with suffixes, it will be noted that some of these prefixes also exist, without a hyphen, as words in their own right – *extra* is perhaps the most striking example, but also *anti*, *photo*, and *ultra*. The list records the senses of these prefixes as they derive from their original meanings in Latin or Greek. In English, they have developed further senses – or perhaps it would be more accurate to say, have been 'copied' by prefixes that are actually shortenings of longer words formed with the help of the original prefix. For example, the word *autocross* has only a distant relationship with 'self'. The prefix *auto-* here is simply a shortening of *automobile*.

There is another set of simpler, shorter prefixes that have not been covered in the above paragraphs. These are particles that have the effect of turning the meaning of a word around completely so that it means its opposite. The commonest of these has already been mentioned: *un-*. Others that perform a similar function include *de-*, *dis-*, *il-*, *im-*, *in-*, *ir-*, *mis-*, and *non-* (*congestion – decongestion*; *appearance – disappearance*; *literate – illiterate*; *perfect – imperfect*; *secure – insecure*; *rational – irrational*; *treat – mistreat*; *stop – non-stop*). (On hyphenation with *non-* see chapter 2, p. 94.) The prefixes *il-*, *im-*, *in-*, and *ir-* are in fact variants of the same word element based on the Latin prefix *in-*. The choice of prefix depends on the first letter of the word to which it is attached: *il-* attaches itself to words beginning with *l* (*legal – illegal*); *im-* to words beginning with *b*, *m*, or *p* (*balance – imbalance*, *material – immaterial*, *pure – impure*); and *ir-* to words beginning with *r* (relevant – irrelevant), while *in-* serves all other initial letters.

On the difference in meaning between words formed with *non-* and words formed with *un-*, see chapter 2, p. 108. On hyphenation with *re-* and *well-*, see chapter 2, pp. 100 and 110.

Back formation

A further way of forming new words is by removing an element from (instead of adding one to) a word, usually leading to a change in word class. An example is that from the noun *editor* came the verb *edit*. Other so-called **back formations** include:

burgle from *burglar*

enthuse from *enthusiasm*

gruntled from *disgruntled*

laze from *lazy*

liaise from *liaison*

televise from *television*.

Eponyms

The final method of word formation to be discussed here is the derivation of words from the name of a person, often the first person to introduce, devise, or invent a particular article. Such words are called **eponymous words**, the word **eponym** being used to refer to the name of such a person. For example, the raincoat known as the *mackintosh* is named after the Scottish chemist and inventor Charles *Macintosh* (died 1843) who patented a process of making waterproof fabrics in 1823. Other examples of eponyms include:

Word	Named after
ampere	André Ampère, died 1836
aubrietia	Claude Aubriet, died 1743
bloomers	Amelia Bloomer, died 1894
boycott	Captain Charles Cunningham Boycott, died 1897
cardigan	James Thomas Brudenel, 7th Earl of Cardigan, died 1868
Celsius	Anders Celsius, died 1744
dahlia	Andreas Dahl, died 1789
diesel	Rudolf Diesel, died 1913
Fallopian tube	Gabriel Fallopius, died 1562
fuchsia	Leonhard Fuchs, died 1566
galvanize	Luigi Galvani, died 1798
leotard	Jules Léotard, died 1870
Morse code	Samuel Finley Breese Morse, died 1872
Pareto principle	Vilfredo Frederico Pareto, died 1923
Parkinson's law	Cyril Northcote Parkinson, died 1993
plimsoll line	Samuel Plimsoll, died 1898
Richter scale	Charles Richter, died 1985
salmonella	Daniel Salmon, died 1914
sandwich	John Montagu, 4th Earl of Sandwich, died 1792
saxophone	Adolphe Sax, died 1894
shrapnel	Henry Shrapnel, died 1842
sousaphone	John Philip Sousa, died 1932
volt	Alessandro Volta, died 1827

watt	James Watt, died 1819
wellington	Arthur Wellesley, 1st Duke of Wellington, died 1852

Borrowed words: history of English

Most people know that modern English has two main sources: *Anglo-Saxon* (or Old English) – the Germanic language of the Saxon invaders who conquered England after the fall of the Roman Empire – and *French*, brought over by the Normans when they in turn conquered the country in 1066. For a while the two languages existed side by side, Anglo-French being the language of the upper classes, Anglo-Saxon that of the lower. By the time of Geoffrey Chaucer (?1342–1400) they had blended into what we now call Middle English, a form of the language easily recognizable as the ancestor of modern English and with many of the same characteristics.

Saxon and French

It is often said – and it is generally true – that the simpler and more basic words in the English language have an Anglo-Saxon (or Germanic) origin, the more complex and refined words a French (or Latin) one. In the first chapter of his novel *Ivanhoe*, set in the reign of King Richard I, Sir Walter Scott introduces two Saxon serfs, one of whom comments bitterly on the fact that, while the animals he has to tend and feed have Old English names, *swine*, *ox*, and *calf*, the meat that comes from them – and is more often eaten by the nobility than by the peasantry – is known by names of French origin: *pork*, *beef*, and *veal*. The same applies, though Sir Walter did not mention them, to *sheep* and *mutton*. The words *house* and *hall* come from Old English, the words *castle*, *mansion*, and *palace* come from French or via French from Latin. The words *sun* and *moon* are of Germanic origin, but the adjectives *solar* and *lunar* are of Latin. The number *two* comes to us through the Germanic route, the nouns *couple*, *double*, *duo*, and *pair* do not.

The most basic words of all – such as the number *two* – can be traced back by language historians to a prehistoric language that is assumed to have been the common ancestor not only of the vast majority of modern

European languages from Albanian through Russian to Welsh, but also of the languages of India and Iran. English belongs to one branch of the Indo-European family of languages, Latin, French, Spanish, and Italian to another, Gujarati, Hindi, and Urdu to yet another. They are all assumed to derive from a tongue known as Proto-Indo-European spoken somewhere in western Asia around 5000 BC.

When, during the thirteenth and fourteenth centuries, the blending and mixing process took place that produced Middle English, it was by no means always the case that where two words for the same thing were available, one of Old English and the other of French origin, one was selected and the other, as it were, was discarded. In a great many cases both were retained and both have been carried down to modern English. Thus modern English includes the word *deep*, which comes from Anglo-Saxon and is very much like the Dutch word *diep*. It also includes the word *profound*, which comes via French from Latin and is very similar to the French word *profond*. It has room both for *holiness* (Germanic) and for *sanctity* (Latin), for *to follow* and *to pursue*, and for *lovely* and *beautiful*. The richness and variety of English vocabulary owes a great deal to the fact that the language had these two main sources to draw on.

The relationship with French has made it comparatively easy for English to absorb words from Latin and Greek. As both ordinary and intellectual life became more complex over the centuries, the tendency was generally to look to Latin and Greek for the material to create new words to denote new realities, especially new scientific and technical realities. There has never been a strong urge among ordinary English speakers or English-speaking scholars to 'translate' imported Greek or Latin terms into 'native English' or 'Saxon' ones. The German word for 'television' is *Fernsehen* – a direct translation into German of the Greek prefix *tele-* (from a distance) and the Latin word *vision*. Had English followed the same procedure, we might sit down to watch programmes on the 'farseer'. Dutch has a word *verrekijker* (literally 'farlooker'), just as English has the word *spyglass* – something a lot nearer to a native English word than the obvious import *telescope* (Greek prefix and Greek root). But, in this case, both the Dutch and the English 'native' terms sound old-fashioned and non-technical in comparison with the word of foreign extraction.

The purpose of mentioning the route that English, generally speaking, did not take is to lead into a brief discussion of to what extent vocabulary deriving from one side of English's heritage is to be preferred over vocabulary deriving from the other. It used to be suggested – notably by the great usage expert H. W. Fowler – that, as a general rule, Saxon words should be preferred to French (Romance) ones on the grounds of their greater simplicity, directness, and clarity. Simplicity, directness, and clarity are major virtues in any kind of verbal communication – this is the main point Fowler was making. But, leaving aside the fact that few people can tell at a glance which side of our linguistic heritage a particular word derives from, the distinction is not clear-cut. Many ordinary words in everyday use come from the French side – including *ordinary* and *use*, and *army* and *chair* and *pain* and *reason*. Nevertheless, it remains true that most of the words that have come into English from French and Latin tend to be not only more complex than Anglo-Saxon ones, but also more abstract, and more formal and literary. As George Orwell demonstrated in his essay *Politics and the English Language*, vocabulary derived from Latin makes pretentiousness, woolly generalization, beating about the bush (or, to use the Latin word, *circumlocution*), and pulling the wool over people's eyes possible in a way that vocabulary of Anglo-Saxon origin does not. Orwell argued that it is easier to think or say *liquidate* than it is to think or say *kill*. In a more modern context, it might be felt that the rather abstract phrase *collateral damage* serves the same purpose of drawing attention away from the reality (buildings destroyed and civilians killed that were not the main target of an attack) and inveigling the listener or reader into a realm of concepts. It is abstract; it sounds technical and therefore vaguely impressive; it is probably easier to think and say. Latin words do often have the effect of seeming to create a greater distance between reality and language than normally exists. But this argument can be taken too far. The Latinate word *homicide* may be slightly less 'direct' or 'immediate' than the Old English word *murder*, but the equally Latinate word *suicide* would, to most people and in most contexts, seem more 'direct' and more 'immediate' than the equivalent *self-murder*. For more on the use of long and short words, see pp. 201–7.

Exotic sources

Although its core vocabulary comes mainly from the Anglo-Saxon and French sources discussed above, English has never been slow to take words from other languages more remote from it both geographically and linguistically when the need to extend its word stock, or fill a gap in it, arose. Thus, foreign words were often imported to refer to things that were originally foreign to the British or North American environment or culture. It should come as no surprise that *matador* comes from Spanish, *tequila* from Mexican Spanish, *kasbah* from Arabic, *kayak* from Inuit, *squaw* from a Native American language, and *sukiyaki* from Japanese. A great deal of musical vocabulary comes from Italian; the vocabulary of ballet comes from modern French. Other borrowings are not so obvious. Arabic gave English not only *kasbah* and *harem* but also *almanac*, *arsenal*, *assassin*, *zenith*, and *zero*. The British suburban scene would likewise be incomplete without *bungalow* and *veranda*, both from Hindi (along with *dinghy*, *dungarees*, and *pyjamas*), *caravan* from Persian, *tea* and *ketchup* from Chinese, and *budgerigar* from an Australian Aboriginal language. The vocabulary of English contains a partially hidden record of the contacts made by English-speaking people with the rest of the world over the course of centuries. The process continues. Political change in the former Soviet Union brought the words *glasnost* and *perestroika* within the ambit of English in the 1980s. Changes in diet, lifestyle, and fashion that have originated abroad or are copied from abroad are continually adding to the debt – which English has amply repaid by exporting as many, if not more of its own, words to other languages.

Semantic development

From whatever source they enter the language, once words have become a part of English they develop in form and meaning as time goes on. The word *assassin*, for example, came originally from Arabic, but *assassinate* and *assassination* were formed by adding common English suffixes (of Latin and French origin) to the original word.

The changes of meaning that words can sometimes undergo as they grow away from their original sense are particularly interesting, and it is helpful to be aware of this. The branch of language study that deals with the meaning of words is called *semantics*. To take one particularly striking example, the word *silly* comes from an Old English word *saelig* with a Germanic root meaning 'happy' or 'lucky', often, under the influence of Christianity, with the connotation 'blessed'. By the thirteenth century the word had come to suggest 'blissful innocence' and from there acquired overtones of pitiableness and undeserved suffering. The Middle English meanings are given as 'happy', 'innocent', 'pitiable', and 'feeble'. These meanings remained current for a considerable time after the word first began to be used in its modern sense of 'foolish', which was probably in the early sixteenth century. The poet Wordsworth, writing at the end of the eighteenth century, quotes from the ballad of the 'Babes in the Wood' – 'These silly children, hand in hand/Went walking up and down' – and it is obvious from the context that the old innocent and pitiable sense is the one intended. Eventually, however, the modern disparaging sense of the word asserted itself overwhelmingly, making it impossible to use the word in the older, more positive one and be properly understood.

This process too continues in the present day. It is possible that the primary modern meaning of the word *gay* 'homosexual' will eventually drive the older meaning 'cheerful, carefree' out of the usable language. If it does, the old meaning, like many other old meanings, will be part of the natural process of evolution that all languages undergo. It used to be the practice in many dictionaries to list the meanings of words in historical order, beginning with the oldest known sense, whether it was still in use or not, and ending with the oldest surviving sense. Most modern dictionaries have abandoned this practice and now list meanings according to their currency in modern English, beginning with the commonest. This is in keeping with a general trend in lexicography to 'describe' English as it is now and to reflect current use and users' needs rather than be storehouses of historical scholarship on the model of the *Oxford English Dictionary*. Traditionalists – and some others who would not necessarily describe themselves as traditionalists – may find it irritating when words are used in a manner that does not accord with their root meaning. The word *decimate*, for example derives from the Latin word for 'ten' and originally meant 'to kill every tenth man' in a Roman legion as a collective punishment for cowardice or incompetence. There are few circumstances, fortunately, in which this original meaning is likely to apply in modern life. If an epidemic were said to have 'decimated' a population, it might be taken that a proportion roughly of the order of one in ten had died, but it is more likely that the word would be being used in a broader and looser sense, simply suggesting that very large numbers of people had been killed or, in other contexts, that a vast amount of damage had been done. If enough people use a word in a particular sense – whether or not that sense is strictly 'correct' – it is very difficult for traditionalists to hold out against them. The example of *silly* is perhaps an instructive one.

Other words that have shown changes in their meaning in time include the following:

Word	Meanings in the word's history	Current meaning
buxom	obedient	attractively plump
	obliging; courteous	
	blithe; easygoing	
gossip	godparent	person who tells facts about others
	close friend	
	acquaintance	
idiot	private or ignorant person	silly person
nice	ignorant	pleasant
	silly, simple	
	wanton, lascivious	
	shy	
	precise, delicate	
vulgar	ordinary, common	indecent

It is a mistake to believe that an earlier meaning of a word is somehow 'more correct' than a later meaning. Language changes and so the meanings of words themselves change.

Sexism and discrimination in language

One of the biggest challenges facing the vocabulary and structures of languages today is to find acceptable non-discriminatory ways of describing and discussing human activity. When modern analysts talk about sexism and discrimination in language nowadays they are not, of course, generally referring to deliberate abuse or deliberate attempts to demean people on the grounds of their sex, race, or physical disabilities. They are concerned with in-built or long-established features of the language or its usage that reflect an 'unreconstructed' attitude to women, other races, or the disabled – in other words, an attitude that is no longer acceptable in modern society.

The aim of removing discriminatory or demeaning language from everyday use and replacing it with neutral language is in itself wholly admirable. The problem often seems to lie in the fact that much of the terminology that is presented as non-discriminatory seems also to be euphemistic or contrived. It is as if the general rule of good language use were to be plain and direct, but that this particular area of language use constituted a special case where other rules apply. Plain terms (of Saxon origin) such as *blind, deaf, cripple, mad, backward* are deemed inappropriate and the more roundabout terms *visually impaired, mentally ill, experiencing learning difficulties*, etc., are preferred. It is sometimes hard to decide whether this represents a collective effort on the part of the well meaning to sugar some particularly bitter pills and be nice to everybody or a genuine attempt to make society rethink its attitude to and treatment of people with disabilities. See also chapter 2, p. 62 **'challenged'**.

It seems that, as far as non-discriminatory language is concerned, English is in a transitional or possibly still experimental stage. People are aware of the problem and endeavouring to tackle it, but the means of tackling it that have so far been devised have either not become quite familiar enough to be used with natural ease by the bulk of the population or are not the best that can be devised and better ones will in time replace them.

One particular legacy of former centuries that currently causes concern in English is what many perceive as its in-built sexism. It is generally agreed that language ought to reflect new social relationships between men and women or even promote a more equal relationship if it does not yet exist. The process of adjusting it to fit this purpose has been going on for some time, but here too by no means all the problems have been solved satisfactorily. It is not simply a question of old habits dying hard. There are some areas where grammar and usage make it difficult to speak or write without an apparent sexual bias.

First among these is the question of which personal pronoun to use when discussing something that applies equally to women and to men. It used to be the case that the masculine pronoun *he* was used when a member of a particular category of people was being referred to in the singular: *When a doctor suspects this to be the case he will generally refer his patient to a specialist.* It is a measure of the progress that has been made that a sentence of this kind seems not only inappropriate but also distinctly old-fashioned.

There are various alternatives. One is to use both the masculine and feminine pronouns *he or she* (or *she or he*) – or, in writing, in a form such as *he/she* or *(s)he.* This can become cumbersome: *... he or she will generally refer his or her patient to a specialist, who will then use his or her discretion ...*, but is often a perfectly adequate solution to the problem. Since the third person plural pronoun *they* is neither masculine nor feminine, it often works to recast the whole sentence using the plural form: *When doctors suspect this to be the case, they will generally refer their patients ...*

It is sometimes possible to use *they* as a singular pronoun. Traditionalists object, but it has long been common in speech, and is becoming much more so in writing, to use *they* to refer back to an indefinite pronoun such as *anyone, everyone, nobody, someone, each, every, either,* or *neither.* The majority of ordinary users of English and most experts would not object to sentences of the following type except in the most formal writing:

> *Everyone needs a friend they can rely on.*
> *Anybody who thinks that needs their head examined.*

It is not usually acceptable to use *they* as a singular pronoun to refer back to a specific noun: *When a doctor suspects this to be the case they will refer ...* does not work because there is too jarring a clash between the definitely singular element (*a doctor suspects ...*) and the plural used as singular (*they will ...*). A degree of care and sometimes ingenuity is needed to produce a sentence that truly and elegantly reflects the fact that a member of a particular group or profession may be either a woman or a man.

The nouns used to denote people in particular occupations or positions are sometimes also a source of trouble. Neutral terms are often available and should be used: *headteacher* instead of *headmaster* and *headmistress, firefighter* instead of *fireman, police officer* (although, given the fact women police officers sometimes have a special role in dealing with female members of the public, the term *policewoman* still has its place), *chair* or *chairperson, flight attendant*, etc. It is generally inappropriate to use terms with a specifically feminine suffix *-ess* or *-ette* or *-trix*. There are a few exceptions to this (in British English it is still quite common for a woman running a shop to be referred to as the *manageress* or a woman serving in a restaurant as a *waitress*), but in the vast majority of cases these forms are regarded as patronizing and are dying out. Terms ending in *-er* or *-or* are considered to be neutral. When available they should be used. The suffix *-person* occasionally has its uses as well, and has become fairly established in combinations such as *chairperson* and *spokesperson*. It is probably not a good idea, however, to use it too generally. The plural form *people* (in a combination such as *business people*) often sounds much more natural than a construct such as *businessperson* or a plural form such as *businesspersons*.

Finally, there is the question of the most appropriate term to refer to human beings as a race. The term for the human species as a species is still *man*. It is evident, however, that in many instances it would be preferable to use a term that did not appear to be favouring human males over human females. The singular form again presents most problems – and again the use of the plural instead of the singular can sometimes solve them (*early* or *primitive humans* (*human beings*) instead of *early man*, etc.). Likewise the substitution of *humanity* or *humankind* for *mankind* is generally to be recommended. The verb *to man* is also sometimes considered contentious and can usually be replaced by *to staff* or *to crew* or by changing a sentence around so that *The switchboard is manned at all times* becomes *There is someone on duty at all times*. American English has a term *humanmade* that is substitutable for *man-made*. That term is not current in British English, but *artificial* or *synthetic* can serve the same purpose.

As with non-discriminatory language in general, this is an area where the process of change, adaptation, and familiarization is likely to continue for some time. It is most unlikely that present social trends towards the equalization of the sexes will be set into reverse. Consequently it is the responsibility of all serious users of English to be aware of the issues and to use care and imagination in dealing with them.

4 Spelling

Introduction

English spelling is notoriously difficult and inconsistent. Other languages have what is known as **phonetic spelling**, in which a word is, roughly speaking, spelt as it sounds, each letter of the alphabet corresponding to one particular sound made by the voice. While many of the simpler words in English (*fat*, *cat*, *mat*, etc.) function in this way, most of the more complex ones do not. The number of possible ways in which the combination of letters *-ough*, to take only one particularly strange example, can be pronounced illustrates how far English has moved away from phonetic spelling (compare *cough*, *dough*, *rough*, *slough* and *thorough* – and there are more!). There are rules governing the way words are spelt, which will be set out later in this chapter, and rules can be learnt. People who are not gifted with superb powers of memory or who do not have a natural talent for spelling, however, are still likely to make mistakes. Even with the benefit of the spellcheckers that are incorporated into almost all modern computers and word processors, official and business letters still arrive with spelling mistakes in them. The spelling (and grammar) of many websites on the Internet is notoriously bad. Spelling mistakes are often hard to spot when you are writing and yet somehow so conspicuous when read later.

Putting aside authorial impersonality for a moment, the writers confess to being far from perfect spellers. We trust in the effectiveness of a spellchecker and the eagle eyes of other editors, proofreaders, etc., and hope to provide an unblemished text. Writing with a pen on paper (especially in a hurry) or typing without the benefit of an automatic error-indicator, it is a somewhat different story. The best and perhaps only guard, apart from mechanical aids, against making mistakes is knowledge of your own weak points and reference to a dictionary in cases of doubt. How many *r*'s in *embarrass*, how many *n*'s in *millennium*? If you have difficulties remembering such spellings as these, at least try mentally to flag these words as dangerous. There are dictionaries available that are specifically designed to show the spellings of words (also often indicating the correct places to make syllable breaks if you should need to hyphenate a word to make it fit a line) and including a very brief definition. However, a dictionary cannot help unless it is consulted, that is, unless the writer is aware that they need help.

Sounds and spellings

While it is true to say that English spelling is not particularly phonetic, there is generally a link between the way a word is pronounced and the way it is spelt. Different sounds are reproduced by different combinations of letters. This is most crucial – and most difficult – with regard to vowel sounds. The nature of a vowel also often affects other aspects of spelling such as the dropping or retaining of a final *e* or the doubling of a final consonant.

There are, of course, five vowels in the English alphabet *a*, *e*, *i*, *o*, *u*. All the other letters are consonants, though *w* and *y* are sometimes referred to as semivowels because they share some of the characteristics of true vowels.

The English language, however, uses rather more vowel sounds than it has letters for and this where the complications arise. Vowel sounds can be pronounced short or long. The vowels in the words *bat*, *bet*, *bit*, *cot*, *put*, and *but* are all short. The vowels in *father*, *be*, and *to* are long. Short vowel sounds are usually represented by a single letter – though the short *e* in *bed* is sometimes represented by *ea* (*head*, *lead* (the metal)). Long vowel sounds can be represented in a number of ways. The *a* sound in *father*, for example, can also be represented by *ar* (*arm*); the *e* in *be* often appears as *ee* (*bee*), *ea* (*bean*), *ei* (*ceiling*), or *ie* (*niece*); while the *o* in *to* may be rendered as *oo* (*too*), *ew* (*flew*), *u* (*flute*), or by *ue* (*blue*).

English is also rich in sounds known as **diphthongs**, combinations of two vowel sounds. If the list of long vowel sounds above seems rather short, this is because many of the long sounds in English are actually diphthongs – for example the *a* sound in *hay* or *rain*, the *i* sound in *lie* or *my*, the *o* sound in *note* or *coat*. The *u* sound in *unit* and *you* is also a combined sound, tacking a *y* onto the long *o* sound.

Spelling rules for vowels: 'i' before 'e'

This chapter gives some of the basic rules of English spelling. One of the easiest spelling rules to remember concerning vowels is one that is – or used to be – taught to every child at primary school: *i before e except after c*. The rule applies to most words in which *ie* represents the long *e* sound: *achieve, believe, brief, chief, diesel, field, grief, hygiene, niece, piece, relieve, reprieve, shield, shriek, siege, thief, wield, yield*. The exception is after *c*: *ceiling, conceit, conceive, deceit, deceive, perceive, receipt, receive*. Exceptions to the general rule include: *caffeine, Keith, Neil, protein, seize, Sheila, species, weir, weird*. And note that the spelling *ei* is used when the sound is *ay*: *beige, deign, eight, freight, neighbour, reign, rein, veil, vein, weigh*.

'y' and 'ie'

The combination *ie* also figures in another useful rule of spelling. Words that end in a consonant followed by *-y* change the *y* to *ie* in order to form most of their inflections (the plural if they are nouns, the comparative and superlative if they are adjectives, and the third person singular of the present tense and past tense and past participle if they are verbs). So, when *fancy* is a noun, its plural is *fancies*; when it is an adjective, its comparative is *fancier* and its superlative is *fanciest*; and when it is a verb we say *he fancies* and *he fancied* (but *fancying*). To give further examples: the plural of *charity* is *charities*; *happy* converts to *happier* and *happiest*; *to vary* makes *he varies, she has varied* (but *varying*).

Words that end with a vowel followed by a *y* do not do this. For the most part they inflect in the normal way. The plural of *boy* is *boys* and of *holiday* is *holidays*; *coy* converts to *coyer* and *coyest*; *annoy* makes *annoys, annoyed*, and *annoying*. The most notable exceptions to this rule are irregular verbs such as *lay, pay*, and *say*, which use *id* to form their past tense and past participle (*laid, paid, said*).

'-os' and '-oes'

Words that end with a combination of a consonant and *o* generally form their plural by adding *-es* (*potato – potatoes*; *tomato – tomatoes*; *echo – echoes*). The same applies to the formation of the third person singular of the present tense of verbs that end in a consonant + *o* (*embargo – embargoes*). When a word ends in a vowel followed by *o*, it simply adds an *s* (*cameo – cameos, studio – studios*).

Some words add *-es* or *-s* for the plural: *banjo – banjos* or *banjoes*; *cargo – cargos* or *cargoes*; *ghetto – ghettos* or *ghettoes*; *volcano – volcanos* or *volcanoes*; *zero – zeros* or *zeroes*. At least the original rule covers *potato* and *tomato* and you would not go wrong in following it for all the words that have alternative plurals!

Dropping or retaining '-e'

English words that contain a long vowel or diphthong often end with a silent *-e*: *hate, invite, nice, note, cute*. When these words are nouns and adjectives they cause few problems – they add *s* to form the plural in the normal way (*hates, notes*) and form the comparative and superlative by adding *-r* and *-st* (*nicer, nicest*; *cuter, cutest*). Another, and more accurate, way of putting that last point would be to say that they drop their own silent *e* and add the standard suffixes *-er* and *-est*. The distinction is quite important because the rule of spelling that concerns these words is usually formulated like this. Words that end in a silent *e* drop it in order to add a suffix that begins with a vowel.

To give some examples. The verb *to note* has the present participle (*-ing* form) *noting* and the past participle *noted*. The *e* is dropped to make the adjective *notable* because the suffix *-able* begins with a vowel. Following the same pattern, from *bore* we get *boring*, from *hope* we get *hoping*, from *precise* comes *precision*. There are a few exceptions where the *e* is not omitted before *-ing*. For example *singeing* ('scorching') to differentiate it from *singing* a song; *routeing* ('arranging a route') to differentiate it from *routing* ('defeating decisively'). There is a growing tendency to omit the *-e* before the suffixes *-able* and *-age*: *lovable* or *loveable*; *movable* or *moveable*; *unmistakable* or *unmistakeable*.

If the word ends with the 'soft' *c* or *g* (as in *nice* or *huge*), the *e* is not omitted in front of *a* and *o*. Thus, *peace* and *service* give *peaceable* and *serviceable* respectively, while the *g* words *courage*, *manage*, and *outrage* produce the adjectives *courageous*, *manageable*, and *outrageous*.

The following words can be spelt with or without the *-e* after *g*: *acknowledgment* or *acknowledgement*; *judgment* or *judgement*.

In front of the suffixes that begin with a consonant, the final *-e* is not usually omitted: *arrange – arrangement*; *bore – boredom*; *complete – completely*; *precise – precisely*. Exceptions include: *argue – argument*; *due – duly*; *true – truly*.

'-our' and '-orous'

One of the best-known differences between British and American spelling affects words such as *humour*, which is spelt with two *u*'s in British and only one (*humor*) in American English. British users need to remember that the extra *u* is omitted when certain suffixes are added to them. The main suffix is *-ous*; others are *-ary*, *-ation*, *-ial*, and *-ific*. Thus *glamour – glamorous*; *humour – humorous*; *labour – laborious*; *colour – coloration*; *honour – honorary*, *honorific*; *armour – armorial*.

'-able' and '-ible'

It is often difficult to decide or remember which of these two forms of essentially the same suffix is the correct one to use when spelling a particular word. Of the two, *-able* is much the commoner. It stands to reason, therefore, that, if pressed, one should opt for it rather than for *-ible*. Moreover, new words are formed by adding *-able* rather than *-ible*: *microwave – microwav(e)able*; *photocopy – photocopiable*.

There are a few rules of thumb, however, which can act as pointers to those words in which *-ible* is the correct spelling.

Cases where the main part of the word to which the suffix is attached is not a complete and recognizable English word in itself tend to end in *-ible*. So we have *ed|ible*, *horr|ible* and *terr|ible* and using the same system: *audible*, *credible*, *incredible*, and *visible* in contrast to, for example, *accept|-able*, *agree|able*, *break|able*, and *work|able*. Unfortunately there are a good many exceptions to this rule, such as *affable, amenable, formidable, inevitable, memorable, probable*, and *vulnerable*.

Likewise, if the main part of the word ends in one of the following letters or combinations of letters then it is likely that *-ible* will be the correct form: a 'soft' *c* (*deducible, forcible, invincible, reducible, irascible*); a soft *g* (*eligible, incorrigible, legible, negligible, tangible*); the combinations *ns* and *ss* (*comprehensible, defensible, responsible, reprehensible, sensible; accessible, admissible, expressible, permissible, possible*). A good many words in which *ct, pt*, and *st* immediately precede the suffix also take *-ible* (*indestructible; contemptible; perceptible; digestible, inexhaustible*, and *irresistible*), but there are several *-able* words of this type as well, for example, *contactable, acceptable, adaptable*, and *detestable*.

Doubling of consonants

The principal spelling problem with consonants in English is to know when to double them. The basic rule is that when a word ends with a single consonant, that consonant doubles when adding a suffix which begins with a vowel. This applies to adjectives when adding *-er* and *-est* to form the comparative and superlative: *big – bigger – biggest; sad – sadder – saddest*. It applies to verbs forming their participles: *stop – stopping – stopped; tip – tipping – tipped*. It similarly applies when adding other suffixes to form different classes of words: *bid – biddable; plod – plodder*. It also applies when *-y* is added to form adjectives from nouns: *fun – funny; jam – jammy; wit – witty*.

All the above examples show words with only one syllable. When a word has two or more syllables, the rule still applies when the last syllable is stressed and the final consonant is preceded by a single vowel: *allot – allotting – allotted; commit – committing – committed – committal; compel – compelling – compelled; forget – forgetting – forgettable; occur – occurring – occurred; regret – regretting – regretted – regrettable*. Examples of words with more than two syllables: *disinter – disinterring – disinterred; intermit – intermittent*.

If the stress falls on an earlier syllable, the final consonant does not double. So *develop* (stress on the second syllable of three) has words deriving from it such as *developing, developed* and *developer; focus – focused; benefit – benefited; target – targeted*. Occasionally, certain of these words may appear with a doubled consonant: *biassed, focussed, benefitted, targetted*, although these spellings are becoming less frequently used in contemporary English.

Exceptions include words that have a final *-l* which is doubled even though the syllable is unstressed: *travel – travelled – traveller; cancel – cancelled; counsel – counselled*. American spelling is more consistent than British in this respect, since all the above words have only one *l* (*traveler, counseled*, etc.) when spelt the American way. Other exceptions: *handicap – handicapped; worship – worshipped – worshipper* (American English usually *worshiped, worshiper*).

Difficult words

To end this section, here is a list of over 150 words, as spelt in British English, many not mentioned previously, that commonly cause problems. Other words that cause difficulty, e.g. *complimentary* and *complementary, disc* and *disk, licence* and *license, practice* and *practise, principal* and *principle*, are dealt with in chapter 2.

accessory
accommodate, accommodation
address
adolescent
advertisement
aggravate
all right
analyse, analysis
annihilate
anonymous
appalling
Arctic, Antarctic
asphyxiate
assassin, assassinate
assessment
attendant
bankruptcy
beautiful, beauty
besiege
bigot, bigoted
bourgeois
buoy, buoyant
caffeine
calendar
calibre
carburettor
catalogue
ceiling
chrysanthemum
commemorate
commiserate
committee
conceit
condemn
conscience, conscientious
conscious
consensus
copyright
corollary
correspondence, correspondent
deceive

desiccated
desperate
dialogue
diarrhoea
diphtheria
diphthong
discipline
ecstasy, ecstatic
eighth
embarrass
exaggerate
excite, exciting
exhilarate
Fahrenheit
fascinate
fatigue
favourite
February
fluorescent
forty
four, fourth
friend
fulfil
gardener
gauge
gorilla
gossip
government
grammar
guarantee
guard, guardian

census
haemorrhage
harass, harassment
height
honorary
hygiene
hypocrisy, hypocrite
idiosyncrasy
illegible
independent
inoculate
instalment
it's (it is)
its (of it)
leisure
liaise, liaison
liquefy
loose
lose
manoeuvre
Mediterranean
millennium
minuscule
miscellaneous
mortgage
moustache
necessary, necessarily
niece
occasion
ophthalmic, ophthalmologist
orthopaedic

descendant
parallel
peccadillo
penicillin
perceive
perennial
personnel
playwright
pneumatic
possess
precede
privilege
proceed
psychiatry
psychology
pursue
questionnaire
queue, queued
receipt
recommend
reconnaissance
reconnoitre
relevant
rendezvous
repertoire
repetition
resistant
restaurant
resuscitate
rhyme
rhythm
right

guerrilla
salutary
schizophrenia
seize
separate, separation
sergeant
sheikh
sheriff
siege
skilful
sober
sombre
straight
subterranean
oscillate
supersede
surgeon
surveillance
susceptible
symmetry, symmetrical
synchronize
syringe
teetotaller
thief
threshold
tranquillizer
treacherous
vaccinate
sacrilegious
vacillate
vacuum
variegated
Wednesday
weight
welcome
welfare
wholly
withhold
woollen
write
yacht
yogurt/yoghurt

5 Punctuation

Introduction

Punctuation breaks up the flow of words and thoughts into meaningful units. Without punctuation, a string of words would often remain just that – a string of words. Punctuation shapes sentences, distinguishes between different types of utterance, and highlights and emphasizes different words or groups of words. In proficiency in a language, knowledge and skill in the use of punctuation is as important as a sound grasp of grammar and a wide vocabulary.

It is easy enough to illustrate the confusion that can arise when punctuation marks are incorrectly used:

The supervisor said John was not doing his job properly.

This is a perfectly good and understandable sentence. Inserting two commas, however, can completely reverse its meaning:

The supervisor, said John, was not doing his job properly.

Adding quotation marks reinforces this interpretation of the sentence:

'The supervisor,' said John, 'was not doing his job properly.'

In dealing with punctuation, of course, we are concerned only with the written language. If sentences such as those used in the example above were spoken, it would be obvious which meaning was intended from the slight pauses that the speaker introduced, the way that their voice rose and fell, and the emphasis they put on different words. The human voice is a very flexible and expressive instrument. Body language and eye contact can also play their part. There are all sorts of ways in which meaning can be conveyed when speaking that are not available to someone who is using a pen or a keyboard and who cannot be heard or seen by the person that they are communicating with. Punctuation cannot be a substitute for all of these, but it can take the place of many of them. Good punctuation can almost put a shrug of the shoulders or a hesitant tone of voice down on paper without having to describe either explicitly. Imaginative and varied punctuation gives individual rhythm to a piece of prose.

Writers nowadays tend to punctuate their work much more lightly than they did in the past. Semicolons and colons were often used in places where nowadays many writers would put a comma, and commas were often used where most modern writers would put no punctuation at all. Dickens' sentences, for instance, sometimes seem to bristle with punctuation. This is the opening of *Nicholas Nickleby*:

> There once lived, in a sequestered part of the county of Devonshire, one Mr. Godfrey Nickleby: a worthy gentleman, who, taking it into his head rather late in life that he must get married, and not being young enough or rich enough to aspire to the hand of a lady of fortune, had wedded an old flame out of mere attachment, who in her turn had taken him for the same reason.

The bristly effect is even more pronounced in writers of earlier centuries. Here is the famous essayist Joseph Addison, one of the most admired stylists of his time, writing about Shakespeare in *The Spectator* in the early eighteenth century:

> Among great Genius's, those few draw the Admiration of mankind of all the World upon them, and stand up as the Prodigies of Mankind, who by the meer strength of natural Parts, and without any Assistance of Art or Learning, have produced Works that were the Delight of their own Times and the Wonder of Posterity.

Lighter punctuation goes with the plainer and rather more informal style adopted by most modern writers. It is perfectly possible to write quite long sentences which are structured so that they require no punctuation at all. The aim of this chapter is to give guidelines on correct and effective punctuation.

The comma

The comma is perhaps rivalled only by the apostrophe for the amount of confusion it can cause. In certain circumstances, including or excluding a comma is largely a matter of taste. There are many contexts, however, in which the correct use of a comma, as of any other punctuation mark, is essential if a sentence is to be properly understood.

Although the main function of punctuation is to separate – sentence from sentence, clause from clause, one meaningful unit of language from another – it can also be seen as a linking device. Commas illustrate this point well. They have several main functions – three that have mainly to do with separation and two that have more to do with linking. Commas separate the items in a list, separate small sections at the beginning and end of sentences, and bracket independent sections in the middle of sentences. But commas also link the clauses that make up a compound sentence and the beginning and end of clauses from which something has been missed out. These five functions will now be dealt with in more detail. Three other specific uses of commas will then complete this section.

Commas in lists

In lists, commas are generally a substitute for the word *and* and sometimes for the word *or*. They are used when a list contains three or more items which are single words, phrases, or sentences:

> *I bought apples, bananas, carrots, and lettuces.*
>
> *French is spoken in Canada, in North Africa, and in the Lebanon.*
>
> *The President speaks French, the Vice-President speaks German, and the Prime Minister speaks Greek.*

To repeat the point, these commas could, at least theoretically, be replaced by *and* (*I bought apples and bananas and carrots and lettuces*). If a comma in a list cannot be replaced by *and*, then it is in the wrong place.

It is becoming more common in British English (and is usual in American English) to place a comma before the *and* that precedes the final item in a simple list (*numbers one, two, three, and four*). A comma used in that position is known as a **serial comma**. This book uses such serial commas.

The more complex a list becomes, the more useful it is to add a serial comma: *The President speaks French, the Vice-President speaks German, and the Prime Minister speaks Greek.* There are also occasions when it is vital to use an extra comma because otherwise the divisions between the various items in the list might not be clear: *I've bought several recordings by Bob Dylan, Paul Simon, and Simon and Garfunkel.* If there were no comma after *Paul Simon*, the reader might be misled into thinking there was a pop group called *Paul Simon and Simon and Garfunkel.*

Commas are also used to divide up lists of adjectives preceding a noun: *The suspect had long, dark, greasy hair.* It would, however, be equally correct in this case to omit the commas from the list entirely and to write: *The suspect had long dark greasy hair.* The use of commas, therefore, is common, but optional, in lists of adjectives that are all of equal value and all refer to the same noun.

Sometimes it is positively wrong to put in a comma. Take, for example, the sentences: *I bought two large, juicy, green apples* and *I bought two large, juicy green peppers.* In the first instance, *and* could be reasonably inserted in the list: *I bought two large and juicy and green apples*, or, more elegantly, *I bought two apples that were large and juicy and green.* All the adjectives refer equally to *apples.* In the second instance, what we assume the speaker bought was *two green peppers that were large and juicy* rather than *two peppers that were large and juicy and green.* In this instance, instead of three equal adjectives, we have two adjectives, *large* and *juicy*, preceding a compound noun *green pepper.*

Further, commas should not be placed between an adverb and an adjective. It is easy to make that mistake with adverbs such as *bright* or *hard* that have the same form as adjectives: compare *a bright, yellow moon* with *a bright yellow envelope.* Neither, generally speaking, should a comma be put in front of a noun used adjectivally in front of another noun: *a red, waxy substance* but a *red wax candle.*

Commas with clauses at beginnings and ends of sentences

When a subordinate clause begins a sentence, a comma is often used to separate it from the rest of the sentence:

When you next go to Paris, come and see me.

Although he didn't like her, he was prepared to tolerate her.

Since you're so clever, why don't you sort the whole thing out yourself?

In these examples there is no great danger of the sense being misunderstood if the comma is omitted.

But where a subordinate clause ends with a verb, and the following clause begins with a noun, the danger of at least momentary confusion is greater. The insertion of a comma in such sentences is vital. Consider the following examples:

If they don't return, the money will be given to charity.

After she had finished reading, the book was replaced on the shelf.

As you see, the situation is desperate.

In each case, the comma indicates that the writer intends the verb to be understood as an intransitive one (with no direct object). Remove the comma and it seems for a moment that the verb has a direct object after all:

If they don't return the money . . .

After she had finished reading the book . . .

As you see the situation . . .

A comma is also often used when an adverb, adverbial phrase, or adverbial clause comes at the beginning of a sentence. Here, too, it is often vital to insert a comma so that the sense can be properly understood. Consider the following examples:

Below, the ocean waves were crashing against the rocks.

Normally, intelligent people can see through such subterfuge.

After eating, the staff went home.

After a period of calm, college students have begun to demonstrate again.

If commas were left out of these sentences, the sense is different:

Below the ocean waves . . .

Normally intelligent people . . .

After eating the staff . . .

After a period of calm college students . . .

Even where there is no real danger of confusion or absurdity, it is usually better to insert a comma than not. Most phrases that are based on the infinitive form of a verb or a participle require one:

To do them justice, they were very apologetic.

Reading between the lines, I think they're getting very worried.

Having dealt with that problem successfully, she immediately turned her attention to the next.

Turning to the other end of the sentence, a comma is often used before a subordinate clause positioned after a main clause:

I'm very fond of him, although I'm well aware that he has his faults.

Barbara couldn't come, because she had a prior engagement.

A comma is not always necessary, however, in such sentences.

Commas are not used before clauses beginning with *that*:

It is possible that the delivery of the goods might be late.

She told me that the rumours were untrue.

There is a good chance that he will be out of hospital next week.

The grammatical reason for this is that the *that* clauses in the above examples are functioning either as complements or, in the second example, as the object of the verb. It is, of course, proper to use commas to separate a series or 'list' of *that* clauses: *He said that he was sorry, that he hadn't meant to hurt anyone, that he'd paid for any damage, and that he hoped we would forgive him.*

Finally, commas are always used after a group of words that makes a statement when a tag question such as *didn't he* or *aren't they* is tacked onto it:

It's nice and warm today, isn't it?

You are coming out tonight, aren't you?

Bracketing commas

One of the most important functions of commas is their use in pairs to separate a piece of information that is obviously additional to the main meaning of a sentence. In fact, such pieces of information are not merely additional; they are, strictly speaking, superfluous to the sentence as a whole. They can be removed from it and the sentence will still make sense.

For example, take the sentence *David Mander, the club's new chairperson, made a speech.* Here the phrase *the club's new chairperson* describes David Mander, but is essentially incidental to the main statement, which is that *David Mander made a speech.* The sentence could be switched around – in this case making the name of the new chairperson the incidental factor – and the punctuation would remain the same: *The club's new chairperson, David Mander, made a speech.* Here are some examples where the insert is much longer, but it is nonetheless incidental to the sentence as a whole and so is enclosed within commas:

> *It's not the most beautiful car in the world, as anyone can see, but it is very economical.*
>
> *The dictionary, first published in 1918 and re-edited at roughly ten-year intervals ever since, has never been out of print.*
>
> *Gone are the days when, because everything Victorian was out of fashion, such buildings were considered to be a joke.*

There are all sorts of little phrases that commonly occur within sentences – *above all*; *as I said*; *in fact*; *of course, what is more*, etc. – that should, in most instances, appear only within commas:

> *He felt, of course, rather foolish.*
>
> *I, in fact, had said much the same thing at a previous meeting.*
>
> *The terms they were offering were, to be honest, less favourable than we had expected.*

In a similar way there are a number of single words, often serving as backward links to what has been said in a previous sentence, to which the same thing applies. *However* is perhaps the most common:

The railway system, however, remains in a state of disrepair.

The board, consequently, has had to revise its previous decision.

We have, nevertheless, to consider the other possibilities.

A major source of trouble with commas lies in their use in what are known as **non-restrictive clauses** – that is, those that describe rather than identify (or define) a person or thing (see also pp. 21–2). Because such clauses *describe* rather than *identify*, they could be omitted, and so they go into commas. The problem is to decide what identifies and what merely describes.

Consider the example: *My sister who lives in Australia is a sales executive.* There are two ways of understanding and, consequently, of punctuating this sentence. The first assumes that the sentence refers specifically to *my sister who lives in Australia.* The implication is that the speaker has more than one sister. One lives in Australia, the others live elsewhere, consequently the phrase *who lives in Australia* identifies and defines which sister is being talked about. The phrase is, therefore, crucial to the sentence and *cannot* be put between commas. The second way of understanding the sentence, however, is that it refers simply to *my sister* – possibly the speaker's only sister – who is a sales executive. In that case, the fact that she lives in Australia is a piece of incidental information and the phrase that expresses this should be enclosed in commas: *My sister, who lives in Australia, is a sales executive.*

When referring to things, non-restrictive (describing) clauses always begin with *which* and restrictive (identifying or defining) clauses may begin with either *that* or *which.* Note too that *that* clauses do not have commas; *which* clauses frequently do.

Here are some further examples:

Mrs Beeton's Book of Household Management, which was first published in 1861, has become an international bestseller.

The clause *which was first published in 1861* gives incidental information and so is a non-restrictive *which* clause, with commas.

The cookery book that I had been given as a birthday present somehow got lost in the move.

This is a restrictive *that* clause – it identifies or defines which cookery book – and so there are no commas.

A further type of descriptive relative clause that is used with a comma is one in which the *which* clause relates to the main clause as a whole.

He failed the exam, which was not surprising.

They helped us move house, for which we were most grateful.

Linking commas

Commas are often used to link together the two parts of a compound sentence, a compound sentence being one that has two main clauses joined by *and, or, but, yet,* or *while* (see pp. 15–16). However, it is as important to know when not to use a comma as when to use one.

When the two clauses have the same subject or initial phrase, whether or not it is repeated, a comma is not usually used:

They speak Italian fluently and (they) can get by in Spanish as well.

On the stroke of midnight Cinderella's fine clothes turned back into rags and (also on the stroke of midnight) her silver coach vanished into thin air.

When the subjects of the two clauses joined by *and* are not the same, however, a comma is generally used:

They speak fluently, and their Italian friends are equally fluent in English.

Is that your final decision, or do you need more time to think things over?

A comma is particularly used when the two clauses form a contrast:

Jan wants to continue the relationship, but Tom wants to walk out and end it.

It seems like a good idea, yet I'm not at all convinced it will work.

The use of the comma has the effect of highlighting the contrast and also making a slight pause between the clauses. Nevertheless, if the clauses are fairly short, the comma is optional: *The car overturned but the driver wasn't hurt.*

If there are two clauses in the sentence, and they are not joined by *and,* etc., then a comma is not usually the correct way to link them. If their meaning is quite closely connected, a semicolon (see also pp. 157–9) should be used instead of a comma: *German-born Schmidt became a British citizen; he later married an Englishwoman.*

Where the meaning is less closely connected, the better alternative is to have two sentences: *The red car was cheaper. The blue car, on the other hand, looked much smarter.*

Commas filling gaps

Sometimes a group of words (usually a verb phrase) that is used in one clause needs to be repeated in a subsequent clause in order to complete its sense. But if repeating the phrase would make the sentence very cumbersome, it can be omitted, and a comma inserted in its place. Take, for example: *They had already made a decision to go; we had already made a decision to stay.* The phrase *had already made a decision* can be replaced in the second clause by a comma, producing a much crisper result: *They had already made a decision to go; we, to stay.* The comma also has the same function in the following sentences:

> *Chelsea had the greater share of possession in the first half; Villa, in the second.*
>
> *The new building was generally considered to be an eyesore, the exhibition, a failure, and the whole enterprise, a waste of public money.*
>
> *To err is human, to forgive, divine.*

Commas and speech

A comma is used between the words of direct speech – the words that are put in quotation marks – and the verb *say* or any other reporting expression:

> *'Come and look at the room,' he said, 'it has a sea view.'*
>
> *'I'm back,' she called out.*
>
> *He ventured the question, 'Do you really love me?'*

For more on this, see pp. 161–3.

Remember, however, that a comma is not used before *that*, etc., in indirect speech:

She called out that she was back.

The committee agreed that they would fund half the cost of the extension.

Commas with numbers

Commas are used to divide large numbers into groups of three digits, to separate thousands, millions, etc.:

65,678

10,137,673

Note that commas are sometimes not used with four-digit numbers and they are never used in dates: *4,517* or *4517*; *in the year 2010*.

Spaces are sometimes used in place of commas, particularly with metric units: *A kilometre consists of 1 000 metres.*

Commas with names

Commas must be used when a person is being addressed by name or when a group of people are being addressed:

Please, Fred, try again.

Sergeant Miller, take those men away.

Ladies and gentlemen, boys and girls, welcome to the show.

I've told you before, Hoskins, this has got to stop.

The reason for this is simple and goes back to what has been said before. Without commas, the name appears as part of the sentence. Compare *I'm fed up with ringing Jane* and *I'm fed up with ringing, Jane.*

The full stop

There are two functions of the full stop. Its main one is to mark the end of a sentence that does not have a question mark or an exclamation mark at the end. This function does not require specific illustration. Most of the sentences in this book end with full stops. It is worth noting, however, that a sentence should never have more than one full stop. This rule mainly comes into play in relation to quotations: see pp. 161–3.

A full stop is also used with certain types of abbreviation, though generally it must be said that full stops are used less with abbreviations these days than in the past. The abbreviation for the 'British Broadcasting Corporation' is now more commonly found as *BBC* than *B.B.C.* Full stops tend to be used more with abbreviations that consist of small letters, particularly when the abbreviated form without the full stops could be confused with an ordinary word: *a.m.* (ante meridiem, before noon), *f.o.b.* (free on board, relating to a shipment of goods); *e.g.* (exempli gratia, for example).

Abbreviations which contain the first and last letters of a word (*Mr*; *St* [Saint or Street]) are generally written without a full stop. For further details, see pp. 175–7.

The question mark

The question mark has one main function: to appear at the end of a direct question and indicate that it is a question:

Which way is it to the station?

So Margot has invited you too, has she?

He did what?

When a sentence ends in a question mark, it does not require a full stop.

There are several different ways in which questions can be phrased in standard English. These are dealt with on pp. 12–13 and pp. 38–9. Any question that is addressed directly to another person needs a question mark. So does any rhetorical question, that is, one to which an answer is not really expected:

How do you do?

Where has the time gone?

How can people live like that?

So too does a question that is reported in direct speech: *'Have you seen my book anywhere?' he asked.* Notice that in this instance the question mark is placed inside the inverted commas.

The only type of question that does not require a question mark is a question that is given in reported (or indirect) speech. (See also pp. 19–21.) It would be incorrect to end any of the following examples with a question mark:

She asked me why I had come.

People are very curious to know how you managed to do it.

We questioned him again as to what had motivated his decision.

The presence of question words (*why*, *how*, *what*) in these sentences does not alter the fact that they are essentially statements giving information rather than questions requesting it.

The question mark has one minor function, which is to indicate that something, often a date or figure, is doubtful or an estimate. When used in this way the question mark usually appears next to (usually in front of) whatever it refers to. Often the question mark is put inside brackets. For example, the year in which the poet Geoffrey Chaucer died is known precisely, but the year of his birth is not, so his dates are often shown in the following form: *Geoffrey Chaucer (?1342–1400)*. Likewise the question mark in the following example shows that the speaker is not precisely sure what number is involved: *According to the rules, 33 per cent of committee members constitute a quorum, that is (?)9 people* (or *?9 people*).

The exclamation mark

The exclamation mark is another punctuation mark with one main function – to indicate that the words that precede it constitute an exclamation:

How splendid!

Give me a chance!

Stand still!

What a disaster!

As with the question mark, a sentence ending in an exclamation mark does not need a full stop. Likewise, an exclamation reported in direct speech ends with an exclamation mark inside the inverted commas: *'What an extraordinary coincidence!' he exclaimed.*

The nature and form of exclamations is discussed on pp. 14–15. Exclamations are usually fairly short expressions of heightened emotion which are often given in a somewhat louder voice than ordinary speech. Since formal writing generally adopts a moderate tone, the use of exclamation marks in formal writing is comparatively rare. In fact, most writers on punctuation discourage the use of too many exclamation marks, suggesting that, if used too frequently, they give a piece of writing an overheated and hysterical or slightly bullying tone. They also frown on the use of more than one exclamation mark at a time (*Goal!!!*). This is good advice for formal writing, though in personal or comic writing this rule can be relaxed.

Exclamation marks are also occasionally used to draw attention to an interruption – often one enclosed in brackets or between dashes – in the general flow of a sentence, especially if the interruption is a slightly ironical one:

On those (thankfully rare!) occasions when we tried to have a serious conversation . . .

Our visitors arrived at noon – Jean wasn't up yet! – having been invited for six o'clock in the evening.

The semicolon

The semicolon, like the colon, is probably underused as a punctuation mark because its correct use is felt to be complicated and difficult. This is not, in fact, the case: the basic rule for using the semicolon is quite simple. It links together clauses which could stand alone as sentences, but which have a close relationship with one another and are more effectively shown as components of a single sentence. Semicolons are not used in conjunction with linking words such as *and* or *but*; they are, however, frequently used in situations where an alternative method of constructing the sentence would be to use a joining word of that kind.

The basic point to remember is that semicolons join clauses that could function as complete sentences. If a clause cannot function as a complete sentence, it ought, generally speaking, not to begin or end with a semicolon. Let us look at a few examples:

> *John was wearing his best suit; Mary was in a T-shirt and a pair of torn jeans.*
>
> *The troops are preparing to attack the city; all foreign journalists have been ordered to leave the area.*
>
> *The prime minister sat down; the leader of the opposition stood up; a sudden hush fell over the chamber.*

In all the above examples, clearly, the elements that make up the sentences could stand alone as sentences:

> *John was wearing his best suit.*
>
> *Mary was in a T-shirt and a pair of torn jeans.*
>
> *All foreign journalists have been ordered to leave the area.*
>
> *The leader of the opposition stood up.*

What may not be quite so clear is why it is desirable to use a semicolon in such sentences instead of full stops or a conjunction such as *and*. The answer lies in the second part of the rule given in the first paragraph of this section. A semicolon links clauses which could stand alone, but which have a close relationship with one another and are more effectively shown as components of a single sentence. To look at it from the opposite viewpoint, the use of a semicolon rather than a full stop implies a relationship between the two clauses which the semicolon joins.

Take the first of the examples shown above. If it reads as follows:

> *John was wearing his best suit.*
>
> *Mary was in a T-shirt and a pair of torn jeans.*

then these two sentences might simply be part of a string of similar sentences describing the clothes worn by all the people present on a particular occasion. Using a semicolon implies that the facts that John was dressing up and that Mary was dressing down are somehow related – perhaps that they are a couple with different attitudes to dress. An alternative way of constructing this same sentence would be to use *and*: *John was wearing his best suit, and Mary was in a T-shirt and a pair of torn jeans.* This is a perfectly good sentence. The only difference between it and the sentence with the semicolon is that it is slightly less crisp and the contrast is slightly less pointed. The semicolon is particularly well adapted to point up the contrast between two otherwise related statements: *It was the shortest day of the year; it felt like the longest day of my life.*

The situation is slightly different with regard to the third example:

> *The prime minister sat down; the leader of the opposition stood up; a sudden hush fell over the chamber.*

This sentence would obviously be rather clumsy if two *ands* were inserted into it. The choice is really between dividing it with semicolons or with full stops. The difference is a slight one, but worth noting. To use full stops would tend to interrupt the narrative flow more, describing, as it were, three separate actions. To use semicolons and keep the description of the three actions within one sentence suggests that they were all part of the same process – one incident with three parts, rather than three separate incidents.

The semicolon is also used as a stronger dividing mark in lists, particularly lists whose component elements use commas for internal punctuation. In this particular case, it is not necessary for the elements divided by semicolons to be possible complete sentences: *There are three courses I can particularly recommend: 'Computing for Beginners', run by Ms Jenkins, which is aimed at absolute novices; 'How Your Computer Works', a course that deals, basically, with the hardware side of things and is run by Mr Watt; 'Intermediate-Level Computing' also by Ms Jenkins, which requires a certain amount of previous knowledge, but should not be beyond your capabilities.*

The colon

The use of the colon in modern English is, like that of the semicolon, rather simpler than it is often imagined to be. The main use of the colon is to separate a general statement from one or more statements or items that give more specific information and illustrate or explain it:

There are three reasons why I'm not coming with you: I haven't the time, I haven't the money, and I don't like skiing.

The general statement (*There are three reasons . . .*) is followed by a simple explanation of what those reasons are.

Economists have a lot in common with weather-forecasters: they are often wrong (The Guardian).

There is no need for the item or items that follow the colon to be complete sentences:

They knew precisely what they were facing: almost certain death.

Two members of the committee have already been named: Mrs Atkinson and Mr Peters.

The effect of the explosion were all too visible: houses burning, glass littering the street, people wandering around in a state of shock.

The colon is also sometimes used to introduce a passage of direct speech: *Mr Harris said, and I quote: 'The whole thing has been a complete waste of time and money.'* This, however, is a convention mainly used in journalism. Most authorities recommend using a comma at the beginning of a passage of direct speech (see pp. 161–3).

Quotation marks

Quotation marks (also known as inverted commas) are primarily used to indicate that the words written between the *opening* (' or ") and the *closing* (' or ") marks are the words that the person in question has actually spoken:

He said, 'I'm ready now.'

'What are you doing here?' she asked.

'Time,' Groucho Marx is supposed to have said, 'wounds all heels.'

Quotations from a piece of writing also need to be placed inside inverted commas:

We felt we were dealing with what St Paul referred to as 'spiritual wickedness in high places'.

In your report you mention 'an undercurrent of hostility towards management among the workforce'. What precisely did you mean by that?

Only the words that were actually spoken or written by the person in question belong inside quotation marks. All the other words should be left outside, even if they come in the middle of the remark being actually quoted and so necessitate the use of two sets of quotation marks:

'Time,' Groucho Marx is supposed to have said, 'wounds all heels.'

'My darling,' he wrote in a letter hurriedly scribbled just before boarding the plane, 'I wish you knew how much I love you.'

For further discussion of the use of quotations in essays, etc., see pp. 289–91.

Double or single quotation marks

There is no difference in meaning or use between single quotation marks ('. . .') and double ones (". . ."). The most important thing is to choose a system and adhere to it consistently. Most British book publishers prefer the use of single *quotes* (quotation marks), reserving the use of double quotes for quotations within quotations: *'What Shakespeare actually wrote,' Harry interrupted, 'was "We are such stuff as dreams are made on", not "made of", as you seem to think.'* If the quotation-within-a-quotation happens to fall at the end of a sentence then two sets of quotation marks will be needed: *She noted, 'I wish he wouldn't call me "duck".'* In the US double quotes are used as the primary level and single quotes are used for the secondary level of quotations within quotations.

Punctuation with quotation marks

While the rules governing what should go into quotation marks are fairly simple, the rules governing how other punctuation should be used in conjunction with them are more complicated.

A comma is used with the verb of reporting to separate the unspoken words and the spoken words:

He said, 'I'm ready now.'

'I've no idea what you're talking about,' she replied.

She leapt up out of her chair and shouted, 'I can smell something burning.'

When the reporting verb is placed in the middle of a quotation, commas perform their usual bracketing function:

'Time,' Groucho Marx is supposed to have said, 'wounds all heels.'

'That,' she replied, 'is a matter of opinion.'

It will be noted that in each of these examples the first comma has been placed inside the quotation marks.

If the words being quoted make a full sentence, then the passage within quotation marks should begin with a capital letter and end with a full stop: *He said, 'You deliberately lied to me.'* The same applies if the words quoted form a question or an exclamation:

She merely smiled and enquired, 'Where have you been hiding all this while?'

The man behind me roared out, 'Stop that infernal noise!'

The full stop, question mark, and exclamation mark all come before the closing quotation mark. It is incorrect to place an additional full stop outside the closing quotation mark.

When the quoted words do not form a full sentence, then there should be no capital letter and the full stop should appear outside the inverted commas because it belongs to the sentence in which the quotation appears, not to the quotation itself:

They both wrote saying that they wanted to 'try and sort things out between them'.

The expression 'to out-herod Herod' means 'to exceed someone in a particular quality', especially wickedness or cruelty.

American usage differs from British usage at this point. In American usage, full stops and commas come inside the quotation marks:

They both wrote saying that they wanted to "try and sort things out between them."

> *The expression "to out-herod Herod" means "to exceed someone in a particular quality," especially wickedness or cruelty.*

In both British and American English, semicolons and colons come outside the quotation marks:

> *A critical phase is reached as the aircraft goes 'transonic'; that is, as it accelerates through the speed band from just below to just above the speed of sound.* (New Scientist)

> *A common method of cheating is to rely on what magicians call a 'stooge': someone who is watching behind a screen and sending secret signals to the psychic by any one of scores of little-known techniques.* (Scientific American)

The position of the question mark and exclamation mark depends on whether they belong to the quoted material or not:

> *Did he really say, 'I wish I hadn't married you'?*
>
> *He asked, 'Is it time for me to go yet?'*
>
> *She had the cheek to say to me, 'I never want to see you again'!*
>
> *The man behind me roared out, 'Stop that infernal noise!'*

Quotation marks and paragraphs

In a passage of dialogue, each act of speech normally starts a new paragraph:

> *'You know,' he said, in an important voice, 'I've thought all along that that pig of ours was an extra good one. He's a solid pig. That pig is as solid as they come. You notice how solid he is around the shoulders, Lurvy?'*
>
> *'Sure, sure I do,' said Lurvy. 'I've always noticed that pig. He's quite a pig.'*
>
> *'He's long, and he's smooth,' said Zuckerman.*
>
> *'That's right,' agreed Lurvy. 'He's as smooth as they come. He's some pig.'*
>
> (from E. B. White, *Charlotte's Web*)

See also 'Paragraphs in dialogue', p. 230.

If a quoted passage consists of more than one paragraph, opening quotation marks are placed at the beginning of each paragraph, but the closing quotation marks are placed only at the end of the complete quotation, i.e. at the end of the final paragraph:

"Woe to you Pharisees, because you give God a tenth of your mint, rue and all other kinds of garden herbs, but you neglect justice and the love of God. You should have practised the latter without leaving the former undone.

"Woe to you Pharisees, because you love the most important seats in the synagogues and greetings in the market-places.

"Woe to you, because you are like unmarked graves, which men walk over without knowing it."

(The Bible, Luke 11:42–4, New International Version, London, Hodder & Stoughton Ltd)

Quotation marks in titles

Quotation marks are also used for certain titles, for example, of essays, songs and of alternative names of musical works:

The Beatles' song 'She Loves You'

Mozart's Symphony no. 38 in D, K504 ('Prague'*)*

David Smith, 'Recent Developments in German', *Journal of Modern Languages, 51 (1995), pp. 143–6*

On the use of quotation marks in references to books, journals, etc., see pp. 291–2.

Quotation marks used to create a distance

Quotation marks are also sometimes placed around words or phrases that were not actually spoken or written by a specific other person, but which represent the point of view of another person or other people rather than the writer's own. The effect of using them is to create a distance from the word or phrase, often, in effect, saying, 'He, she, or they may call it that, but I wouldn't.' For example: *Apparently his 'hobbies' include bungee-jumping and fire-walking.* The implication is that those two activities are most peculiar things to call hobbies. The use of quotation marks in this way often suggests disapproval of, or an ironic or sarcastic attitude towards, the thing or phrase in question: *I've never been anyone's 'significant other', to the best of my knowledge, and I don't intend to start now.*

Highlighting particular words

Quotation marks are also used to highlight a particular phrase and, as it were, extract it from its immediate context:

> *'People' is a plural noun.*
>
> *It is possible to use either a singular or a plural verb with the word 'statistics'.*
>
> *Are there two m's in 'accommodation'?*

The dash

The function of the dash is similar to that of the bracketing comma, in that it is frequently used in pairs to separate an inserted item or interruption from the rest of the sentence. A dash is, however, a far stronger punctuation mark than a comma, and a more eye-catching one. It is best used for fairly dramatic and large-scale interruptions in the middle of sentences: *The thieves – there were four of them, all masked and brandishing heavy iron bars – forced the terrified sales assistants to lie down on the floor.* The size of the insert (*there were four of them, all masked and brandishing heavy iron bars*) and the fact that it constitutes a complete sentence on its own make it impossible to accommodate within commas. Consequently, dashes are needed. Here is a similar example: *Mr Brown – Why is there someone like Mr Brown in every single class I ever teach? – was still having trouble finding the shift key.* There is no other way, apart from using round brackets, of accommodating a complete question within another sentence.

The dash is not, however, limited to use with such lengthy inserts:

> *There was no reason – at least, none that I could see – why we had to go through the whole rigmarole again.*
>
> *The point is – and this is the crux of the matter – that if we don't get additional funding, we shall have to close.*

A dash can also be used singly to separate the end of a sentence: again, usually in order to establish a fairly marked contrast, between it and what has gone before. It marks where there is a change of tone (or where there would be a change in the speaker's tone of voice if the sentence were spoken):

> *It would be a complete and utter disaster if they did that to us – not that I think for a moment that they will.*
>
> *It was a murder with an obvious motive and an obvious suspect – or so we thought.*

In all these instances, the dash is used with a space at either end of it. It can also be used, without spaces, to indicate a range of numbers or values, for example, when indicating a person's lifespan (*Charles Dickens, 1812–70*) or the duration of a period (*the Jurassic period 208–146 million years ago*). Note that when the dash is used in this way, there is no need to use a construction with *from* and *to* or *between* and *and*. Write either *The compound contains 10–14 per cent potassium* or *The compound contains from 10 to 14 per cent potassium*, not *from 10–14 per cent.*

The hyphen: word-making

A hyphen makes words by joining together two existing words either permanently or, as it were, temporarily.

As is mentioned elsewhere in this book (pp. 115–16), the number of words with a permanent hyphen in English is tending gradually to diminish. It was not so long ago that even a word such as *today* was often spelt *to-day*. That spelling is now considered old-fashioned, but until very recently it was usual for prefixes that ended in a vowel to be attached with words that began with a vowel by means of a hyphen. This is no longer the situation: modern dictionaries give *antiaircraft* not *anti-aircraft*, *cooperate* before *co-operate*, *rearm* not *re-arm*, *socioeconomic* not *socio-economic*. The process is not complete, however. Apart from *cooperate* and *coordinate*, the tendency is still to hyphenate compound words where the prefix ends with the same vowel that the main word begins with (*anti-inflationary*; *pre-exist*; *re-establish*). Not that it is wrong to use a hyphen in words such as *anti-aircraft*, it is simply that the modern trend is against it and the tendency is either to make one solid compound word or to use two words. If in doubt, consult a modern dictionary.

The hyphen, however, is still widely used for 'temporary' word construction. By 'temporary' construction is meant for such words as *word-making* that has been used in the title of this section. It is a convenient and perfectly understandable term, made by joining two existing words together, but it would not appear in any dictionary. The particular word-making process involves taking material that might usually appear after the noun in question and placing it in front of it:

hyphens that make words – word-making hyphens

a child who is two years old – a two-year-old child

a region that produces grain – a grain-producing region

a company that is not in business for profit – a not-for-profit company

When they are used before a noun, such constructions should have hyphens. Probably the best-known and best-established words of this type in English are the *well* compounds. When they appear after a verb they have no hyphen; when they appear before a noun, they have one:

She is well known as a singer – She is a well-known singer.

The fact is well established – a well-established fact.

The insertion of hyphens when such combined words are used in front of nouns is a very helpful guide to the reader, who in this way knows what belongs together.

On the use of the hyphen with words beginning *non-*, see chapter 2, p. 94 and with words beginning *re-* (e.g. *re-cover* ('cover again') and *recover* ('recuperate'), see chapter 2, p. 100, '-re'. See also pp. 120–24.

Word-breaking hyphens

The word-breaking function of hyphens is usually more of an issue for a typesetter than for the ordinary writer. If a word will not fit onto a line, it is customary to break it with a hyphen, leaving part of the word and the hyphen on the first line and putting the remainder of the word on the next. This only applies to words of more than one syllable, and there are rather complicated rules determining at which points words may or may not be broken. Some ordinary dictionaries show the correct syllable breaks in words; all specialized spelling dictionaries do.

Hanging hyphens

There are two other minor uses of the hyphen. If, for any reason, a writer only wishes to show part of a word, or a word component such as a prefix or a suffix that is not complete in itself, than a hyphen is attached to the beginning or the end of it:

> *The same applies to the prefix 'pre-'.*
> *Another common noun suffix is '-ment'.*

A hyphen can also be used when two words that share a common second element are used close together, to shorten the first and avoid the necessity of writing them both out twice. For example, instead of writing *both the pro-hunting and anti-hunting lobbies*, the following shortened version is acceptable: *both the pro- and anti-hunting lobbies*. Likewise, instead of writing *She tried to explain the distinction between metapsychology and parapsychology*, the following shortened version is acceptable: *... the distinction between meta- and parapsychology*.

Brackets: round

The function of round brackets (also known as *parentheses*) is much the same as that of dashes and bracketing commas. They always appear in pairs and put what is contained within them slightly apart from the rest of the sentence. They are particularly useful for marking asides from the writer to the reader:

> *It is said (though not by historians) that the tree was planted by King Charles I.*
>
> *If in doubt, consult a (modern) dictionary.*

They are also frequently used to enclose a small piece of explanatory or interpretative material:

> *Charles Dickens (1812–70)*

He showed me the recipe for Sachertorte *(a type of Austrian chocolate cake).*

The World Health Organization (WHO) has its headquarters in Geneva.

Square brackets

The most frequent function of square brackets is to enclose a brief comment inside a quotation, to clarify or specify something that is left vague or unspecified in the piece quoted:

The two authors she most admired [Charles Dickens and Sir Walter Scott] dealt with subjects very different to the ones she chose.

Square brackets are also used to indicate that a mistake in the passage was made by the original author, not by the writer quoting the original text. The formula *[sic]* is used for this purpose:

He wrote, 'We are planning a big celebration for the millenium [sic].'

'There is [sic] still a great many things to discuss.'

The apostrophe: plurals

The apostrophe is never used to form the plurals of ordinary nouns. It seems to be becoming more and more common to see signs advertising, for example, *lettuce*'s or *sausage*'s or, perhaps slightly more forgivably, *CD's*. Apostrophe plurals have been occasionally spotted in subtitles for the television news. They are all incorrect. Ordinary nouns, even personal names, even names or nouns ending in *s*, do not need an apostrophe to form their plurals:

There are three other Janes in Jane's class.

The team contained three Joneses and two Evanses.

Abbreviations, when they have a plural, do not need an apostrophe either: *CDs or C.D.s.* Apostrophes are generally not now used, at least in British

English, when referring to a particular decade of a century: *the 1990s; the 1820s.*

The only occasion on which an apostrophe should be used to make a plural is when one needs to refer in the plural to individual letters of the alphabet:

How many i's are there in 'Mississippi'?

Are there two m's in 'accommodation'?

There is obvious scope for confusion if the plurals of *a, i,* and *u* were to be written as *as, is,* and *us* respectively.

The apostrophe and the possessive

An apostrophe *s* (*'s*) is used to form the possessive of ordinary nouns in English: to show, in other words, that a particular thing or quality belongs to or is connected with someone or something. In the sentence *There are three other Janes in Jane's class, Janes* is the plural form of *Jane,* while *Jane's* is the possessive form.

The apostrophe *s* can be added to the end of almost all singular nouns (including those that end in *s,* add *-es* to form the plural, or consist of more than one word); *Jess'* (or *Jess's*) *notebook; the bus's numberplate; the church's one foundation; his mistress's voice; the vice captain's role; the Bath Investment and Building Society's head office.* Abbreviations too can take an apostrophe *s*: *an MP's salary; the TV's wiring system.*

When a noun forms its plural in the normal way by adding an *s* or *es,* the possessive is formed by adding an apostrophe only: *my parents' house; the parties' election manifestos; the Petersons' party.* The same goes for the plurals of abbreviations: *MPs' salaries.* If a noun has an irregular plural that ends in a letter other than *s,* then an apostrophe *s* is added as for the singular: *women's attitude to work; children's toys; the bureaux's permanent staffs; the media's coverage of the event.*

There are two exceptions to these general rules. The more important one relates to personal possessive pronouns. *Hers, ours, yours* and *theirs* have no apostrophe. They may sound as if they might have (*hers* = *her* + apostrophe *s*), but they do not. If in doubt, remember that *his* and *mine* are the other two members of this particular class of words and there is no way in which either of them can accommodate an apostrophe. Remember also that a word with an apostrophe usually comes before the noun, whereas *hers*, *ours*, etc., come after it:

The handwriting is definitely hers.

Those seats are ours.

This last point is not invalidated by the existence of a rather unusual construction with *of* involving the possessive form, which is the second exception to the general rule: *a friend of mine*; *a photograph of Cecil Beaton's* (that is, taken by or belonging to Cecil Beaton, in contrast to *a photograph of Cecil Beaton* – that is, depicting him).

'Its' and 'whose'

For many people, the most difficult possessive forms are *its* and *whose*. Because *its* is used before a noun, the temptation to give it an apostrophe is sometimes almost overwhelming. It does not have one:

The dog has lost its bone.

Half its bits are missing.

What have you done with its cover?

There is a word *it's*, but it is a contraction of *it is*: see pp. 172–3. Similarly, there is a word *who's* meaning *who is* or *who has*, but the possessive form is *whose*:

Whose book is this?

Whose are those gloves on the table?

The people whose names are on the list . . .

Names ending in '-s'

Usage varies with names ending in *s*. The style with only the apostrophe is possibly slightly more common than that with the apostrophe *'s*: *Robert Burns' poetry* or *Robert Burns's poetry*; *Henry James' novels* or *Henry James's novels*; *Keats' poems* or *Keats's poems*; *Diana Ross' recordings* or *Diana Ross's recordings*.

Apostrophes with nouns as modifiers

Finally, with the increasing use of nouns as modifiers before other nouns in modern English, it is difficult sometimes to decide whether there should be an apostrophe in a combination such as, for example, *trousers pocket*. Since you can say *the pocket of my trousers* it might be reasonable to suppose that *trousers' pocket* was correct. You could equally well say *the pocket of my jacket*, but nobody would say *it's in my jacket's pocket*. On the basis of comparison and analogy, therefore, it is reasonable to conclude that if *jacket pocket*, *coat pocket*, and *shirt pocket* are correct, then *trousers pocket* is correct as well. On the other hand, the combination *girls' changing room* is preferable to *girls changing room* on the basis that you would not speak of a *women* or *men changing room* but of a *women's changing room*.

The apostrophe and contractions

The other main use of the apostrophe, besides indicating the possessive form of nouns, is to show that a letter has been missed out of a word. There are two main types of contraction. First, words in which the word *not* is next to a verb and part of *not* has been left out: *can't* = can not; *isn't* = is not; *don't* = do not, etc. Secondly, words in which a personal pronoun has been run together with a simple verb and part of the verb has been omitted: *I'm* = I am; *you've* = you have; *they'll* = they will, etc. All these forms are characteristic of speech and less formal writing. The apostrophe is a vital component of all these words: they are incorrectly spelt without it. In several cases there are other words with the identical spelling apart from the apostrophe: *were* and *we're*; *cant* and *can't*; *shell* and *she'll*; *hell* and *he'll*, etc. Although the spelling is different, there is perhaps an even greater risk of confusion between *you're* and *your*, and between *they're* and *their*, because these words are pronounced in the same way.

There are a number of other words which need an apostrophe of this kind – the commonest being *o'clock* (reduced from 'of the clock'). On the other hand, well-established cut-down forms of longer words do not need apostrophes: *bra*; *cello*; *flu*; *hippo*; *phone*. Other examples of words that need an apostrophe include *cat-o'-nine-tails*, *ne'er-do-well*, and *will-o'-the-wisp*. A number of archaic poetic forms require an apostrophe (*'tis* (it is); *'twere* (it were); *e'en* (even); *e'er* (ever); *ne'er* (never). So, at the other end of the scale, do representations of very casual speech: *'Fraid I can't help you there; S'pose so.*

6 Abbreviations

Introduction

An **abbreviation** is a shortened form of a word, phrase, or title, used for convenience and to save space. Abbreviations take several forms. People in fact frequently shorten words in any way that takes their fancy when, for example, writing to friends or colleagues in the reasonably sure knowledge that what they write will still be comprehensible to the recipient. This chapter deals with the standard abbreviations in use in English, of which there are a great many, and with the standard conventions for presenting them.

The first rule for using abbreviations is to use them only if you are sure that the person you are writing to or for will understand them. Some abbreviations are likely to be recognized throughout the English-speaking world (*Dr*, *AD*, *BC*, *UN*, *UK*, *USA*, etc.); some will be known to most British people (*BBC*, *ITV*, *MP*, *QC*, etc.). It will usually be clear from the text whether *BA* stands for *British Airways* or *Bachelor of Arts* and *PC* for *Police Constable* or *personal computer* (or *politically correct* or *Parish Council(lor)* or *Privy Council(lor)*) – but if there is any doubt, then the full form should be used. Technical writing is often a trial to lay people, even when it is ostensibly addressed to them, because they cannot understand the abbreviations used in it. It is good manners in writing to be clear and not to put the reader to unnecessary trouble. It is perfectly in order to use abbreviations as long as it is made clear what is being referred to – for instance by spelling out a term on its first appearance and putting the abbreviations in brackets after it: *Comparatively few speakers of English perhaps actually use received pronunciation (RP) all the time. RP is . . .* On the use of *AD* and *BC*, see chapter 2, p. 54.

Acronyms and contractions

Acronyms are a special class of abbreviations made up of the initial letters of other words and forming a pronounceable name or word. Common acronyms include the titles of organizations such as *NATO* (North Atlantic Treaty Organization), *UNESCO* (United Nations Educational, Scientific, and Cultural Organization), and *BUPA* (British United Provident Association). Most acronyms consist of strings of capital letters. A number of words that began life as acronyms have become fully integrated into the language as ordinary words and are spelt in small letters throughout. The best-known of these are probably *radar* (radio direction and ranging) and *laser* (light amplification by stimulated emission of radiation).

It is sometimes difficult to know whether an abbreviation is an acronym (and thus usually pronounced as a word) or not. *AID* (artificial insemination by donor), for example, is an abbreviation and referred to as A-I-D, whereas *AIDS* (or *Aids* – acquired immune deficiency syndrome) is an acronym. The solution is to consult a dictionary. Most modern dictionaries now cover abbreviations in alphabetical order among their entries for full words. Acronyms are labelled as such, and pronunciations are often provided for them. There are some abbreviations that are sometimes pronounced as acronyms and sometimes not, for example *VAT* (value added tax, sometimes V-A-T and sometimes pronounced *vat*) and *UFO* (unidentified flying object).

Contractions are abbreviations in which the first and final letters of the full form are retained: *Mr, Dr, Rd, St.*

Abbreviations and full stops

The situation with regard to the use of full stops in abbreviations in modern English is, to say the least, fluid. Some commentators have suggested that there is no longer a consensus, that different publishers decide on a set of rules that will apply to their own publications, and that individuals are equally at liberty to adopt their own conventions. A glance at three British dictionaries published in the same year (1999) backs up this suggestion. What is important, however, is that whatever system is adopted should be followed consistently. This means for example that a decision should be made to adopt either *eg* or *e.g.* and this policy should be followed throughout an article, book, etc., or, as appropriate, a series of articles, books, etc. The following guidelines represent what seems to be the majority opinion among modern authorities.

It seems generally to be the case that the full stop is being used less and less, particularly in British English. Sets of initials consisting of two or more capital letters are generally written without full stops in both British and American English, though sometimes retained in the latter: *BC*, *JP*, *BBC*, *USA*, *RSPCA*, etc.; *Washington DC* or *Washington D.C.* Full stops are always omitted from acronyms: *NATO*, *BUPA*, *radar*, *laser*. Full stops are also usually unnecessary where the initials consist of two or more small letters (*asap* (as soon as possible), *bps* (bits per second – in computing), *mph* (miles per hour), *wg* (wire gauge)). But whereas a string of capital letters is easily recognized as an abbreviation and unlikely to be confused with an ordinary word, the same is not true of a string of small letters. Sets of small-letter initials that have the same form as an existing words should be separated by full stops, therefore *a.m.* (ante meridiem), *f.o.b.* (free on board – relating to a shipment of goods) and *f.o.r.* (free on rail).

Contractions are generally written in British English without a full stop: *Mr*; *Mrs*; *St* (Saint or Street); *Wg Cdr* (Wing Commander); *yr* (year). American English does, however, usually use a full stop after such abbreviations.

There is more likely to be a full stop when the abbreviation is only the first part of the word: *Col.* (Colonel); *Prof.* (Professor); although here also the modern trend is to omit it: *Rev* (Reverend); *Feb* (February).

Abbreviations of people's first names can take a full stop or not: *D H Lawrence*; *Richard M. Nixon*.

Full stops are not generally used when a letter stands for part of a word rather than a whole word or for the abbreviation of weights and measurements: *TB* (tuberculosis); *TV* (television); *km* (kilometre); *mg* (milligram).

The symbols for chemical elements and the abbreviations for points of the compass are never shown with full stops: *Ca* (calcium); *Pb* (lead); *NbNW* (north by northwest); *SE* (southeast).

On the use of *e.g.* and *i.e.* see chapter 2, p. 71.

Finally, if a sentence ends with an abbreviation followed by a full stop, it is incorrect to add another:

> *We agreed to meet at 10 a.m.*
>
> *The capital of the United States is Washington D.C.*

Inflections of abbreviations

Some abbreviations have plural and possessive forms like ordinary nouns. In many cases the plural is formed simply by adding *-s* or *-es* in the normal way: *two MPs*; *three FRSes* (Fellows of the Royal Society). If the abbreviation has more than one full stop, the *-s* is tacked on after the final full stop: *two V.C.s.* Where there is only one full stop, the *-s* is generally placed before the full stop: *Cols. Cody and Sanders*; *vols. 2 and 3*. An apostrophe *s* should not be used to form the plural of abbreviations, since it is used to form the possessive in the normal way: *a JP's signature*; *MPs' salaries*; *the G.M.C.'s code of conduct.*

Some single-letter abbreviations form their plurals by doubling: *p* (page) becomes *pp* (pages); alternatively, *p.* becomes *pp.* Terms for weights and measures tend to retain the singular form when the plural sense is intended: *150 km* (kilometres), *6 oz* (ounces). A few common abbreviations have irregular plurals, notably *Mr*, which becomes *Messrs.*

Part Two

7 Communication, preparation, and revision

Introduction

Writing is a form of communication, and all communication involves a sender, a receiver, and an intervening space that has to be bridged. When you sit down to write, however, that intervening space often seems particularly large and formidable.

Compared with communicating by speech, communicating in writing is more of a process whose outcome cannot easily be foreseen. When speaking to someone face to face you can make at least a rough assessment of what that person is like, and, as the conversation develops, you can adjust your approach to take into account what you learn from the responses they give. You can also use a whole repertory of body language and facial expressions to help communicate your message. When you are writing to or for someone, you cannot see them, hear them, or receive feedback. It is rather like speaking into a microphone for the benefit of a radio audience. You know that there is probably someone out there, but you do not know who is switched on and who is switched off, who is carrying on a conversation with someone else, who is making coffee, and who is hanging on your every word. Furthermore, as a writer, you have nothing to communicate with except the words that you write down on the page – no tone of voice, no smiles and grimaces, no nods and winks, no little movements of your hands. All the meaning signified by these little gestures has somehow to be put into the text, or what you have to say must be perfectly clear without them. It is no wonder that for some people staring at a blank piece of paper or a blank screen is a very intimidating experience.

The invisible writer

Despite the difficulties just mentioned, almost everyone can, and almost everyone does, make contact in writing. The situation outlined in the previous paragraph has its advantages as well as its disadvantages. Chief among them is the fact that you are, generally speaking, far more in control when wielding a pen or tapping away at the keyboard than when holding forth extempore. You have time to prepare what you want to communicate; even more important, you have time to look at what you have prepared, think about it, revise it, and correct it. When speaking, you commit yourself at once. When writing, in contrast, you do not have to commit yourself until you are quite sure that what you have written is precisely what you want to say and that you have said it exactly in the way that you wanted to.

Similarly, you can control not only how your message comes across, but how you come across as a person. When planning or revising a text, it is worth asking yourself, 'How does this make me look?' You are under no obligation to show yourself warts and all. Creative writers often appear to have a different personality on paper from the one they show in real life – sometimes a better and wiser one, sometimes one that is more exciting and adventurous. But the same is true, to a greater or lesser extent, of everyone who writes. You may want to reveal a lot about your personality in a personal letter. In more formal writing, the usual aim is to appear as a mature, dignified and reasonably knowledgeable adult – with an individual personality, but without too many idiosyncrasies on show. The crucial fact is you are in control, able to define your own image, quietly, in your own time, just as you define your message.

The invisible reader

In writing, as in conversation, communication is much easier when you already have, or when you have managed to establish, a rapport with your opposite number. Writing a letter to a close friend is generally one of the easiest and most pleasant kinds of writing there is. It is not too difficult, usually, to get an imaginary conversation going with them, because you already know what they are like, what they are likely to be doing, and how they are likely to react when reading your letter. All this in turn makes it much easier to write in your own voice, to write as you speak, with an individual turn of phrase or personal colour and tone. Ideally, some of this relaxed confidence and some of this personal flavouring should go into writing of a more formal kind as well.

'Know your reader' is a maxim that is constantly being drilled into writers. If you know nothing, try to find out something, or try to imagine what he or she might be like. If nothing else, imagine how you yourself would respond if you received a piece of writing of the kind that you are about to send to someone else. This is a good first step to opening the outward channels of communication and to getting yourself started. It helps to have a target to aim at; it helps to have at least an imagined ear to speak to.

The message has to be adjusted to suit the person for whom it is intended. It is obviously inappropriate to write to the Archbishop of Canterbury in the same way that you would to the manager of a local supermarket. Language, however, is an extremely versatile instrument. It can be made to express an enormous range of tones and to imply a wide variety of relationships between the writer and the addressee. Which style language to use on what occasion is a question that will be dealt with in chapter 8. For the moment is suffices to point out that until you have identified your reader, there are no sure grounds for deciding what tone of approach to adopt.

Whoever the reader happens to be, it will often be the case – especially in a work situation – that he or she will not have a great deal of time to spend on reading what you write. A friend may be happy to sit down and devote half an hour to rambling along with you. Customers and colleagues have other demands on their time. Imagining your reader also involves realistically assessing how much of his or her attention you are likely to be able to take up. This will vitally affect how you construct and express your message. Be clear – that is the golden rule, and be brief. Say what you have to say in as few words as you can without sacrificing clarity.

What constitutes clarity depends to some extent on the context in which you are writing. What is clear to a fellow professional or colleague may be anything but clear to a lay person. To explain something to a child may require far more effort than making it understandable to an adult. Again, you have to know your reader or imagine your reader, before you can decide, for example, how much technical terminology he or she can cope with.

Clarity and brevity are courtesies that the writer pays the reader, especially the reader who is pressed for time. But there are other courtesies as well. Communication is not solely about the passing on of information, although most of the types of writing that will be discussed in this book have that purpose mainly in mind. 'Passing the time of day' with someone is a legitimate form of communication too, though it often has no information content at all. It fills a vacuum, gives a friendly or courteous context to a meeting, or establishes a mildly friendly relationship between people. Even functional communications benefit from the human touch. Modern living involves a considerable amount of 'talking to machines', but the final thing to be said about the invisible reader is that he or she is not a machine. He or she will not take kindly to being addressed as one or apparently being addressed by one. If you have the confidence to retain your own natural and personal 'voice' while writing and the skill to refine and adjust it as the circumstances demand, then you will be able to bridge the communication gap effectively and satisfy most readers.

You must know what you want to say. That is the subject of the next section.

Preparations

'Where were you fellows when the paper was blank?' – said by American comedian Fred Allen to some writers who had heavily edited one of his scripts.

Getting started

One of the most common ways of getting started with any piece of writing is to wait until the deadline for delivering it is so close that a combination of guilt and despair drives you to put something – anything – down on paper.

It does not have to be like that, and indeed it ought not to be like that, because doing the job in a great hurry robs you of an advantage of writing mentioned in the previous section – time to think and correct. A piece of writing should be a considered opinion, not an opinion off the top of your head. Before you even begin to plan what you write, you need to plan your time so that you are able to do the job properly.

There are some people, whether operating under time constraints or not, who find it very difficult to plan things in advance. They need to do something, to move a pen over paper or put characters on the screen, simply in order to get their creative juices flowing at all. There is some validity in this approach, and something like it is often recommended for producing a first draft (see p. 191, 'Drafting'). But 'How do I know what I mean till I see what I say?' is not a question that people with a more orderly mindset are likely to ask. Rushing in can waste a great deal of time and effort. If time is scarce, and it usually is, it should be used wisely and that means taking a more deliberate and more systematic approach.

Thinking

One of the wisest uses of time is to think about precisely what it is that you wish or need to say. Especially in those cases where a quick scan is all that your piece of writing may receive, it is absolutely vital to be clear in your own mind what you want the reader to pick up. Obviously, if what you are saying is not clear to you, the chances of its being clear to the reader are very slim indeed.

Consequently, a systematic approach to writing demands that thinking about the topic – researching it, taking notes, and clarifying in your own mind precisely what information you want to convey or what point of view you wish to express – should precede any attempt to get things down on paper. In fact, it may be better to actively resist the temptation to pick up the pen or switch on the computer until you feel clear and settled about why you are writing and what you are saying. Then you may find it useful to compose a statement of intent, setting out in one sentence, or two or three at most, precisely what your purpose is in writing. Typical statements of intent might be the following:

> *To ask the council to move the zebra crossing in the High Street to a new and safer position.*
>
> *To cancel the existing order for type B gaskets. To replace it with a similar order for type C gaskets.*

To make my boss see the advantages of getting time off in lieu in contrast to being paid overtime.

I want advice on how to make changes to my will.

The statement of intent does not have to be a proper sentence or one that you can incorporate into the piece as it stands – though it may be helpful if it is. Its purpose is to give you a starting point and a guideline. You may even want to change it later if, having thought more about it, you decide that your actual purpose is something different from what you thought it was at first. In any case, once your purpose and your ideas are clear, the time has come to consider how to organize your material in such a way as to carry out your task successfully.

Organization: Why plan?

All but the most informal and spontaneous pieces of writing will benefit from being planned in advance. Planning assists both writer and reader. A piece of writing with a clear and logical structure is easier for the reader to take in than one which is confused, rambles, repeats itself, or is connected in a way that makes perfect sense to the writer but which no other person is able to follow.

For the writer, likewise, the benefits of careful preparation are enormous. Filling the blank page or screen is much easier if you know not only what you want to say, but have worked out a way of saying it. Making a plan also forces you to clarify your message further. It should help you to distinguish between the more important and less important among the various things you have to say. It also makes it easier to see which items belong together.

Once a plan has been made and been found to be generally satisfactory, it also serves as a guide to progress. You can see how far you have reached and how much remains to be covered. Teachers frequently stress the importance of a plan, if only a rough one, for candidates writing essays in examinations. With the aid of a plan, examinees can pace themselves, ensuring that they leave enough time to cover all the crucial points. Few other people are forced to write against the clock in quite the same way as examination candidates, but there are often other constraints on one's writing. For example, space. If you have only 2000 words at your disposal, then planning should enable you to allocate them sensibly. Finally, for those who have particular difficulty with beginnings, the construction of a plan enables you to start somewhere else. Begin with what comes easiest. Use it to get yourself going. Once the writing process has begun and you have achieved something, it is psychologically easier to go back and start to fill in the blanks.

Making a plan

How, then, do you go about making a plan? First, for all but the briefest and most informal writings and for all but the most organized and retentive of minds, a written plan is far better than a plan made in the head. Pieces of paper can get lost, but ideas that are not put down on paper can get lost far more easily.

What can be used to help make a plan? If what you are writing is based on something else – if, for example, you are replying to a letter – your plan may simply reflect the shape of the other document. Planning is easy if your purpose is to answer a letter, query, or complaint point by point. If what you are writing relates to a topic that has already been given to you – if, for example, you are writing an academic essay on a subject set by a teacher or examiner – then the key words in the title will probably act as cues. An essay title such as 'The effects of colonial expansion on British foreign policy between 1748 and 1815' contains four basic concepts 'effects', 'colonial expansion', 'British foreign policy' and 'the period 1748 to 1815', all of which provide focal points for clusters of ideas. If you have had to research your subject, then the notes of your findings are the obvious source of the ingredients for a plan. Another useful strategy is to enter into an imaginary conversation with your potential reader. Ask yourself the kind of questions that what you are intending to say might arouse in his or her mind. A short cut to this procedure is simply to jot down a series of question words: what? why? how? who? when? and where? The answers, as they relate to your particular topic, will frequently provide a useful basis for your plan. If, however, none of these is appropriate, and you are starting from scratch merely with an intention to write on a particular subject, then the best policy is usually to jot down any thoughts or ideas you have had on the subject in any order, and then try to sort them out.

Ordering ideas

It is very likely that as ideas come, they will begin to form themselves into groups and even to line themselves up in the order in which they might be presented. If they do not, then the next stage in the process is to shape them into order.

The structure that you choose for a piece of writing varies according to the kind of communication that you are preparing. Certain kinds of writing – such as the academic essay and the report – have a standard form which you depart from almost at your peril. Business letters also tend to follow a standard pattern. These patterns will be discussed later in the appropriate sections ('Business letters', pp. 242–51; 'Reports', pp. 269–73; 'Essays', pp. 283–91). There are a few general rules, however, which are applicable in a large number of cases, especially in functional writing.

The sooner you start your main intention, on the whole, the easier it will be for your reader to grasp the thread and to hold on to it through the rest of your writing. Start, writers are sometimes advised, with your conclusion. State the information that you have to give or the opinions that you wish to express straight away. Spend the rest of the time and space that you have available in providing support for the information or opinions. The reader, especially the reluctant reader or the reader under time constraints, will often thank you for encapsulating your message in a pithy opening sentence or paragraphs, not least because he or she is thus given the choice of whether to read on or not. Your opening, in this case, is like the headline of a newspaper report. As in a newspaper report, the logical order to follow is to place the points that support this conclusion in their relative order of importance, beginning with the most important and ending with the least. Readers can stop at any point once they know all they feel they need to know.

For example, take one of the statements of intent given on pp. 185–6. You intend to write a letter to the council asking them to move a zebra crossing. You have noted the facts that:

> *There was nearly an accident on the crossing last Thursday;*
>
> *You know the crossing as a pedestrian and a motorist and don't feel it's safe from either point of view;*
>
> *The crossing is on a bend;*

> *The cars and lorries parked on both sides of the road make the crossing difficult to see;*
>
> *Children use the crossing going to and from school;*
>
> *You are willing to support a public protest.*

It might seem tempting to begin the letter with the first point, especially if witnessing the near accident and being shocked and angered by it is what has compelled you to write. You might feel that the council need alerting to the fact that there is an accident waiting to happen and begin '*There was nearly an accident . . .*' or '*Did you know there was nearly an accident . . . ?*' But your primary purpose is not to report the near accident but to urge that the crossing should be moved. You could begin with the accident, mention the other points, and conclude with something like: '*For all these reasons the crossing must be moved.*'

However, the better tactic is to begin with the main point, which can itself be strongly stated: 'I feel very strongly that the zebra crossing in the High Street should be moved from its present position, which is very unsafe. I feel so strongly in fact that I should be willing to organize or support a public protest . . .' The person who reads the letter should be left in no doubt as to what you are writing about or how strongly you feel. The best continuation then would probably be to set out why this crossing is always going to be dangerous – its position on a bend, the parked cars and lorries – and only then mention the specific event last Thursday.

Even if you want to keep your reader with you to the end, a statement of your aims and intentions or why you are writing still makes a useful starting point. There are many other possible ways of arranging material apart from listing supporting arguments in descending order of importance. A chronological or sequential approach will often make sense if you are talking about a process that proceeds step by step. An analytical breakdown of the main points of an argument or proposal may well provide a suitable framework. Here the technique of holding an imaginary question-and-answer session with the reader particularly comes into its own. Alternatively, a comparative structure may suit the subject. The events or performance of one year can be placed against those of another or the advantages and disadvantages of a particular course of action can be set out against each other. In cases where your task is to persuade or demonstrate something, then a logical and deductive sequence might be the best option. If A is the case, then the consequences are likely to be B and C and therefore the best course of action to adopt is D.

There are many more types of possible plan than can be discussed here. What is important is to note that the material should be clearly marshalled to suit the writer's purpose and to assist the reader's understanding.

Types of plan

The way that you choose to lay out your plan on paper depends partly on circumstances and, in particular, whether you have to show the plan to anyone else. The principal purpose of an outline is to serve as an aid to the writer. As such it can be in any form that the writer chooses and as rough or smooth as he or she decides to make it. The most obvious form of outline is a list of points. If a list of points is compiled on computer, it is relatively easy to rearrange them, to make a subpoint into a main point and vice versa. The list of points can, if the writer wishes, be converted into a series of headings to form a skeleton for the piece and an easy reference guide for the reader. Each main point in the list should be followed by a list of subpoints which, ideally, would correspond to the paragraphs in a particular section. Especially in the earlier stages, a diagrammatic form may help to show how the various points relate to one another. A 'web chart' with the key words or points in boxes and radiating lines extending outwards to related concepts is one useful format. Presentation in the form of a flow chart may look better than a simple list and give a sense of onward progression in the writing. Some people recommend that, even at the planning stage, everything should be written in proper sentences. This may be a useful discipline – especially where a plan has to be submitted for someone else's criticism or approval – but in most cases notes will suffice.

Post-planning

Having constructed a plan, it is vital to check it. Check it first against your statement of intent if you made one. If your original intention and your initial plan vary, then one or the other must be changed. It may well be that the thinking that has gone into your plan has clarified your sense of what you want to say or your sense of priorities. If so, all well and good. If, however, your original intention remains paramount and a self-critical analysis suggests that the plan you have devised does not represent the best way of putting it across to your reader, then the plan must be changed. Making minor adjustments may be sufficient, but it may have to be discarded completely. Another structure or another approach may have to be tried. The only consolation in all the labour of these early stages of writing is that false starts usually lead to respectable endings. Preparing the piece may take as long as writing it, but preparation time is seldom wasted time. The benefits of having a reliable working plan outweigh all the agonies of trying to get it right.

Drafting

In a stage-by-stage process of producing a written document, the stage following the construction of a plan is that of writing a draft, a draft being a version of the document written out in full and approximating to what you eventually intend to present to the reader.

A piece of writing usually goes through several drafts before it reaches its final form. The precise number of drafts will depend on the status of the work, the perfectionism of the writer and, not least, the time remaining to complete the task. A book, a shorter piece of creative prose or verse, or an important report will probably go through three, four, or even more drafts before reaching its final form. One draft will usually suffice for a letter, unless this first attempt shows major flaws.

When a draft is complete, it should be looked at very carefully, errors should be corrected, parts added where necessary and, perhaps more important, parts left out which are superfluous. Once a draft has been thoroughly revised, a new draft should be written incorporating all the satisfactory parts of the previous one together with any new additions. The drafting, revising, and editing process should continue until you are satisfied that the writing fulfils all your intentions, and then a final copy can be made.

The first draft

The function of the first draft is to put flesh on the bones of your original plan. Ideas, notes, and plans are all very well, but the finished product has to appear in the form of connected sentences and paragraphs. The first draft marks the transition from the preparation stage to the stage of execution.

It is at this point that you are finally confronted by the dreaded blank page or screen. A writer who has gone through an extensive preparation process before beginning, however, is now generally at an advantage over one who starts from scratch. If you have thought about your subject matter, are confident about what you wish to put across, and have armed yourself with a detailed plan, then the chances are that you will have little difficulty in beginning at the beginning. But if for any reason the opening paragraph or section is a difficult one – and the beginning is vital, not least because it has to catch the reader's interest and compel him or her to read on – then, as has been mentioned before, provided you have a plan, it is always possible to start elsewhere.

The first draft also provides the writer with something to work on. Once the draft is there, the page or screen is no longer blank. And, though editing and revising may sound like a chore, for many people working on or with something that is already in existence is far easier and more rewarding than plucking ideas or words out of the air. A potter slaps down a lump of clay on the wheel and the most productive and satisfying part of the job is fingering and moulding the material until it reaches the desired shape. The writer has no comparable material to work with until he or she has put down many words on paper. Then, what is for many the most interesting part of the task commences – making it into an effective and elegant expression of your thoughts and intentions.

Producing a first draft usually falls into the category of activities carried out for the writer's own benefit. The first draft is for his or her eyes only. It is an opportunity to discover problems and make mistakes. It is also generally recommended that the first draft should be written as far as possible in your own words and in your own voice. 'Your own voice' is the way of writing that comes naturally to you, writing as you personally would speak. Many, perhaps most, people 'hear' the words in their heads before or as they write them. If the inner voice speaks, follow it when writing the first draft. For all that has been said about knowing and making allowances for your reader, at this stage the important thing is to implement your plan and to get something down on paper or on the computer. You need not necessarily try too hard to achieve precisely the correct tone first time, certainly not if it involves any cramping of your own style or stemming your own flow. Adjustments can come later, when revising.

Bearing all this in mind, it is usually better that a first draft should be written in fairly long stretches and at a reasonable speed. The important thing is to get something continuous down on paper or on computer, and anything that militates against this should be avoided. For this reason, it is usually better to make editing a separate process rather than something you do as you go along. There are often practical problems involved in writing for a longish time at a stretch. Freedom from distractions is not always easy to come by in the modern office or the modern home. But much more can be achieved when you get a flow going than can be achieved in fits and starts. In particular, when the first draft has to be written, when what have been points and notes become paragraphs and sentences and what has been an outline or skeleton becomes a piece of extended prose, a period of quiet, concentrated time is of great importance.

The purpose of a draft is to allow for editing and improvement, so it is important to present it in such a way that corrections, deletions, and additions can be clearly made. This usually means typing with double spacing or leaving substantial gaps between the lines of a manuscript. It is far less convenient to have to make editorial notes on a separate sheet of paper, which, apart from the fact that it may get lost, then has to be put together with the actual text. For the same reason, when working on a computer, it is usually better to print out the text so that you can write over it rather than trying to do all the editing on screen.

Revising

Revision is not only an essential but also a creative task. If the right word or the best way of putting something did not come in a flash of inspiration, then the revision stage is the point at which you may arrive at it by thinking and reflecting or perhaps by consulting a reference book such as a thesaurus. There are a number of technical checks that need to be undertaken when revising, especially a careful examination of spelling, grammar, and punctuation. These are matters dealt with at length in the first part of this *Writer's Manual*. A further task is to work on the details of sentence and paragraph construction and general style. These too are subjects that deserve more than a passing reference; the next chapter in this book is devoted to them. Perhaps what needs stressing most at this stage is that revision need not be a chore. A good deal of the hard work is already behind you. You have decided what you want to say, you have planned how to say it, indeed you have already said it after a fashion. Now is the time to ensure that it truly conveys your meaning to the reader and does so in a way that not merely presents no bar to communication but also, where appropriate, gives him or her a positive pleasure.

A few practical hints with regard to the revision stage. It is, as has been said, usually easier to edit on paper than on screen. Printing out your work also gives you a broader overview – not many double-spaced lines appear on a computer screen at any one time – and, furthermore, shows you how the piece will look when it goes onto paper. Where circumstances allow, it helps to leave an interval of time between the writing of a draft and its revision. After time spent doing something else, you may well be able to come back to your writing with fresh eyes and a greater willingness to be self-critical. Not only that, but the unconscious mind tends to work on in secret, while your conscious attention is directed elsewhere. You may find that, by allowing a period of time to elapse, you have solved some of the problems that you encountered on the first draft. For an even fresher view of the situation, show what you have written to someone else – preferably someone you trust and whose judgment you respect – and ask for his or her comments. It is not always advisable to do this with a first draft, which is in many cases made in order to be discarded; but a second or third draft, which you have already gone over carefully yourself, will probably benefit from a friendly but critical assessment by someone else. Finally, writers, like everyone else, must learn when to let go. It is possible to get into an obsessive state aiming at a degree of perfection that is always just beyond your grasp. Prepare, draft, correct, revise, redraft, and polish again, but then release your writing to the world.

8 Style

True ease in writing comes from art, not chance,
As those move easiest who have learn'd to dance.

Alexander Pope, 'An Essay on Criticism'

Introduction

The aim of this section is to identify and discuss the characteristics of good writing. It is not intended simply as an abstract discussion. At the end of chapter 7, the step-by-step account of the writing process had reached the revision stage. Once the essential qualities of good writing have been established, they can be used as a set of basic principles to guide a writer when he or she is revising a piece of work.

The general heading for this chapter is 'Style', one of the words most commonly used in discussions of the art or business of writing. According to *The New Penguin English Dictionary* 'style', among its many senses, means 'a distinctive or characteristic manner of doing something' and 'a manner of expression in writing, painting, music, etc., *esp* when characteristic of an individual, period, etc.'. The emphasis in both these definitions is on individuality and distinctiveness. Style is essentially a personal thing, something peculiar to each individual. As you are, so you write. Personality will out. And this is true. Each one of us, writing at whatever level, does have his or her own personal way of using words.

At the same time, however, when people talk about 'good style' they are usually referring to something more general. The rules of style attempt to define the characteristics that are typical of all good and effective writing. If style were an individual characteristic only, a person would be born stylish or unstylish and that would be that. In order to achieve a valid style all the writer would have to do would be to listen carefully to his or her inner voice and follow it faithfully.

Nothing in the real world is ever that simple or that subjective. But there is sufficient tension between the individual and the general in the concept of style to warrant a brief discussion of some questions relating to style as such, before the topic of the qualities that distinguish a good style is addressed.

Can good style be learnt?

Yes, it can. Having a tidy, logical mind and being careful and self-critical by nature helps to produce good-quality writing, just as it helps to have a vivid and offbeat imagination to write a fantasy novel. But just as you can train yourself into and out of certain patterns of behaviour, so you can also train yourself into and out of particular ways of thinking and writing.

How do you learn good style?

Like any other art, writing is learnt by doing and by looking at what others have already done. Practise writing and also practise reading, but not simply this book or other books on the craft of writing. Read widely, especially in the type of writing that you want to do yourself, but above all read carefully. And, where appropriate, copy what other people have done. Someone who is learning to paint can obviously learn much more by trying to copy a Rembrandt exactly than a would-be writer can by copying out large chunks of Shakespeare word for word. But many dramatists have learnt from Shakespeare how to structure dialogue or a scene, just as many politicians have tried, admittedly with varying degrees of success, to learn from Winston Churchill on how to address the nation in times of trouble. The point of copying is always to learn a technique and move on to use it for yourself. You should rightly shrink from copying whole sentences or paragraphs from a source. It is possible, however, by reading carefully, to recognize a technique in the abstract and separate it from its encapsulation in a particular form of words. Succeed in doing that, and you can reuse the basic pattern with a good conscience in your own work.

How does style relate to content?

When trying to describe the writing process step by step, it is quite easy to give the impression that style is something additional to the text. It is sometimes presented as if it were an extra decorative or finishing layer on top, as if the actual message were the floor and its style were the ornate carpet laid over it. If that were so, then style would be only on the surface and the reader could reverse the process and roll away the covering to reveal the rough boards underneath. It is sometimes necessary for readers to go through some such process when writers 'dress up' their ideas in fancy language. The idea of style as an additional layer is, however, fundamentally misleading.

To begin with, the process of revising in general or 'revising for style' often means taking away rather than adding. It is probably more common to use too many words and to express yourself in too roundabout a way than to be unnecessarily terse. The stylish version may be something that is hidden inside the rough version and only revealed by pruning away the excess.

The metaphor of 'polishing', which is a long-time favourite with writers on the art of writing, is a better one, so long as the polish is not thought of as an extra layer, but as a means of bringing out the essential qualities of what is already there. A polished floor is still made of wood; it is wood, as it were, made good. In the same way, what is called 'good style' in writing should not, ideally, be separable from the message or content. The poet and writer on style, Alexander Pope, knew this in the eighteenth century:

> But true Expression, like th' unchanging Sun,
> Clears, and improves whate'er it shines upon,
> It gilds all objects, but it alters none.

Style should not be separable from the individual's way of putting the message across either. This is where the individual and general aspects in the concept of style are reconciled. The rules of style are not intended as a means of stifling self-expression, but as a means of enhancing it. It takes time and effort to bring out the best in particular pieces of writing. It takes even more time, effort, and practice to develop style as a personal attribute that will 'gild' every piece of writing to which you turn your hand. But such effort is worthwhile.

Good style

The general notion of what constitutes a good writing style has probably not changed greatly over the centuries – at least, in English, not since the latter part of the seventeenth century. The same qualities characterize good style in the twenty-first century as in preceding ones: they are clarity, simplicity, economy, variety, vigour, and suitability.

Clarity

Clarity takes precedence for the reason that successful communication depends on the reader being able to receive the writer's message without undue effort. As has been said before, clarity depends to a large extent on knowing what you want to say and carefully preparing how you are going to say it. It also depends on a knowledge of basic grammar. Ambiguity arises as often from incorrect or sloppy grammar as from an unfortunate choice of words. Grammar is an agreed framework. The reader will expect sentences to fit together in the usual way and to be decodable according to the normal rules. If this expectation is not fulfilled, then the message may not be properly understood. But a correct grammatical structure is only the basis for clear expression. Clarity needs to be a guiding light in the choice of words and choice of tone as well.

Simplicity

Simplicity is usually the best means to achieve clarity. In case simplicity should seem a somewhat low-grade virtue, it is worth pointing out that it is generally reckoned to be much harder to write simply and elegantly than to write pretentiously and impenetrably – especially on a difficult subject. In fact, it is frequently suggested that the more difficult and complex the subject, the more you need to make the effort to write simply. Anyone who has struggled to make sense of the operating instructions for a piece of technical equipment will surely agree with that.

Economy

Economy is a further courtesy paid by the writer to the reader. Economize on words to save readers' time. What has been clearly thought out should usually be expressible in few words. But economy is an aesthetic virtue as well. There are no words in the English language that have the meaning 'using a great many words' and that are also terms of praise.

Variety

Successful communication also demands the reader's attention is held. The riveting nature of what you have to say, when clearly, simply, and economically expressed, will, you hope, do that by itself. But variety in the choice of vocabulary, in the length and shape of sentences and paragraphs, and sometimes in the tone you adopt with the reader, helps enormously.

Vigour

Vigour has a great deal to do with personal involvement. It is not always possible or even desirable for writing to leap off the page, but limp, lacklustre prose that has seemingly crept onto the page in order to die there is unacceptable. Even dignified, formal, and conventional writing can accommodate some rhythm and life.

> You praise the firm restraint with which they write—
> I'm with you there, of course:
> They use the snaffle and the curb all right,
> But where's the bloody horse?
>
> Roy Campbell 'On Some South African Novelists'

Word choice and sentence structure again come into play, but putting 'the horse' in your writing also has a lot to do with keeping in touch with your personal voice and allowing an element of conversational style to show through.

Suitability

It is possible to imagine occasions on which one or other of these five qualities might not be a virtue. For most normal purposes, however, writing which is clear, simple, and concise, but also varied and lively, is good writing. To cover exceptional cases, a final overall quality might be added, that of suitability. The reader has to be kept in mind at all times. What you write should be adjusted, as far as possible, to suit the reader's capacity to understand, his or her interests and existing knowledge, and your relationship with him or her.

Writing with style

Recognizing the qualities that make for a good style is one thing, realizing them is another. The all-important question of how to write with style will, for the sake of convenience, be considered under four main headings. Three of them correspond to the units that make up all writing: words (below), sentences (p. 222), and paragraphs (p. 229). The fourth deals with the somewhat more elusive matter of tone (p. 216).

Choosing the right word or expression

The right word or expression on every occasion is the one that expresses the writer's meaning most clearly, simply, and concisely and that has sufficient force to convey any emotion attaching to what he or she has to say. This much follows from everything that has been said before. English, however, has a massive vocabulary. Chapter 3 on *Vocabulary* in the first part of this book contains a brief discussion of the history of the English language and explains how it came to be particularly rich in synonyms, that is, different words that have a similar meaning. Where there is a choice between a number of different words or expressions, any of which would express a meaning more or less adequately, how do you arrive at a decision? There are various criteria.

Simple versus complex

Generally speaking, where two words offer themselves for consideration, one a simple everyday term and the other a longer or more complicated one, the right word to choose is the simpler one.

What, it might reasonably be asked, is wrong with long words? It sometimes seems difficult to find anyone who writes about writing who has a good word to say for anything over three syllables. Many manuals on writing provide lists of terms to avoid (*accordingly* when used instead of *so*, *ascertain* used for *find out*, *erroneous* for *wrong*, *implementation* for *carrying out*, and many more). At the same time, however, a recent survey (September 2000) has voted *serendipity*, a word of six syllables, the favourite word in the English language – among British people who took part in the survey, at least. According to *The New Penguin English Dictionary serendipity* is 'the faculty of discovering pleasing or valuable things by chance'. Why this word was chosen is clear. It is a delightful, quaint, rather musical word expressing a charming idea, apparently denoting a factor that many people see as playing a major part in their own lives.

Writers on style and related matters run the risk of sounding like linguistic puritans and killjoys. Isn't it part of the fun of writing to use long, unusual words? Ought not the expressive powers of English be relished? Isn't a good mouth-filling word something to rejoice in especially? *Serendipity* and *prestidigitation* and the word T. S. Eliot chose to start one of his (shorter and lesser) poems *polyphiloprogenitive*, not to mention *supercalifragilisticexpialidotious*.

> Professor Edgeworth, of All Souls' [College, Oxford], avoided conversational English, persistently using words and phrases that one expects to meet only in books. One evening, [T. E.] Lawrence returned from a visit to London, and Edgeworth met him at the gate. 'Was it very caliginous in the Metropolis?'
>
> 'Somewhat caliginous, but not altogether inspissated,' Lawrence replied gravely.
>
> Robert Graves *Goodbye to All That*

If Professor Edgeworth had simply asked 'Was it foggy in London?' and T. E. Lawrence had merely replied 'Quite foggy, but not exactly a pea-souper' there would have been no story to tell.

Everyone would be the poorer without the quaint rough music of tortuous words and the strange regions of human activity and thought that they lead to. But it is a question of keeping things in proportion. Long words are often fun in themselves and a source of humour or wonder. More than that, especially in the higher reaches of particular disciplines, a longer word is often the only word. There are, probably, no simpler synonyms for *aeromagnetometer* (a measuring instrument), *hyperparathyroidism* (a medical condition), or *thigmotactically* (in relation to responses to touch stimuli). If these were the words that were needed and that fitted the context, then you would be perfectly justified in using them. But, at the same time, you would have to take into account the number of readers you were excluding from a full understanding of the text by using them without an accompanying explanation.

Where the word that correctly describes or expresses something is a long one, then it should be used. Nevertheless, where there is a choice, as a general rule and when your intentions are serious and practical rather than humorous or extravagant, the choice should be in favour of the simpler term.

What then are the virtues of short, simple words and why are they usually said to be more effective than long complicated ones? For a start, they are part of almost everyone's vocabulary. It is not a good idea to send a reader off to consult a dictionary every five minutes. It breaks his or her concentration, and if a reader does not bother to look up the word in question then a significant part of the message may not be communicated.

Simple words are clear and direct. They suggest that the writer knows what he or she is doing. Instead of being a sign of great cleverness and sophistication, the use of long words can sometimes be seen as a cover for a lack of clear thinking and careful preparation. Simplicity is often a sign of self-confidence, whereas people who use many long words are, it may be felt, setting out to impress and must have something to prove.

Simpler words are generally more concrete than longer ones. They suggest something specific to the imagination. The words *rain*, *fog*, *hail*, *sunshine*, etc., call up particular pictures in the mind based on experience. The phrase *weather conditions* does no such thing. It covers everything –

that is its virtue, it might be said – but the choice of such a phrase suggests nothing in particular, and that is its weakness.

Finally, at least since the days of George Orwell's famous essay on *Politics and the English Language* (which was referred to also in the chapter on *Vocabulary*), the use of vague, generalized terminology has also been associated with having something to hide. The masking effect of terms such as *collateral damage* and *liquidate* has already been mentioned (p. 128). It does not take people long to see through the euphemistic phrasing to the unpalatable reality underneath. But if a writer's purpose is not to mislead but to present a case directly and forcefully, it is wise to avoid the type of vocabulary favoured by those who wish to pull the wool over people's eyes.

All of this does not mean that everything has to be written in monosyllables. There is a the-fat-cat-sat-on-the-mat style of writing in some types of literature which, in the long run, seems just as affected as one in which every second word has six or more syllables. People do not like the feeling that they are being talked down to any more than the feeling that they are being blinded with science. There has to be a balance – but with a preference for simpler words where possible.

An example will perhaps help to make the point. If the instructions for returning a piece of equipment to the manufacturer contain a sentence such as the following:

> Please endeavour to ensure that a container of suitable size is available to accommodate the machine together with the requisite amount of packaging material of sufficient durability to protect it in transit.

then the reader would surely be justified in thinking that the writer was making excessive use of longer words. Why choose words like *endeavour*, *accommodate*, *requisite*, and *durability*, when there are simpler and plainer alternatives to hand? The longer words add a spurious air of importance to what is basically a simple instruction or piece of advice:

> Please make sure you have a big enough box to put the machine in and enough strong packing material to keep it safe in transit.

Notice too that one long word somehow seems to draw on another. Starting with 'endeavour' makes it more likely that other multisyllable terms and wordy phrases will be used. Consistency of tone is generally a very desirable thing, but the tone should start off at the right level.

Why, it might be asked, should anyone choose to write this message in the former style when it could just as easily be written in the latter? It seems to happen quite often. It may be that, in the modern world where voice communication is the norm, any act of writing is seen as formal and thus inevitably demands a more elevated vocabulary than might be used, say, over the telephone. It may seem more respectful to the reader or more professional on the writer's own part to adopt a rather impersonal, lofty tone. More will be said on this subject later. For the moment it is enough to say again that simple language and a straightforward approach are not in the least unsuitable for written communications. They do not sound impolite; in fact most readers will appreciate being written to by someone who has his or her feet on the ground and expects them to have their feet in the same place.

Another reason to express caution in the use of longer words is that they tend to create a distance between the reader and the writer, and also between both the reader and the writer and reality. This is particularly the case with abstract nouns.

Abstract nouns – nouns which describe qualities or processes and frequently end in suffixes such as *-ance*, *-ity*, *-ness*, or *-tion* – are by definition general and non-concrete. It is obviously untrue to say that you cannot experience the qualities or processes denoted by abstract nouns. 'Kindness', 'generosity', and 'frustration' are all abstract nouns and represent things that most people have no difficulty relating to. But the tendency of abstract nouns, when used too lavishly, is to lift things out of the realm of the tangible into a world of shadowy generalities.

The following serve as examples of complex abstract expressions that have been simplified. They are taken from Trent Buses' driving manual, which was rewritten in 2000 by Guy Gibson, its training officer, to the acclaim of the Plain English Campaign:

> *Before: Ensure location factors and conditions in which manoeuvres are to occur are considered with regard to safety, minimal disruption to other road users, residents, legal constraints and regulatory requirements.*
> *After: Look where you are going, check mirrors, etc.*
>
> *Before: Ensure the vehicle is effectively manoeuvred to change direction.*
> *After: Turn the steering wheel when you reach a bend.*

Before: Ensure awareness and anticipation of other road users in the vicinity of the manoeuvre is maintained.
After: Look where you're going.

Before: Ensure vehicle is started from and stopped at a designated point.
After: Use the bus stops.

Here is a brief list of words that are often decried as being unnecessarily complex, together with some simpler equivalents.

Complex	*Simple*
accede to	allow, grant
accordingly	so
accustomed to	used to
acknowledge	thank someone for
acquaint oneself with	find out about, get to know
acquiesce	agree
additional	more, extra
address (an issue)	deal with, tackle
advise	inform, tell
affirmative	yes
aggregate	total
alleviate	lessen, reduce, ease
allocate	assign
append	add, attach
apprise	inform, tell
ascertain	find out, see
authenticate	prove
calculate	work out
cognizant of	aware of
commence	start, begin
concept	idea
conceptualize	imagine
concerning	about
constitute	form, make up
determine	find out, decide

detrimental	harmful
disburse	spend
discontinue	end, stop
dispatch (despatch)	send
elucidate	explain
endeavour	try
envisage	expect
equitable	fair, just
erroneous	wrong, mistaken
establish	set up, create, find out, work out
eventuate	result, come out
evince	show, display
expedite	speed up
expiration	end
facilitate	help, make something easier
failure to	if you do not
functionality	what something can do
furnish	give, provide, supply
herewith	with this
hitherto	up to now
impart	give, pass on
implement	carry out, do, put into effect
increment	rise, increase, step
initiate	begin, start, prompt
in lieu of	instead of
institute	begin, start
instrumentality	means
manifest	show
necessitate	need, make necessary
notwithstanding	even if, despite, still, yet
obtain	get
peruse	read, study
principal	chief, main
prior to	before
purchase	buy
purport	claim, pretend

regarding	about
reimburse	pay, pay back
relinquish	give up
remittance	payment
remuneration	pay, salary, wages
repercussion	effect, results
request	ask
requisite	needed, required
reside	live
residence	home, address
stipulate	lay down
sufficient	enough
supplement	add to
supplementary	extra, more
terminate	end, stop
thereafter	afterwards
utilize	use
verify	check

The fact that a word appears in the *complex* column is not equivalent to saying that it is a bad word and ought not to be used at all. But if your writing contains too many words of that type, then it may sound over-formal or pompous.

Jargon

Jargon is private language, the language of an in-group. There is nothing intrinsically wrong with jargon when it is confined to communication between the members of a particular group. If a doctor writes a prescription to be made up by a pharmacist, a few scrawled scientific abbreviations may be all that is needed to get the message across. Likewise a doctor discussing a case with a colleague might well do so using a Latinate technical language which means very little to someone outside the medical profession. When the doctor has to explain either a prescription or a condition to a patient, he or she must, however, use different and simpler language in order to be understood.

It might be assumed that it is easier to use everyday words rather than technical terms to discuss things. Unfortunately, this is not the case. People become entrenched in their own particular spheres of activity. They take it so much for granted that their world is everyone's world that they are often unable to make the leap of imagination required to realize that outsiders do not operate within the same linguistic environment as they do and so cannot understand what they are talking about.

A private language is not necessarily made up mostly of long, unusual and technical terms. Here, for example, is a piece of jargon from the Internet:

> A Sole Grind is another of the basic grinds that any skater needs to know how to do. Essentially, you are grinding on the bottom of your boot, next to your frame, and in between the two middle wheels of your other skate. Like with the other grinds, practising to stall before grinding is always helpful. You will want most of your weight on your sole foot. It might be helpful to skate alongside the kerb and lock your sole foot onto the kerb and grind the kerb with one skate while rolling on the other skate.

The jargon words in this case are very ordinary simple words used in a specialized sense. Other online skaters visiting the site presumably know what a *grind* is, how you *stall* on a skate and which foot is your *sole foot.* Outsiders who are not familiar with this basic vocabulary have only a very rough idea of what is going on (e.g. *grinding* is sliding on the frame of the skate rather than on the wheels).

The same problem can be encountered in almost any specialist kind of publication. If, as a writer, you happen to be writing only for other professionals or specialists, then you are free to use the specialist terminology that only they will properly understand. If not, then in choosing words you need to be particularly aware of the reader and of the possible limitations of his or her understanding of the subject. If you need to use a term that the lay person is likely to be unfamiliar with, then you should give guidance when introducing it by, for example, fitting in a brief definition in simple language or spelling out the full form of an acronym: *Insert the Scart plug (a plug with two rows of small pins) into the socket in the back of the VCR (video cassette recorder)* . . . Finally, if you are unsure whether something is jargon or not, you should ask someone from outside your own profession or sphere of interest to check it.

Clichés and buzz words

In making an effort to keep things simple and remain safely within the limits of what your reader is familiar with, it is all too easy perhaps to fall into using clichés. A cliché is a hackneyed, well-worn phrase or expression. For example:

> At the end of the day, it's a game of two halves and when the chips are down and their backs are against the wall they can always be relied on to pull something out of the bag.

At some time or other, usually in the long-distant past, clichés were picturesque new ways of saying something. Unfortunately, they have become victims of their own success. Too many people have used them and as a result they have become stale and rather ridiculous. George Orwell (see *Politics and the English Language* again) is particularly hard on users of clichés, describing them as a sort of reach-me-down for the lazy writer and a substitute for thinking. It is as if, by using a cliché, you were saying to the reader, 'I'm sorry, I can't be bothered to decide precisely what I mean or think of an original way of saying it, so, here, have this ready-made phrase instead.'

Many clichés are figurative expressions. Orwell's particular hates in the 1930s were 'explore every avenue' and 'leave no stone unturned'. The fact that these two venerable favourites are still with us is a sign, perhaps, of how limited the effectiveness of even the most eminent writers on language questions actually is. On the other hand, the fact that they are figurative would suggest that by remaining with direct and simple language they can be avoided. Someone who says or writes '*We shall do everything we can*' is perhaps more likely to be believed than someone who asserts that '*We shall leave no stone unturned.*' Likewise, people perhaps react more positively to someone who declares that '*They play better when they're losing*' than to someone who parrots, '*They come out fighting when their backs are against the wall.*'

Here are a few more expressions that now sound very corny and should only be used tongue-in-cheek in serious writing:

> *a ballpark figure*
>
> *a quantum leap*

at the cutting edge
at the end of the day
at this juncture
at this moment in time
at this point in time
because you're worth it
in this day and age
it's a whole new ball game
no gain without pain
put something on the back burner
take on board
the bottom line is . . .
when it comes to the crunch . . .
when push comes to shove
when the chips are down
whichever way you slice it

Most of these phrases come originally from American English. America is as inventive and productive linguistically as it is in most other ways. The average British person nowadays requires some understanding of American idiom in order to follow the dialogue in films and television programmes produced in the USA. It is inevitable and quite right that some American words and expressions should be adopted into British English, even though you have to go a long way in the UK to see an actual ballpark. But the vanguard position and perceived superior vibrancy of American culture, business, and street life mean that Americanisms often come in as buzz words and end up as clichés. When writing in Britain for an ordinary British audience, treat anything that very obviously betrays its American origins with care.

Buzz words – new words, or old words with a new meaning, that all the smarter people seem to be using at a particular time – present a slightly different risk. It is the same with buzz words as with any other new invention: the rate of uptake is different among different sections of the population. Some adventurous people immediately seize on them and start talking with abandon about *networking*, *cascading*, or *empowerment* while the mass of the general public still has very little idea of what these words exactly mean. Gradually, everyone else catches up and the new word or sense may in time enter the established vocabulary of the language. Dictionaries are revised and reissued much more frequently nowadays than previously and their dust jackets are frequently resplendent with many of the new words that the user will find inside. But by then the caravan has moved on, and the really smart people are saying something else.

For ordinary purposes, therefore, buzz words or any new words need to be used with care and treated more or less as if they were a form of jargon, which indeed they are. If you are not certain that your reader will understand, choose another way of putting what you have to say. Remember also that buzz words – like slang – tend to date and therefore to date the person who uses them.

Informal language and slang

There is a difference between informal or colloquial language and slang. Informal language is essentially the language of everyday casual speech:

> *You peel the spuds and I'll do the rest of the veg.*
>
> *There's nothing on the telly tonight, so why don't we get a video?*
>
> *Jane says she can't make Thursday, but would Friday be OK?*

It is characterized by the use of contracted forms of the commonest verbs (*I'll*, *he's*, *can't*, *don't*, etc.), of all-purpose verbs such as *do* and *get*, and of familiar terms for common objects that are often shortenings of the full form (*veg*, *telly*). It is homely rather than racy and the familiar terms it uses are not particularly modern. Most ordinary speakers of the language will know them.

Because informal language is primarily a spoken form, the scope for using it in writing is limited. It inevitably carries with it the tone of casual conversation. Consequently it is only really appropriate when the relationship between writer and reader and the context in which communication takes place allow a high degree of familiarity. It is fine in a letter to a friend or in an internal memorandum to a close colleague; it is likely to be out of place in a business letter, an essay, or a report. But, it may be suggested, it is obvious that you should not write words like *spud* or *telly* most of the time, but does the same really apply to *can't* and *don't* and to verbs like *do* and *get*?

This is a matter for judgment. The usual convention in writing is to write verbs out in full – *you will, he does not*. It is safer to stick to that convention, except again when writing to friends.

People often are – or at least used to be – told at school to avoid all-purpose verbs and in particular not to use *get*. A blanket ban, however, makes little sense. Nothing is gained by writing *as I become older* in place of *as I get older*, in fact the former seems stilted. A sequence such as *I get up, get washed, get dressed, get into the car, get to work and get down to the task in hand* is extremely unlikely to occur in real life but shows how all-pervasive *get* is in modern English – and how indispensable in many contexts. You could write *I rise, wash, dress, enter the car*... but, here again, while *wash* and *dress* are neat and perfectly acceptable, to replace *I get up* with *I rise* would seem pompous in the vast majority of contexts, as would *I enter the car*. Where *get* or an extended form of it such as *get up* or *get down to* is the natural verb to use, then it should be used. In the context of a formal letter of application for a job writing a sentence such as '*I did English at Exeter University and got a second-class degree*' sounds rather casual. The fuller verbs *studied* or *read English* and *was awarded a degree* might well be preferable.

Slang is a degree lower in the scale of formality than colloquial English and usually far less universal. On both these counts it is best not used at all in ordinary writing. Technical slang, the humorous or familiar words coined by members of a profession for the objects and procedures they use daily, is subject to precisely the same restrictions as jargon and has the additional disadvantage, for the serious writer's purposes, of being meant to be racy and elliptical. Slang in more general use also dates rapidly.

The difference in the degree of formality of words with roughly the same meaning can also be shown by means of a table such as the following (although there is always a degree of subjectivity in how particular words are allotted to particular categories):

Formal	*Standard*	*Informal*	*Slang*
affray	brawl, set-to	punch-up, scrap	
bemuse, confound	baffle, puzzle	bamboozle, flummox	do one's head in
dentition	teeth		choppers, gnashers
deranged	mad	loony	barking
devotee	fan	buff, fiend	nut
dissipate	squander	blow	
impecunious	poor	broke, stony	skint
inferior	bad, poor	useless, no good	pants
motor car	car		limo, wheels
reside, dwell	live		hang out
	umbrella	brolly	gamp (*old*)
unintelligent	stupid	dense, dim, thick	out to lunch, a brick short of a load, two sandwiches short of a picnic

Emotive or neutral

One simple way of introducing vigour into writing is to make a deliberate effort to choose emphatic and colourful words in contrast to quieter and more run-of-the-mill words. For example:

> *The sea was very rough and Jan was seasick all the way.*

seems rather tame compared with:

> *The ship was tossed about by enormous waves and Jan spent the whole crossing throwing up over the rail.*

Similarly:

> *The atmosphere at the meeting was very noisy and unfriendly so that the chairman eventually left.*

might seem to understate the event, whereas:

> *There was such a tremendous uproar and the atmosphere became so hostile that the chairman eventually walked out.*

gives a clearer idea of the fact that there were strong feelings on both sides.

There is nothing wrong in – indeed there is a great deal to be said for – giving vividness and an air of excitement to a description where appropriate. The general rules still apply. The simple, direct, and specific words are more effective, generally speaking, than the vague and generalized ones. If you write that unless particular action is taken 'people may die', it is more likely to concentrate the reader's mind than if you write 'fatalities may follow'. The important thing is that the goods should live up to the packaging. It is one thing to do justice to the significance or excitement of an event, another to enliven something mundane and ordinary by describing it as if it were epoch-making: *Another triumph for people power – cracked paving stone replaced outside post office.* In other words, there is seldom a case for 'writing up something' – deliberately making it seem grand, important, and exciting by describing it in over-colourful or pretentious prose.

There is, however, a distinction to be made between vivid and exciting language and *emotive* language. *The New Penguin English Dictionary* defines 'emotive' as 'arousing or appealing to emotion, *esp* as opposed to reason'. Language that carries an in-built emotional charge and is intended to create a corresponding emotional response in the reader is a vital asset in many kinds of writing. If you are writing in order to persuade, encourage, warn, or reprimand someone, then you need to find words that are strong enough to spark the appropriate feeling. But, because it is meant to sway the reader's emotions, emotive language implies a judgment of some kind. There is a difference, for example, between describing someone as a *servant* and describing that same person as a *flunkey*, *lackey*, *underling*, or a *retainer*. The first is a fairly neutral term describing someone's job and status. The next three all have negative associations of one kind or another. *Flunkey* implies a servant looking faintly ridiculous in a fancy uniform, *lackey* a servant who fetches and carries in a servile way, while *underling* strongly suggests the lowness and inferiority of the person concerned. If, on the other hand, you refer to a servant as a *retainer*, the word conjures up a far more positive and dignified image.

It is always important to be aware of the undertones or overtones that a particular word conveys. You may not necessarily want to suggest approval or disapproval of a person or thing merely by your choice of a word to describe them. There are varieties of writing in which it is vital not to prejudge the issues and to maintain a neutral stance. Sometimes it is very difficult to find the inoffensive middle way without slipping into banality. The laudable side of the movement for political correctness (itself now anything but a neutral term) lay in its efforts to find neutral or positive terms for people who felt that the existing ones carried demeaning or offensive associations. But those efforts have not been entirely successful. (For more on this subject, see pp. 131–4 'Sexism and discrimination in language' in chapter 3.)

This particular difficulty – finding the neutral way of expressing things – is by no means confined to those areas of life which involve considerations of political correctness. There are several ways, for example, in which you might describe the actions of someone who did not want to pay any more tax than was absolutely necessary. You might say that he or she was trying to *avoid (paying) tax* or *evade (paying) tax* or *get round having to pay tax* or *get out of having to pay tax*. Of these four (the first two more formal, the second two more informal) the last three all suggest varying degrees of dishonesty or a possible unwillingness to comply with a civic duty. If you said that someone was trying to *wriggle out of paying tax* the suggestion of undignified and dubious behaviour would be even stronger. Using any of these forms of words might prejudice the upright citizen reader to some extent against the person whose activities were being described. This might be your intention. If it was not, then you would have to find a neutral form of words (*avoid*, *not pay*) that suited the purpose.

Here are some more emotive terms contrasted with their more neutral equivalents:

Emotive	*Neutral*
axe	cancel, omit, remove
bizarre	odd, uncommon, unusual
blast	criticize
blunder	mistake
boost	encourage, improve, increase
bungle	make a mistake, mishandle
clash	argument (argue), dispute, quarrel
covert	confidential, private, secret
crony	associate, friend

cut	lessen, reduce
devastated	sad, saddened
dump	drop, leave out, omit
fanatic	enthusiast, devotee
feeble	weak, inadequate
fury	dissent, opposition
gaffe	lapse, mistake
immense	great, large
magnate, mogul	businessman, industrialist
moan	complain
outrageous	unfair, unreasonable
plummet, plunge	decrease, drop, fall
poverty-stricken	poor, hard-up
rocket	increase, rise
rubbish, trash	waste, nonsense
slash	lower, reduce
soar	increase, rise
split	disagree; disagreement
storm	controversy, dispute
terrific	excellent, outstanding; large; intense
thrash, trounce	beat, defeat

Most of the words in the *emotive* column are shorter and simpler, as well as punchier, than their equivalents. Although the general rule is to choose the simpler word, there has to be an element of balance in all things. If your purpose is to remain strictly objective, then the simpler word may occasionally have to be passed over in favour of a slightly longer and less colourful one.

But questions of emotion and neutrality are not confined to the matter of individual word choice. They also relate to the broader topic of tone.

Choosing the tone

Tone in writing is approximately equivalent to tone of voice; the same words said with different voice inflections can sound serious or ironic, calm or anxious, encouraging or off-putting. Tone also conveys the attitude of a writer or speaker both towards the subject that he or she is writing or speaking about and towards the reader or listener. Tone, in writing as in speaking, can be respectful or rude, friendly or distant, approving or disapproving. But, as was said at the beginning of chapter 7, in writing all that you have to communicate with are marks on paper: the tone has to be deducible from what is on the page.

It is possible to describe tone directly:

> *'Give me that book,' she said threateningly.*
>
> *I am not exaggerating when I say that this is the worst crisis the country has faced since the Second World War.*

More often than not, however, tone is conveyed by choice of words. The following all express roughly the same meaning:

> *In the event of fire leave the building at once by the nearest exit.*
>
> *If there is a fire, get out of the building as fast as you can using any exit.*
>
> *If you hear the fire alarm, run like hell.*

But each sentence expresses the meaning in different tones and with various degrees of formality, so implying slightly different relationships between message-giver and message-recipient. Choosing informal words and constructions automatically implies a fairly relaxed attitude to your subject and some familiarity with the person you are writing to. Choosing to use jargon implies, or should imply, that you take the reader to be on a roughly equal footing with yourself, a fellow professional or enthusiast. Adopting a formal approach signifies greater distance, and for a great deal of functional writing a fairly formal tone is normally required.

The previous paragraph talks about the writer 'choosing' or 'adopting' a tone. This might suggest that it was possible not to do so, that tonelessness was an option. It is not. No writing is – nor should it be – toneless. There is such a thing as a 'neutral tone', in which emotive words of the kind discussed in the preceding section are studiously avoided, and an 'impersonal tone', the advantages and disadvantages of which will be discussed on pp. 219–21, but these are not default options. If you follow your own 'inner voice', the words still come out in some tone or other, probably a fairly conventional one coloured by your attitude to the subject and the person you are writing to.

Tone is one more aspect for the writer to be concerned with: it is a further weapon in the writer's armoury. Giving no thought to this aspect of the task simply means that your tone is left to chance. It is much better to make a deliberate choice. The right tone is the one that suits the subject matter, your feelings towards it, and the relationship between you and the person you are writing for. On that basis you can decide to be more or less formal, more or less approving, more or less personal, and adjust your word choice and sentence construction accordingly.

This can be expressed in another way. If, as a writer, you are unsure of your tone, how is the reader to know how to take your message? There is nothing worse for a reader than to be uncertain how to respond: is he really angry with me?; is she joking?; are they really going to take us to court or are they bluffing? The possibility that people will read something into what you have written which was never intended to be there can never be ruled out, of course. It is also possible that as a writer you might want to keep your reader guessing. Generally speaking, however, clarity demands that you decide on a particular tone and then remain with it.

Consistency of tone

Consistency is important. It does not work to lurch from the formal to the informal and back again:

> *We will not tolerate any interference in our private affairs. Get that? Any more of your meddling and we shall be obliged to take legal action to secure our rights.*

Either remain on the higher level:

> *We will not tolerate any interference in our private affairs. Be warned: if there is any further interference we shall be obliged to take legal action to secure our rights.*

Or pitch the whole thing in a different key:

> *Keep out of our affairs. Get that? Any more meddling and you'll end up in court.*

It is more difficult to sustain a tone that is at odds with your natural way of communicating. Be aware of that before embarking on anything too lofty and impersonal. For general purposes a tone and use of language based on your natural voice and vocabulary is the best and the easiest to maintain at a constant level.

Personal and impersonal

A good deal of functional writing, as has been said, requires a fairly formal tone. Not perhaps as formal as was the norm in the past, but nonetheless not chatty. Some people believe that the best way of achieving the degree of formality, neutrality, and objectivity required by, say, commercial or academic writing is to make what they write as impersonal as possible. If they avoid directly suggesting that the ideas they are putting forward are their own, or are indeed attributable to any particular person or group, then they feel that either gives the ideas extra weight or cleanses them from the dross of subjectivity. The commonest way of doing this is to put verbs into the passive and to begin sentences with *it* or *there*:

> *It might be thought that . . .*
>
> *It is sometimes argued that . . .*
>
> *There are grounds for believing that . . .*

On the whole, however, this is not a good idea. There are few advantages and many disadvantages in avoiding personalities, and especially in avoiding the use of a personal pronoun (*I*, *you*, *we*, etc.) as the subject of a sentence. (Active and passive verbs will be discussed in the next section.) A good many years ago now, the Inland Revenue in Britain changed its style and began to write, for example:

> *I will send you my calculation of your tax if you have asked the Inland Revenue to do it for you.*

In previous years it might have written something along the lines of

> *A calculation of the tax owing will be sent to taxpayers who have requested the Inland Revenue to make such a calculation.*

It is not clear whom the *I* refers to on a modern tax form, but the majority of people feel more comfortable about being involved in an apparently personal dialogue between an *I* and a *you*, than they would be about being caught up in the definitely impersonal interaction between *the Inland Revenue* and *taxpayers*. And this is generally the case. It is better to use personal pronouns and, if you are stating your own position, to use *I* rather than to write a great many words attempting to avoid doing so. This means that:

> *I believe the situation to be serious and advise you to take immediate action.*

should usually be preferred to:

> *The situation is serious, in my opinion, and my advice is that immediate action should be taken.*

There is an old and generally sound warning against beginning too many sentences with *I*. It is apt to make the writer sound too full of himself or herself. It is better to take corrective action by varying the construction of sentences than by abandoning the first person altogether. Instead of:

> *I have considered the evidence carefully. I think disciplinary action is called for. I am writing to the managing director. I expect to have his reply by Thursday.*

you could write:

> *Having considered the evidence carefully, I think disciplinary action is called for. I am writing to the managing director and expect his reply by Thursday.*

This is much more effective than trying to depersonalize the sentences:

> *The evidence has been carefully considered and there seems to be grounds for disciplinary action. The managing director has been informed by letter and his reply is expected on Thursday.*

Two further points: it is best not to use *we* if you mean *I*. If something is being written by an individual on behalf of a group, then it is appropriate to use *we*:

> *The committee appreciate your difficulties and will make allowances for them. We nevertheless expect the work to be finished on time.*

Otherwise it should be avoided. Likewise, *one* is a useful way of generalizing something without having to resort to too many passive verbs, though in the long run it can sound pompous or affected:

One finds oneself wishing one had thought of that oneself.

Using *you* is perfectly acceptable in most cases.

Active and passive verbs

The hinge of a sentence is its verb. Chapter 1 of this book explains how verbs can be used not only in different tenses, but in what are known as the active and the passive voice (see pp. 46–7). An active verb is one in which the subject of the sentence carries out the action in question:

The boy broke a window.
The newspaper published the story.

When a verb is passive, the subject is affected by an action – it does not do something, it has something done to it. The passive forms of the examples given above would read:

The window was broken by the boy.
The story was published by the newspaper.

This much is grammar. As far as style is concerned, the general recommendation is that writers should prefer active verbs to passive ones on the grounds of directness and vigour. Sentences containing active verbs are shorter and more direct than ones with passive verbs. The passive voice tends to make everything impersonal and general:

A crime has been committed by a person or persons unknown.

This could be taken as a classic instance of the use of the passive voice: there has been a crime, and everyone is still in the dark about the perpetrator. But, generally, it is better to attribute an opinion to someone – in other words to provide an active subject for the sentence and put the verb into the active voice – than to leave things entirely open. If you use the passive and omit to mention who actually carried out the action in question, you are depriving the reader of information.

Take, for example, the sentences from the previous section (p. 220):

The evidence has been carefully considered and there seems to be

> *grounds for disciplinary action. The managing director has been informed by letter and his reply is expected on Thursday.*

All the actions seem to have taken place by magic or as if some inevitable process were working itself out. If the writer is not the person who examined the evidence, there seems to be no reason for not indicating who did.

> *The committee [or 'board' or 'assessors', etc.] have examined the evidence and there seems to be grounds for disciplinary action. They have written to the managing director and his reply is expected by Thursday.*

This both provides information that the reader might legitimately need and makes for a clearer and more robust text.

This is not to say that the passive form should or can be avoided altogether. In some cases it may be desirable to give prominence to someone or something that has been the target or victim of a particular action. In such cases the sentence can begin with the thing or person:

> *The car, which had been stolen the previous week, was later used by ram-raiders and abandoned at the scene of the crime.*

There would be no point in trying to recast that sentence into the active mode unless you wanted to shift the emphasis away from the vehicle and talk instead about the thieves.

Sentences

> **I got into my bones the essential structure of the normal British sentence – which is a noble thing**
> Sir Winston Churchill, *My Early Life*

For a grammatical description of the essential structure of normal sentences, see the first part of this book where it is described in some detail (pp. 5–6, 12–16). The concern here is to try to deal with the question of how to write good sentences within the rules prescribed by grammar.

A sentence is 'a unit of language that makes sense and is complete in itself'. It may consist of a single word; it may contain a hundred words or more. It generally has a main verb. The important thing is that it should be complete in itself – and, to be an altogether satisfying and noble thing, it should have a rhythmic shape that as far as possible matches the completeness of the thought.

Sentence length

There is no optimum length for a sentence. Like most other aspects of writing, a sentence should be as long or as short as it needs to be to fulfil the purpose for which it was intended. Most authorities suggest that shorter sentences should be preferred to longer ones. It is sometimes suggested that an average length for sentences should be around fifteen to twenty words. But that is only a recommended average. There is no point in meticulously counting words and struggling to fit everything into fifteen-to-twenty-word units. The principle of variety needs to be remembered here. It is good not to keep to the same sentence length, because remaining with a single pattern can be monotonous. Unless there is some reason why the writer has to keep things very simple, the occasional long sentence, as long as it is clearly thought out and logically structured, need not put undue strain on the reader's powers of concentration and understanding. Short sentences generate a fast pace. They give a sense of urgency. They can snap a reader back to attention. They are easy to keep under control. But a succession of simple statements of ten words or less can become as boring as long sentences that spin their thread too finely and straggle away into nothingness. Sentences of varying length are most satisfying for both writer and reader.

Having said that, however, it is still appropriate to recommend special care when your sentences are at the longer end of the spectrum. The following, taken from a book on perception, is not untypical of what can happen as sentences start to draw out:

> The message was plain. There must exist an additional level of understanding at which the character of the information-processing tasks carried out during perception are analysed and understood in a way that is independent of the particular mechanisms and structures that implement them in our heads.
>
> Marr, D. (1982) *Vision: A computational investigation into the human representation and processing of visual information*: San

Francisco, Freeman, cited in Gregory, R., Harris, J., Heard, P., and Rose, D. eds. (1995) *The Artful Eye* Oxford University Press, p. 9.

The message, unfortunately, is anything but plain – although, admittedly, the subject under discussion is a very complex one. What quite often happens when sentences get longer and more complicated is that writers lose touch with the early part of the sentence and are drawn into grammatical errors. In this instance the writer seems to have forgotten that 'character' is the subject of the first subordinate clause beginning 'at which' and has used a plural verb instead of a singular one: . . . *the character . . . are analysed and understood.* This can easily occur when a phrase such as 'the character of the information-processing tasks' is used; you latch on to the plural 'tasks' as the most important word, losing sight of the fact that it is grammatically dependent on the singular word 'character'.

It probably does not help either that having used 'carry out' in the first subordinate clause, the writer does not feel able to use it again in the third and uses the slightly more technical word 'implement' that has essentially the same meaning. The result is that it is not immediately clear that the phrase 'that implement them' refers back to 'the information-processing tasks'. The sentence would probably be a lot clearer to the lay person if it were restructured and split in two:

> The message was plain. An additional level of understanding must exist at which the information-processing tasks carried out during perception are analysed and their character is understood. Such a level of understanding must operate independently of the mechanisms and structures that actually carry out those tasks in our heads.

It is good to avoid repetition, but it is better to repeat words or phrases than to be unclear.

One of the main tasks of someone who is revising a piece of written work is to work on his or her sentences as sentences, in addition to checking over the individual words that make them up. Some sentences will need lengthening, some shortening. You should never be afraid either to run what first came out as two separate sentences together into a single unit, or to break down what was drafted as one long continuous sentence into two or more shorter ones. To take an example. Imagine that someone has to write a short letter or memorandum, has made notes of what he or she wants to say, converts those notes into sentences and puts them in the correct order. The initial result looks like this:

> Janet has volunteered to make the bookings for the whole party. She says that she can do that on the Internet. That means that she will have to pay for the tickets by credit card. She is perfectly willing to do that. We all have to pay her back, of course. She would much prefer it if we did this before the end of the month. She does not want to run up any interest charges on her card. Could you please send her a cheque for £32. She does not want cash.

All the relevant information is there, written down in grammatically correct sentences. But the whole thing reads extremely choppily and simplistically. What can be done to improve matters? The answer is to make three or four longer sentences out of the existing nine short ones. The fact that so many of the nine have the same subject (*Janet* or *she*) also indicates that some economizing can be done.

There are three main elements in the message: what Janet has volunteered to do; what 'we' have to do; Janet's wishes regarding how she is to be paid back. The passage could then be recast in three sentences, if possible, devoting one sentence to each idea:

> Janet has volunteered to make the bookings for the whole party, which she can do on the Internet, and she is perfectly willing to pay by credit card. We have to pay her back, of course, so please send her a cheque for £32 before the end of the month. She needs to be paid before the end of the month to avoid interest charges on her credit card and she does not want cash.

There is some improvement here, especially in the first sentence. The redundant and clumsy 'she says that' and 'that means that' have been removed. You could cut the sentence down still further if you felt that the little salute to Janet ('perfectly willing') was unnecessary: '*Janet has volunteered to make the bookings for the whole party over the Internet and pay by credit card.*' The second and third sentences are not so successful. In trying to express the three main ideas in order, the sequence of events seems slightly wrong. As a result the third sentence now begins with an explanatory '*She needs . . . to avoid paying interest charges*'.

Adopting a more businesslike tone would mean removing: '*We have to pay her back, of course*'. It goes without saying that we will pay her back, so why bother to say it? All the person directly addressed has to do is to send a cheque for £32 before the end of the month. What we as a group have to do is obvious. On that basis, the final version can be reduced to:

> Janet has volunteered to make the bookings for the whole party over the Internet and pay by credit card. Please send her a cheque for £32 before the end of the month so that she does not have to pay interest charges. She does not want cash.

If that for any reason seems too businesslike, it could be revised slightly along the following lines:

> Janet has volunteered to make the bookings for the whole party over the Internet and is perfectly willing to pay by credit card. We each owe her £32, which she would like before the end of the month so that she does not have to pay interest charges. Please send her a cheque as she does not want cash.

It can as easily happen, however, that one's first draft comes out not in short choppy sentences but in a long and slightly breathless ramble. For example:

> The results of the survey clearly show that, far from being on the decline, small-business start-ups are actually on the increase and have been so since well before the present government took office in 1997, suggesting either that the economic climate has been particularly favourable to small-scale enterprise since the mid-nineties, especially with the growth of home and teleworking aided by computer technology and increasing access to the Internet, or that the break-up of or lay-offs from larger companies have compelled individuals and small groups to seek their salvation in small-scale enterprises, the data can be interpreted either way.

This is the sort of sentence that brings a modern word-processing program out in a rash of jagged underlining. The sentence never becomes totally incomprehensible, but by the end the writer has lost touch with the starting-out point and despairingly reaches back for it in the final clause. Here the sentence needs to be broken down into smaller units. What are the elements of the existing sentence? A survey has been carried out and its results, according to the writer, can be interpreted in two ways. Small-business start-ups are increasing not declining. This is either because the economic climate is favourable to small business or because big business is declining. The existing material could be expressed in three sentences:

> The results of the survey are clear, but they can be interpreted in two different ways. They clearly show that, far from being on the decline, small-business start-ups are actually on the increase and have been so since well before the present government took office in 1997. This may indicate that the economic climate has been particularly favourable to small-scale enterprise since the mid-nineties, especially with the growth of home and teleworking aided by computer technology and increasing access to the Internet, or, alternatively, that the break-up of or lay-offs from larger companies have compelled individuals and small groups to seek their salvation in small-scale enterprises.

The improvements made so far are small. In particular, the last sentence is still too long and really needs breaking in half:

> This may indicate that the economic climate has been particularly favourable to small-scale enterprise since the mid-nineties, especially since computer technology and increasing access to the Internet have assisted the growth of home- and teleworking. Alternatively, the fact that larger companies have broken up and laid off employees may have compelled individuals and small groups to seek their salvation by going it alone.

This is considerably better, especially since the awkward phrases such as *'the break-up of or lay-offs from'* have been tidied up. That leaves the first two sentences of the second version, which were far from satisfactory since a repetition of 'clear' had crept in (*The results . . . are clear . . . They clearly show . . .*). A little juggling can improve matters:

> The results of the survey clearly show that, far from being on the decline, small-business start-ups are actually on the increase and have been since well before the present government took office in 1997. This may indicate that the economic climate has been particularly favourable to small-scale enterprise since the mid-nineties, especially as computer technology and increasing access to the Internet have assisted the growth of home- and teleworking. Alternatively, the fact that larger companies have broken up or laid off employees may have compelled individuals and small groups to seek their salvation by going it alone. The data could be interpreted either way.

The 'third draft' has in some respects returned to the format of the first. Once the afterthought has been raised to the level of a complete sentence and the intervening structure has been clarified, there is no longer a feeling that the writer is desperately reaching backwards to get in touch with the original subject of the sentence. One unit has become four and the whole thing reads much more easily and elegantly.

Sentence rhythm

The sentence from Winston Churchill used at the beginning of this section notes that he got the structure of the sentence 'into his bones'. This is a telling phrase. It suggests that through diligent reading and writing he internalized a sense of what constitutes good style; it became a matter of instinctive feel. A feeling for the rhythm of prose sentences is precisely that, a feeling, an instinct. It can be acquired, but it is difficult to learn.

Good prose has a rhythm, like poetry. Unlike most poetry, it does not have a regular repeated rhythm. It should have a rhythm of a subtler, less obtrusive kind; it is made up of a satisfying sequence of longer and shorter, emphatic and less emphatic words and syllables. Here is a sentence of poetic prose, but nonetheless prose, by James Joyce:

> His soul swooned slowly as he heard the snow falling faintly through the universe and faintly falling, like the descent of their last end, upon all the living and the dead.
>
> James Joyce, *Dubliners:* 'The Dead'

It uses alliteration (*s*oul, *s*wooned, *s*lowly) like poetry. It uses a phrase (*His soul swooned slowly*) that is almost impossible to *say* fast because of its *s* sounds and long vowels to establish a slow pace. Although the sentence is made up of short words, its mood is hushed and sombre, its rhythm being calculated to bring it, and indeed the whole story from which it comes, to a quiet end.

Here, by contrast, are two definitely unpoetic sentences by George Orwell:

> Serious sport has nothing to do with fair play. It is bound up with hatred, jealousy, boastfulness, disregard of all rules and sadistic pleasure in witnessing violence; in other words it is war minus the shooting.
>
> George Orwell, *The Sporting Spirit*

Orwell is intending to say something unconventional and rather shocking. The first sentence briefly states his main idea. It does not end on a falling tone. The second sentence picks up the idea and quickly builds tension by placing four emphatic nouns one after the other: *'hatred, jealousy, boastfulness, disregard . . .'* with no small words in between. The effect is, almost literally, like someone hammering the point home. The tension is partly released by allowing a few small words in before the semicolon is reached. What the sentence now needs is something neat and original to finish it off – *it is war minus the shooting.* Orwell's intention was to shock. Had he used more words 'it is war waged without weapons and with comparatively little letting of blood', for instance, the force of the thought and the sentence would have been dissipated.

Rhythm need not be confined to literary prose. As you gain experience as a writer, sensitivity to rhythm can help you to detect whether ordinary sentences work well or not. A sentence such as:

> *One of the most attractive things about South Africa is the fact that it has such a variety of different scenery.*

has a kind of stutter in the middle because so many short words follow one immediately after the other. This would be very evident if it were read aloud. Cutting it down makes it run much more smoothly:

> *One of the most attractive things about South Africa is the variety of its scenery.*

Conversely, a sentence such as this (from a record club catalogue) is rhythmically as well as grammatically slack:

> *This remastered recording is amazing for its clarity and impressive performances of the soloists and tightness of the orchestra.*

Putting in commas and slightly breaking the flow makes a definite improvement:

> *This remastered recording is amazing for its clarity, the impressive performances of its soloists, and the tightness of the orchestra.*

Paragraphs: what are they?

Nobody, it would seem, has yet spoken of the English paragraph as a noble thing. The construction of paragraphs, unlike that of sentences, is not governed by grammatical rules. Nevertheless, paragraphing is a vital element in the preparation of a piece of writing. The space between paragraphs is like a mental intake of breath. To read a continuous series of sentences with nothing to interrupt the current would be a little like speaking without ever pausing to breathe. The end of a paragraph provides a place at which the reader can, if he or she wishes or needs to, take a pause for thought.

A paragraph should contain the material for a thought – a sentence or, more often, a group of sentences that encapsulate one idea. It may be an idea that forms part of the development of a larger theme or that is merely one of a sequence. The rule of thumb is one idea, one paragraph.

Another way of looking at the paragraph might be to say that it is a sentence writ large. A sentence is a sequence of words making up a statement or question that is complete in itself; a paragraph is a sequence of sentences making up a longer statement that is also complete in itself. What was said about the length of sentences is equally valid for the length of paragraphs. There is no set length. It is usual to have two, three, or four paragraphs per page in a serious discursive work. But shorter paragraphs, like shorter sentences, produce a less dense texture, a faster pace and a simpler read. Tabloid newspapers, for example, frequently use one-sentence paragraphs. Paragraphs too can possess a kind of rhythm, though this is even more difficult to exemplify and analyse than the rhythm of sentences.

Paragraphs in dialogue

The words spoken by each speaker in a dialogue should be placed in a separate paragraph. In other words, the rule for dialogue is: one speaker, one paragraph:

> 'I am Leutnant Günter Weber, with the Grenadiers at Lixouri. I saw your party, and I thought that I would come and introduce myself.'
>
> 'Ah,' said Carlo, winking, 'you wanted to come and look at the women.'
>
> 'It is no such thing,' lied Weber stiffly. 'Naturally one has seen such things before.'
>
> 'I am Antonio Corelli,' said the captain, 'and naturally, one cannot see enough of such things if one is a man.'
>
> Louis de Bernières, *Captain Corelli's Mandolin*

For more on the use of quotation marks and paragraphs, see p. 163.

Paragraphs and editing

When planning a piece of writing, especially a comparatively short one, it is best to draw up the plan on a paragraph-by-paragraph basis. If, nevertheless, you get carried away while writing a first draft and produce a large block of undifferentiated text, how should you go about dividing it up into paragraphs? Here, as an example, are two pieces of unparagraphed text dashed off by the authors.

The first is written in a fairly light style, so the obvious thing to do is to put it into relatively short paragraphs:

> The idea of being able to travel through time has stirred the human imagination for centuries. Now, at last, the possibility has become a virtual reality. The means of achieving a transfer back to a previous age is not, however, the bullet-shaped machine of science fiction that whisks the intrepid voyager through the years at twice the speed of light. Instead, it is a room in the Department of Teletransportation at the University of San Miguel in southern California. The room is the brainchild of the head of the Department of Teletransportation, Professor Stanislaus Poniatowski, familiarly known as 'Scottie'. Building on techniques used in the film industry that enable real-life actors to appear in old newsreels apparently interacting with historical figures – remember Tom Hanks as Forrest Gump showing his injured backside to President Lyndon B. Johnson – Professor Poniatowski and his dedicated band of researchers and technicians have created a virtual-reality environment known as Watergateworld 73. Using security-camera footage from inside the White House together with some of the notorious sound tapes from the period and computer enhancement, the environment re-creates the Oval Office as it was in the early days of President Richard M. Nixon's second term. More amazingly still, it allows time-travellers to hold conversations with President Nixon and members of his administration and staff in what Professor Poniatowski calls 'apparent historical time'. 'We think of this primarily as a tool for historians,' he says, 'but realize that it may have commercial potential as well.' He denies, however, that he and his staff are currently working on the construction of a second and similar environment focused on the days of the Clinton administration to be known as 'Monicaworld'.

Working according to the rule one idea, one paragraph, the first task is to identify the sequence of thoughts on which the passage is built. It starts by introducing the topic in a general way and the pun on 'virtual reality' at the end of the second sentence provides an obvious first stopping place. The actual subject of the piece is then introduced and the creator of the device is identified. These are two separate operations and so demand two short paragraphs. The next three sentences describe what the device does. It would be reasonable to put them together into one paragraph, although in a tabloid newspaper they might each appear separately. Professor Poniatowski's actual words should be highlighted by being placed in a paragraph of their own. This leaves us with a final paragraph containing the one remaining sentence. The end result looks like this:

> The idea of being able to travel through time has stirred the human imagination for centuries. Now, at last, the possibility has become a virtual reality.
>
> The means of achieving a transfer back to a previous age is not, however, the bullet-shaped machine of science fiction that whisks the intrepid voyager through the years at twice the speed of light. Instead, it is a room in the Department of Teletransportation at the University of San Miguel in southern California.
>
> The room is the brainchild of the head of the Department of Teletransportation, Professor Stanislaus Poniatowski, familiarly known as 'Scottie'.
>
> Building on techniques used in the film industry that enable real-life actors to appear in old newsreels apparently interacting with historical figures – remember Tom Hanks as Forrest Gump showing his injured backside to President Lyndon B. Johnson – Professor Poniatowski and his dedicated band of researchers and technicians have created a virtual-reality environment known as Watergateworld 73. Using security-camera footage from inside the White House together with some of the notorious sound tapes from the period and computer enhancement, the environment re-creates the Oval Office as it was in the early days of President Richard M. Nixon's second term. More amazingly still, it allows time-travellers to hold conversations with President Nixon and members of his administration and staff in what Professor Poniatowski calls 'apparent historical time'.
>
> 'We think of this primarily as a tool for historians,' he says, 'but realize that it may have commercial potential as well.'
>
> He denies, however, that he and his staff are currently working on the

> construction of a second and similar environment focused on the days of the Clinton administration to be known as 'Monicaworld'.

The next example, however, demonstrates a slightly more complicated editorial task. The block of text has been deliberately disorganized and some redundant and repetitious material has been added so that, as often in real life, the task of paragraphing becomes part of the more general task of organizing the material. Dividing up the text goes hand in hand here with deciding what to retain, what to do away with, and what to add.

> Set between steep escarpments rising on either side of the River Avon, Bath is rapidly becoming the victim of its own geography. It is impossible to build a bypass around it. Not that anyone could seriously contemplate building a bypass through the lovely landscapes and quaint villages that surround the city. If ever a city cried out to be extensively pedestrianized, that city is Bath, which is a major British tourist attraction and a World Heritage Site. A beautiful and unique urban environment, it deserves to be enjoyed by visitors and residents alike in leisurely tranquillity. But heavy local traffic mingles with a continuous stream of through traffic close to the city centre and congestion is a frequent problem. The local council has yet to seriously grapple with that problem. Some argue that pedestrianization would kill off business in the city centre, but others, like former local councillor Gilbert Strick MBE, cite evidence from other European cities to show that the provision of a safe, pollution-free central area freed from the stress of traffic actually increases trade.

What the passage seems to suffer from is a lack of focus. The fact that it begins with references to the geography of Bath and its surroundings detracts somewhat from its main theme: the question of whether pedestrianization of the city centre would be beneficial. That this is the basic subject is suggested by the reference to the council and to the conflicting opinions on whether pedestrianization would harm the city's trade. The city's environment contributes to the traffic problem because the beautiful, hilly surroundings prevent a bypass being built. But that is a subordinate point.

Roughly reorganizing the text on that basis, and giving the main subject prominence by announcing it in the opening paragraph, would result in something like the following:

> If ever a city cried out to be extensively pedestrianized, that city is Bath,

> which is a major British tourist attraction and a World Heritage Site. A beautiful and unique urban environment, it deserves to be enjoyed by visitors and residents alike in leisurely tranquillity. But heavy local traffic mingles with a continuous stream of through traffic close to the city centre and congestion is a frequent problem.
>
> Bath is the victim of its own geography. The steep escarpments rising on either side of the River Avon have made it impossible to build a bypass. Not that anyone would contemplate building a bypass through the lovely landscapes and quaint villages that surround the city.
>
> The local council has yet to seriously grapple with the problem. Some argue that pedestrianization would kill off business in the city centre, but others, like former local councillor Gilbert Strick MBE, cite evidence from other European cities to show that the provision of a safe, pollution-free central area freed from the stress of traffic actually increases trade.

This is a definite improvement, but still leaves a lot to be desired. For one thing, it does not explicitly state that traffic is what is spoiling the 'leisurely tranquillity'. With a sentence to that effect added, a little pruning, and some general tidying up, the passage might read:

> If ever a city cried out to be extensively pedestrianized, that city is Bath. Its beautiful and unique urban environment has made it a major British tourist attraction and a World Heritage Site. It deserves to be enjoyed by visitors and residents alike in leisurely tranquillity. This is impossible while its elegant streets are clogged by traffic.
>
> Bath's geography is partly to blame. The steep escarpments rising on either side of the River Avon, together with the lovely landscapes and quaint villages that surround the city, make it almost impossible to build a bypass. As a result, a continuous stream of through traffic mingles with heavy local traffic close to the city centre, frequently causing serious congestion.
>
> The local council has yet to seriously grapple with the problem. Some people argue that pedestrianization would kill off business in the city centre. But many, like former local councillor Gilbert Strick MBE, cite evidence from other European cities to show that the provision of a safe, pollution-free central area freed from the stress of traffic actually increases trade.

Each paragraph now begins with what is often called a 'topic sentence', a sentence that briefly announces the subject of the paragraph. A reader who was really pressed for time could read the first sentence of each paragraph in a passage like this and get the gist of the whole.

If you follow the method adopted in these last two examples, that of first identifying the sequence of ideas in a passage or the most appropriate sequence of ideas for a passage, then topic sentences will usually suggest themselves quite easily. If topic sentences are appropriate, and they often are, they also serve as markers to the writer, indicating what the paragraph is about and, therefore, what belongs inside the paragraph and what does not.

Revising for style: conclusion

The overall aim is clarity: this point cannot be emphasized too much. Clarity in paragraph division assists in achieving clarity in sentence structure and word choice. But finding the right words in a particular context makes it much easier to shape sentences and paragraphs. Some people find it easier to begin their revision by concentrating closely on the individual words. Other people work on the principle that if you look after the paragraphs, the sentences will look after themselves. Each individual needs to discover the method that suits him or her best. The important thing is to consider every aspect, in turn or simultaneously, giving equal attention both to the larger structures that shape the piece of writing and to the smaller units that in the end determine its meaning and tone.

9 Letters and other communications

I have made this letter longer than usual only because I have not had the time to make it shorter
Blaise Pascal, *Provincial Letters*

Letters: Introduction

No one who has read the earlier sections of this book should find this introductory quotation paradoxical. First attempts frequently ramble. To be both clear and concise usually takes revision, which takes time. What the quotation therefore implies is that a letter should be treated as seriously, and given as much care and thought, as any other piece of writing. Another philosopher, the German Friedrich Nietzsche, appears to have been in the habit of drafting even something as apparently casual as a postcard – at least an item labelled 'draft of a postcard' appears in an edition of his complete works. Letters need planning and preparation. The recipient's personality and situation, as far as you know them, should always be borne in mind when deciding what tone and language to adopt. The letter should be structured and written in such a way as to achieve whatever purpose lies behind its sending. A letter is a form of self-presentation and sometimes of self-advertisement, and so you should aim to express yourself in a way that creates a good, or at least the appropriate, impression. In short, all the advice given in the earlier sections of this part of the book applies equally to letter-writing. For example, the more formal and important the letter, the more crucial it is to plan it with care and execute it with skill.

A letter, unlike a phone call and most e-mails, is something that can be kept, on file in an office or in a drawer at home. A really good or significant letter is something to be treasured. It is worth devoting some time and effort to something that, even in the throwaway society, may not be thrown away.

One further general point about letters: they should be answered – in spite of all the witty sayings that if you keep letters for ten days, a fortnight, etc., they will answer themselves. Have the original in front of you as you write the reply. It is annoying to raise an important point in a letter or deliver a significant piece of news and then find that the recipient has ignored it or forgotten it completely. Keeping and using the original also often makes planning your response much easier: you can follow its structure or at least adapt it to your own purposes.

Personal letters

A personal letter is becoming a comparatively rare thing nowadays – not necessarily more welcome than a phone call, but more special, perhaps, because of its rarity. When you write to a close friend or someone you love, the strict rules of writing and style do not apply. Nothing takes precedence over conveying something of yourself to them along with any news, expressions of thanks, requests for information, etc. Such a letter may be all the better for being spontaneous, chatty, warts-and-all and about nothing in particular. It may not matter if it has very little in the way of punctuation or paragraphing and has spelling mistakes. The important thing from the receiver's point of view is that someone has taken the trouble to write.

On the other hand, however, since a letter is something special, if you have taken the trouble to write, perhaps you should also take the trouble to try to write well. Formality rarely goes down well in personal correspondence, nor does a sense that the writer is trying to show off. But formality is not the same as good style and if the purpose of a letter is to give news, then the news can just as well be passed on succinctly and in paragraphs as in a long undifferentiated outpouring. And many personal letters are not about nothing in particular; they have a purpose. Often the purpose is a serious one, even if it needs to coexist with a generally informal tone. It is important to get that purpose across.

The following sections illustrate two different types of personal letter with a purpose that people sometimes find difficult to write: replies, apologies, and thank-you letters, and letters of condolence. (For a discussion of the actual layout of typed or handwritten letters, please see 'Business letters', pp. 242–6, and 'Layout in business letters', pp. 246–51.)

Acceptances, apologies, and thank-you letters

Grateful replies range from the extremely formal to the completely informal. To begin with the more formal, a response to a formal invitation of the kind *Mr and Mrs George Hubbard request the pleasure of the company of . . .* should be handwritten in the same formal third-person style:

> Ms Ruth Brooks thanks Mr and Mrs George Hubbard for their kind invitation to their daughter's wedding on Saturday 12th July and has much pleasure in accepting.

or alternatively:

> Ms Ruth Brooks thanks Mr and Mrs George Hubbard for their kind invitation to their daughter's wedding on Saturday 12th July, but very much regrets that she will be unable to attend.

Less formal acceptances and apologies can be a little longer and should be less formulaic:

> Dear Jane and Peter,
> Many thanks for the invitation to your party on November 20th. We wouldn't miss it for the world. Look forward to seeing you then.
> Love
> Sally and Richard

or alternatively:

> Dear Jane and Peter,
> Many thanks for the invitation to your party on November 20th. Unfortunately, we have already had an invitation for that evening and won't be able to come. It's a great shame, as we would have loved to be there. We hope you have a wonderful time on the 20th and look forward to seeing you soon.
> Love
> Sally and Richard

Thanking people for their hospitality is another frequent task for the letter-writer:

> Dear Barbara,
>
> Just a note to thank you very much for having us to dinner last Saturday. You were the perfect hostess, as ever, the meal was delicious, and it was a real pleasure to meet some of your other friends. That's not something you can always say, but it was truly a most relaxed and enjoyable evening.
>
> We look forward to having you here very soon. Thanks again.
>
> Love
>
> Nigel and Gwen

The next example is intended to serve for occasions when you have not had a particularly good time, but courtesy demands that gratitude should nevertheless be shown:

> Dear Samantha and John,
>
> Thank you very much for an enjoyable evening last Saturday. It was nice to see your new house and meet your new neighbours – they seem a very interesting group of people. Good luck with the rest of your settling-in, and let's hope it isn't too long before we see you again.
>
> Best wishes
>
> Jack and Sue

You cannot, of course, say that you didn't like the new house and that the new neighbours were uniformly boring, but you can keep it fairly cool without being rude.

Finally, letters thanking people for gifts they have sent. People are usually very concerned to know that you like what they have bought and that it will be useful. Reassurance on that matter is a vital part of such a letter. If they have sent money, a token, or a voucher, then some indication of what you intend to use the gift for is generally appreciated. Here are two letters of thanks: the first for a wedding present from the list (it is crucial, incidentally, to keep a note of who has sent what):

> Dear Mrs Worthington,
>
> Thank you very much indeed for the set of saucepans you sent us. They are exactly what we would have chosen ourselves and would grace any kitchen. If anything ever goes wrong there, we certainly won't be able to blame it on the pots and pans.

We're so glad you are able to come to the wedding and look forward very much to seeing you there.

Yours sincerely

Emma and David

This assumes that the thank-you letter is written before the actual day. If you are writing after the wedding, then the letter might end:

We were so glad you were able to come to the wedding. It was a wonderful day for us both, especially being surrounded by so many good and kind friends.

Do come and see us soon.

Yours sincerely

Emma and David

This letter replies to a birthday present in the form of a cheque:

Dear Uncle Dennis and Aunt Jean,

Thank you very much for the cheque you sent for my birthday. I haven't quite decided what I'm going to use it for yet, but I'm either going to be a proper student and spend it on two books I need for my course or extravagant and lash out on a pair of really smart boots I saw in River Island. Either way, I'm going to make the most of feeling flush for a moment.

I hope you are both well and look forward to seeing you at Christmas.

Love

Sam

Letters of sympathy and condolence

Of all personal letters, letters of condolence and sympathy are perhaps the most difficult to write. It is easy to join in expressions of joy, less easy to find the right tone to speak to someone who has just experienced disappointment or loss. It is tempting to believe that the sufferer would rather be left alone or would rather not be reminded of what he or she has just experienced. This is seldom the case. Reluctance to write on these occasions is often due more to the writer's own inhibitions and a feeling of embarrassment than to a genuine concern for the reader. And in sad times letters have an advantage over phone calls because they do not force the receiver to respond at once. He or she has the comfort of knowing that the writer cares, but does not have to reply or try to express deep and often complicated feelings immediately.

A simple and sincere message is usually best, especially if you are writing shortly after the death. There is time later for reminiscences about the life of the person who has died. Likewise, in the immediate aftermath of a bereavement, words of consolation can easily sound hollow except to a sincere religious believer. In most cases the essential thing is to express your own feeling of loss, but in the perspective of the greater loss felt by the people closest to the person who has died.

Two specimen letters of condolence are included – the first appropriate for the death of a relation or someone the writer knows very well, the second for the death of a more distant acquaintance:

Dear Josie,

Ray phoned us yesterday evening with the terrible news about Jack. We are absolutely overwhelmed with shock at the suddenness of his death and devastated at losing such a good friend.

I can imagine that you must be feeling completely numb and heart-broken at the moment. I just want to say that we are here, and that if there is anything we can do – anything at all – please do ask. We are thinking of you and the children at this very sad time.

Jack was a wonderful man. We shan't forget him.

Love
Rita and George

Dear Mr Saunders,

We have only just heard the sad news that your wife died recently. Please accept our sincerest sympathies on your loss.

Although we have not been in very close touch now for some years, we remember the many kindnesses that we received both from Irene and you when we were near neighbours in Southsea. If, when you have recovered from the worst of what must have been a terrible shock, you feel that a change of scene would do you good, please come and visit us. You would be most welcome.

We shall be in touch again soon to find out how you are. In the meantime you are very much in our thoughts.

Yours sincerely
Bruce and Linda Cunningham

Some people prefer to use euphemisms in place of the more direct words *death* and *die*. Thus the first paragraphs of these letters could read:

Dear Josie,

Ray phoned us yesterday evening with the terrible news about Jack. We are absolutely overwhelmed with shock at the suddenness of what happened and devastated at losing such a good friend.

Dear Mr Saunders,

We have only just heard the sad news that your wife passed away recently. Please accept our sincerest sympathies on your loss.

Here is a letter of sympathy that might be suitable for an occasion where someone has suffered a severe setback or disappointment. It is somewhat easier to strike a hopeful note for the future:

Dear Mike,

I've just heard that you've been made redundant. That really is the most appalling bad luck or a terrible injustice. If it had had anything to do with me, you are absolutely the last person I would have wanted to let go. This has happened to so many good people recently. It's a terrible thing, and my heart goes out to you.

I'm sure you are feeling very depressed at the moment and the future probably looks pretty bleak. All you can think of are the problems and all you can feel is a sense of failure and hurt. But you are still the same person. I know you've got the inner strength to get through this time of trouble. And you have the skills and experience and adaptability to find another job.

In the meantime, don't forget that your family and all your friends are rooting for you. If there's anything at all I can do to help, just let me know, even if you just want someone to talk things over with.

I'll give you a ring in a day or two to see how you're getting on. In the meantime, bear up.

All the very best

Jim

Business letters

Business letters are subject to many more conventions than personal ones. These relate mainly to the material placed at the top of the letter, to the greeting (also known as the salutation) and the ending (also known as the complimentary close), and to the general layout. These will be dealt with separately first, working down the page. Example letters are shown in the section 'Layout in business letters', pp. 246–51.

Addresses in business letters

Unless you are using stationery with a printed letterhead, you should write your own address at the top on the right-hand side of the first sheet followed by your telephone number, fax number, and e-mail address, if appropriate. The date goes underneath all these, also on the right. It is best to write the name of the month in full to avoid any possible confusion between the British dating system, in which 9th October 2001 is usually rendered as 9.10.(20)01 (day first), and the American, in which the same date would appear as 10.9.(20)01 (month first).

The topmost line on the left-hand side, level with or just below the date, should show a reference number or code if there is one. If you are writing in a private capacity, you are unlikely to use a reference system, but most businesses do. When replying to a letter with a reference number it is essential to quote it: Your ref JS/JD/CURT07 (or Your ref: ... depending on which layout you are using – see below). The reference is followed by a reference number of your own, if there is one, then by the name and address of the person you are writing to.

The end result should look something like this:

85 Sir Malcolm Sargent Way
Harpville
Hants
SO34 7PF

Tel 023 8112345

9 October 2001

Your ref MC1/COLL1/990-2

Customer Services Department
Universal Umbrella Insurance
Arkwright Trading Estate
Coaltown
Notts
NG67 9QQ

Dear ...

Names in business letters

The guidelines on the use of names and titles in greetings have been relaxed in recent years.

The form of the name that you choose will depend on how the reader has addressed you or has signed himself or herself or on the informality or formality of your relationship. If you know the reader's first name, then it is best to use it:

> Dear Susan . . .
>
> Dear Tony . . .

The more formal style of greeting is usually reserved for dealing with members of the public or with customers:

> Dear Mr Griffiths . . .
>
> Dear Mrs Patel . . .

Unless a man is entitled to a different style, such as *Dr* or *Rev.*, he should be addressed as *Mr*: Mr Stephen Curtis or Mr S. J. Curtis. The title *Esq.* nowadays seems slightly old-fashioned, though it is by no means entirely defunct. It probably goes best with a set of initials (S. G. M. Ridge Esq.) and should never be used together with *Mr*.

When writing to a woman, the position is more complicated. If you do not know how a woman wishes to be addressed, then the safest option is to use either her name (Dear Susan Smith or Dear Susan) or her name and the title *Ms* (Dear Ms Smith). On the use of *Ms*, *Mrs*, or *Miss*, see chapter 2, p. 93.

The problem, however, is not simply one of the choice of styles open to any individual woman. Formal etiquette demands that a married woman should be known by her husband's name and initials until she is widowed or divorced. Thus if Sarah Jones marries Peter Andrew Smith, according to strict etiquette she becomes Mrs Peter Smith or Mrs P. A. Smith. To write to her as Mrs Sarah (or Mrs S.) Smith might imply that she was divorced. It is a moot point how many ordinary people are actually aware of this rule. Nevertheless, it remains something to be wary of, especially in circles where etiquette counts.

In recent years the styles of using both names (Dear Stephen Curtis) –

a form that is particularly useful if it is impossible to ascertain what sex a person is from their name – or only the first (Dear Sally) are becoming increasingly common. This latter style is thought by some to be too informal for someone with whom you have not communicated before.

The formal styles 'Dear Sir', 'Dear Madam', or 'Dear Sir or Madam' are impersonal and are being used less and less nowadays.

Greetings and endings in business letters

Below the recipient's name and address comes the greeting (Dear . . .). The greeting also determines the form of the ending. Modern business practice has reduced the rules governing the beginnings and endings of formal business letter to two. If it begins *Dear Mr Manser*, *Dear Martin*, or *Dear Martin Manser*, it should end *Yours sincerely*. If the letter begins *Dear Sir*, *Dear Madam*, or *Dear Sir or Madam*, it should close with *Yours faithfully*. Less formal letters which use a first name in the greeting also frequently end with the formula *Best wishes* or *With best wishes*. This style is, however, best reserved for people with whom you have had quite close contact in the past. In business correspondence it is preferable to err slightly on the side of formality. Nevertheless the extreme and rather self-abasing formality of old-style complimentary closes (*Your most obedient servant*, *Yours respectfully*, etc.) are for normal purposes completely outdated.

The closing formula should be followed by a signature, with the sender's name and job title, if he or she has one, typed underneath:

Yours sincerely(,)
(signature)

Sharon Redman
Human Resources Manager

Headings in business letters

It is usual to give a business letter a heading. Headings come immediately after the greeting and should be separated from the body of the letter by spacing or centring and should be underlined or typed in **bold.**

Dear Sir or Madam

<u>Closure of current account no. 40299768</u>

or

Dear Rita Sowerby

Your invoice no. 34 of January 25th 2001

Headings should be brief, but as specific as possible so that the reader can see immediately what the main topic of the letter is. A heading that reads, for example **Changes to existing insurance cover** is more useful than one that simply reads **Insurance.** Time is money and the sooner the reader can start getting to grips with what you are writing about the better.

Layout in business letters

There are two standard types of layout for business correspondence. They are known as the blocked (or fully blocked) and the indented (or semi-blocked) layouts.

In a blocked letter, everything except for the sender's address and the date is set up against the left-hand margin. Paragraphs are separated by a blank line, with the new paragraph beginning against the margin. The blocked style also uses 'open punctuation', that is to say, no punctuation at all outside the body of the letter. There are no commas, for instance, at the end of lines in the address and no full stops (and no *-th*, *-st* etc.) in the date. Here is an example of a letter written in blocked layout:

85 Sir Malcolm Sargent Way
Harpville
Hants
SO34 7PF

Tel 023 8112345

9 October 2001

Your ref MCI/COLLI/990-2

Customer Services Department
Universal Umbrella Insurance
Arkwright Trading Estate
Coaltown
Notts
NG67 9QQ

Dear Sir or Madam

Possible alterations to motor insurance policy XXE-7685-COLL-97

My daughter, who reaches the age of 17 in about two months' time, wishes to learn to drive using my car. I am writing to ask how much it would cost to add her name to the list of named drivers already covered by the policy.

I should also be grateful if you could tell me whether it would be possible to protect my no-claims bonus by paying an additional premium and how much the additional premium would be.

Yours faithfully

(signature)
Ian Collins

The blocked layout is becoming the norm for modern business correspondence because of its simplicity: it makes very few demands on the person typing the letter. The format can also be used for handwritten letters, in which case the heading, here given in bold, can be written in block capitals or underlined.

The indented layout is, however, still valid. It is, as the name suggests, characterized by indentations, which make it rather more difficult to type. The sender's address and the complimentary formula are 'progressively indented' and the heading and signature are centred. Full punctuation is used in addresses, etc.

27 Birchfield Crescent,
Plomley,
Yorks.
YO7 3XD

18th September 2001

Your ref: J786/99

Mr Arthur Cowley,
Cowley Roofing Contractors,
24 Handmill Lane,
Brothford,
Yorks.
BD12 8TC

Dear Mr Cowley,

Quotation for roofing work at 27 Birchfield Crescent

Thank you very much for sending us the quotation that we asked you for so promptly.

I am sorry, however, that we cannot accept it as it was somewhat higher than one of the other quotations we received. As I told you, our insurance forces us to accept the lowest estimate.

Nonetheless, thank you for coming round in person and for your commiserations on our accident.

Yours sincerely,
(signature)
Glenda Milnthorpe

Body of the letter

Since there are any number of subjects on which business letters might be written and any number of degrees of relationship that may exist between the people corresponding, there are no fixed rules for the correct tone to adopt for business correspondence. Business letters should be well ordered and err on the side of formality, but not to the extent of sounding completely impersonal. In avoiding the false familiarity of a good deal of modern advertising, you should not revert to the ponderous and old-fashioned phrases that used to characterize commercialese. They still seem to spring all too readily to hand especially at the beginnings and endings of letters, but can easily be replaced by simpler, more modern expressions.

Instead of 'We acknowledge receipt of yours of 15th ult.', use 'Thank you for your letter of 15 September'; instead of 'With reference to (or Re) your recent communication . . .', 'I am writing in answer to your recent letter/phone call'. Replace 'Enclosed/Attached herewith' with 'I enclose/attach' and 'Assuring you of our best attention at all times' with 'Please contact us again if we can be of further assistance'.

Structure

The basic structure of a business letter is simple. It should begin within a paragraph stating why you are writing and introducing the main topic that you are writing about. The next paragraph or paragraphs should deal with the facts of the case or develop an argument, following the general rule of one idea, one paragraph. The letter should end with a concluding section that sets out your own feelings on the question clearly and suggests what should be done. It is important, wherever possible, to end with an action point, a positive statement that spells out what you think ought to be done. In this way, a response is called for on the part of the receiver, either to follow up the suggestion or to come back with an explanation of why some other course of action is necessary or preferable.

The language of business communications, besides being plain and simple, should also on the whole be objective rather than emotive. It is seldom, perhaps, that passions run very high in more formal correspondence, but if, for example, you are writing to complain to someone there is often a temptation to express yourself fiercely. That temptation should be resisted. People are probably more likely to respond to a complaint in a way that is satisfying to the complainer if they have not been subjected to a barrage of abuse or made to feel totally inadequate and incompetent.

Here is a specimen letter of an unduly vehement complaint from someone who bought a computer by mail order and found that when it was set up it would not work properly. (The blocked layout is used for this and for all subsequent example letters.)

Archway Editorial Services
Unit 5
Kingsway Industrial Estate
Chilcompton
Somerset

Tel 0117 895 636
e-mail arched@bvl.com
13 January 2001

Penny Wise
Customer Services Manager
Gridlock Computers
PO Box 3456
Stevenage
Herts
SN1 YO3

Dear Penny Wise

Gridlock ZZ633 computer, serial no AB3/YYT/9007 – complaint

This computer was delivered to me by courier yesterday afternoon (Friday). I was unable to assemble it immediately because of pressure of work and stayed behind after normal office hours to make sure that it was up and running before I begin work again next week. I had no difficulties in following the instructions and connecting up the different units, but when I switched on, nothing appeared on the monitor. I checked and refixed all the connections and switched on again, but still the screen remained blank. After further checks, I came to the conclusion that I was not doing anything wrong, but that there was a fault with the machine. That, I have to say, is only the start of my quarrel with you.

Your advertising material promises on-site maintenance during the guarantee period and a twenty-four-hour helpline. I rang the helpline and discovered that there was no chance of any on-site assistance over the weekend or indeed until the end of next week. I was further told that, as it was now past normal office hours, I could not get one-to-one assistance over the phone, but would have to join a conference call.

As you can perhaps imagine, I was not particularly pleased at this. But, to cut a long story short, I joined the conference call and, after listening to other people's problems, was told by the technician running the service that the problem probably lay in the fact that my video card had come loose in transit. She said that I should unscrew the lid of my processor unit, remove the video card and replace it more firmly.

Ms Wise, I am not a computer expert, not even much of a handyman. When I have just spent over £1500 on a computer I do not expect to have to start fiddling about in its insides to make it go. I appreciate that equipment may get shaken about while being transported, but it is surely Gridlock's responsibility to ensure that goods are properly packed and that, if accidents do happen, your customers can get immediate and effective help.

I need this computer to upgrade my business. I should like to hear from you immediately as to how I can get my machine set up properly and checked by someone who knows what they are doing. If this cannot be done within two or three days, I shall reluctantly have to return the machine to you and find out if there is some way in which I can be compensated for the time, effort and anguish that I have wasted on it so far.

Yours sincerely

Edward Wilcox
Archway Editorial Services

Job applications and CVs

Any letter almost inevitably puts the writer on show. This is never more crucially the case than when you are trying to make a favourable impression on a possible employer. Moreover, many employers are actually looking for people who 'can communicate effectively'. A large part of effective communication takes place on paper. Letter-writing skills are therefore an asset to an applicant, so the letter of application is doubly important because it gives the applicant an opportunity to demonstrate those skills.

In many cases, a letter of application will be accompanied by a curriculum vitae (CV) giving details of your background, education, previous experience, etc. The two should be thought of together. Part of the purpose of the letter is to point out key aspects of the CV, but it can also include material that does not fit within the schematic framework of a CV as well as giving a more general impression of your personality, interests, and capabilities.

Preparations

You will need to give serious thought to the question of what precisely it is that makes you a suitable candidate for the job for which you are applying. There are three basic questions to ask: what training and experience do I have?; what skills have I acquired in addition to my formal training?; what is it about me as a person that would make me an asset to this employer? These questions can be used to produce notes that will form the basis of both the letter of application and the CV.

The answers to the first question should cover the whole of your formal education and training and the jobs you have had. You should also note any activities, such as voluntary work or periods of foreign travel, that have filled the time when you were not actually being educated or employed. The second question should be used to state in a rather more detailed way what you actually did in each of the positions you have been employed in and what you gained by doing them. When I worked as an A for B, in addition to the usual work of an A, the job involved C and I learnt how to do D. Organizational, supervisory, or training skills, for instance, are often acquired in the course of doing a job, even though the original job description did not include any of these. It is also quite possible that you have acquired other skills outside work. Acting as, for instance, a school governor or a referee for local sports teams might have enabled you to acquire skills that could be usefully transferred to the working environment.

The third question is in some ways the most difficult to answer – at least for people who prefer to be self-effacing and are inhibited about putting themselves forward. A list of adjectives that honestly and accurately describe your positive personal qualities will usually suffice: I am honest/hard-working/painstaking/easy to get on with, etc. It may help to ask a trusted friend for his or her honest opinion.

Having made these notes, you are in a position to compose your letter of application and CV.

Letters of application

The general guidelines for writing business letters apply equally to letters of application. Letters of application should be carefully written, preferably typed or word-processed, and presented on good-quality paper. The opening paragraph should refer to the particular post for which you are applying and mention where you saw the advertisement for the job or who or what prompted you to apply. The main body of the letter should be devoted to giving as positive a picture as possible of your own abilities and suitability for the post, and of the job itself. It is important to give reasons why the job appeals to you. Finally, you should end by mentioning anything enclosed with the letter that has not been mentioned before and state your willingness to attend an interview and to provide any further information that might be necessary.

All this, however, should be kept short. You need to make an impression without taking up too much of the reader's time. A typical letter applying for an advertised post might look like this:

99 Western Road
Aylesbury
Bucks
HP19 9QY

Tel 01296 123456

23 May 2001

Mr Christopher Wray
Personnel Manager
ZPT Enterprises
273–278 Lincoln St
Royston
Herts
CB27 8HY

Dear Mr Wray

Post of personal assistant to financial director

I am writing to apply for the above position advertised in last Wednesday's *Guardian*.

As you will see from my CV, which I enclose with this letter, I have considerable experience as a secretary and personal assistant. I am currently working as personal assistant to Mr John Clarke, managing director of Perkins and Hodge Ltd in Aylesbury. My work there includes running the company's payroll database in addition to organizing Mr Clark's appointments and general secretarial duties. I have a full range of secretarial skills, including shorthand and audio-typing, and have also been on several courses to improve my knowledge of computers, especially the handling of databases.

Two aspects of this post attract me in particular. First, I should like to gain more experience on the financial side to build on the skills which I have developed in running my present company's payroll. Secondly, I should like the greater scope and responsibility offered by a larger company with international connections.

I believe that I have the qualifications for this post. In addition, I am efficient, hard-working and – so other people tell me – easy to get on with. I would welcome the chance to discuss the job further with you at an interview. If you require any further information, please get in touch with me at my home address, given above.

I look forward to hearing from you.

Yours sincerely
Judith Greene

The situation is slightly different if you are writing speculatively, perhaps writing to several companies in the hope that one of them has a vacancy. The basic principles remain the same, however. The following is the sort of letter that a school- or college-leaver might usefully write when trying to find an opening.

6 Harbour View
Newport
Pembrokeshire
Wales
SA43 3PF

22 April 2001

The Editor
East Wales Observer
PO Box 9987
Pontypridd
CA36 8JJ

Dear Editor

I am writing to ask whether by any chance there is a junior post at the *East Wales Observer* for which I might be suitable and could apply.

I have just completed a course in English and Journalism at the University of the West of England and gained a 2.1 degree. While I was at school and college I took every opportunity that came my way to gain experience as a journalist. I edited my school magazine and, after working previously on the social and sports pages, also became editor of the university newspaper in my final year. I have had work experience with several newspapers and magazines, including a three-month placement with the *Bristol Evening Echo*.

My special interest is in sport, particularly rugby. My ultimate aim is to become a sports correspondent or sports editor, but, to be frank, I have never wanted to do anything else but be a journalist. I should be willing to consider any post that would enable me to get a first foot on the ladder. I am energetic and hard-working, I think I have an eye for a good story, and I am never late for deadlines.

I should also mention that I hold a full driving licence and am fluent in Welsh.

In addition to my CV, I enclose two specimen pieces that I have written reporting on events in the Newport area. If you have an opening – even the merest chink in a door – I would be most grateful if you would get in touch.

Yours sincerely
Neville Johns

CVs

A CV is a visiting card for employment purposes. You should always have one to hand, and it should always be up to date. For suggestions on how to begin compiling a CV, please see the previous section in this chapter, 'Preparations', p. 252.

Unless you are applying for several identical jobs at the same time, each individual job application should be accompanied by a slightly different version of your CV, one that is specifically angled, as far as possible, towards the job in question. Do not simply copy out your basic or most recent CV. Check it carefully to make sure that it is up to date. Then check it again to see whether, by making small adjustments to what you say about yourself, you can highlight aspects of your training or experience that are particularly relevant to the post you are applying for.

For this reason, it may be helpful to keep your basic CV in a skeleton or all-purpose form that you know has to be filled out or rearranged before you send it out. You should keep a copy of every version that you do send out – together with a note of who you sent it to – both so that you know what interviewers have in front of them if you are called for interview and to save time if you apply again for a similar job. All this is much easier to do if you use a computer or word-processor.

A CV is a potted history of your educational and working life. The standard layout for a modern CV lists your educational achievements and professional appointments in **reverse** chronological order. The point of listing these in reverse order is to give prominence to your most recent and presumably most senior appointment. At the mid-point of your career, you will not want what you did at school or the series of small and relatively junior jobs that you did after leaving school or college to head the list. You should also briefly list your interests outside work and give the names of two referees (having first checked with the people involved that they are willing to provide a reference – see 'Job references', pp. 259–62). If, for any reason, you do not give the name of a referee from the organization that you are currently working for, it is usually advisable to explain why in your letter of application.

The whole CV should, if at all possible, fit onto one side of a sheet of A4 paper. A typical CV might look like this:

Catherine Seaton
92 Cooper's Hill
Eastbury-on-Severn
Glos
GL29 9VY
Tel: 01249 335768
e-mail: CSeaton@freebee.co.uk

Experience

1997–present
Manager of call centre for telephone banking with HTA Bank in Bristol. Responsible for supervising a staff of 50, including many part-timers, organizing shifts and ensuring 24-hour coverage. Also responsible for dealing with particularly difficult queries and complaints from customers and for liaising with bank head office. Managing annual budget of £100,000.

1990–1997
Deputy manager with BCB Market Research in Leicester. In charge of setting up a telephone research section and then running it with staff of 15. Mainly concerned with researching customer satisfaction with newly purchased cars.

1984–1990
Market researcher with Proby Research in Loughborough. Field researcher and later supervisor of small telephone research team.

1978–1984
Trainee cashier, cashier and customer service officer with HTA Bank in Leicester.

Qualifications and training

Diploma in market research, University of Loughborough (external)
RCA diploma in computing and database management
A Level English and Business Studies
O Level English Language, English Literature, Maths, French, Geography, Art

Interests

Sport, especially tennis, former county junior team captain
Foreign travel
Cooking

Referees

Mr V. A. Hill
Customer Services Manager
HTA Bank Ltd
197 Wapping Way
London EC11 8ZZ

Ms Denise Warren
Managing Director
BCB Market Research
PO Box 789
Leicester LE1 9UA

This form of CV works to best advantage if you have a reasonably long and continuous working life behind you. It may look a little sparse at the beginning of your career. Likewise if, for any reason, there have been gaps in your working life, then a chronological presentation will tend to highlight them.

There is an alternative. It involves abandoning chronology, grouping your experience under different headings, and including a brief personal profile. At this stage in your career, what you have done is not very much and what you are really selling to an employer is your personal ability and potential. Thus, the personal profile takes pride of place. The resulting document might look something like this:

Mark Baker
Flat 321
Charles Bradlaugh House
Hale Road
Tottenham
London N17 B68

Tel: 020 8808 1657
e-mail: marcus@tottenham.fiendish.com

Profile
Imaginative website designer with wide-ranging IT skills. Enthusiastic and energetic, used to operating independently but also as part of a team. Able to explain complicated technical matters in simple terms. Also used to problem-solving. Currently still working for an agency in an IT capacity, but looking for a permanent job, preferably in website design.

Training
Diploma in Website Design from North London College
NVQ in computer skills and database management

Skills

Website design
Website management
Computer graphics
Database management
Computer maintenance
Data inputting

Experience

Voluntary work in website design for children's charity
Agency work (3 years) in London in database management and data inputting, especially six months with Winchester Wines setting up and running customer database
Work experience with UVP Electronics, Battersea

Education

A levels	Information Technology Craft Design and Technology
GCSEs	5 at level C or above: English, Maths, IT, Art, Religious Education

Activities

Leader of church youth group
Member of brass band

Interests

Cinema
Surfing the Web

Referees

Mrs Diana White
Technocratics Agency
874 Seven Sisters Rd
Finsbury Park
London N8 4RT

Rev. Peter King
84 Gilpin Road
Edmonton
London N16 2UK

Job references

Employers and educators are not the only people who are called upon to write references to support job applications. Young people especially often call upon those they know to help them by providing what are basically character references for potential employers, so that writing a reference for someone is a task that could fall on almost anyone.

Writing to referees

First a brief word to applicants. It is vital to check before you send in your CV that the person you want to act as a referee is willing, or is still willing, to do so. If you write to them and expect them to write back to indicate whether they are willing or not, it may be courteous to enclose a stamped self-addressed envelope (SAE). You should give them a brief explanation of why you are applying for the job and say that you will let them know how your application turns out. Such a letter might look like this:

> Dear Mrs Thomas,
>
> I am in the process of applying for a new job and am writing to ask whether you would be kind enough to act as referee for me.
>
> I have been in my present job for three years now, and I think that the time has come to move on. The job I am applying for is that of a junior manager with Willoughby plc in Northampton. It would give me more responsibility than I have now as well as a higher salary and better prospects.
>
> My present boss, John Higgins, is supplying a work reference. I would be most grateful if you could say something about my general character and abilities.
>
> I hope this won't cause you too much trouble. Please let me know as soon as possible if you can help. I enclose an SAE for your reply.
>
> Yours sincerely
> Margaret Collins
>
> PS I will, of course, let you know how I get on.

Writing references

When writing a reference for someone, the most important thing is to be honest. If you cannot honestly recommend someone for a particular position, then you must say so – or, if you cannot bring yourself to spoil someone's chances, decline to act as a referee.

It is always possible that a reference will be 'followed up' by the employer. This may simply be to check that you exist and that you are who the candidate says you are – some applicants are not above faking references. But you may have to explain in more detail what precisely you meant by something you said or why you omitted to mention anything about this or that aspect of the applicant's work record or character. Not for this reason only, a reference needs to be written with care. Letters of reference should also be marked 'Confidential'.

In the majority of cases, fortunately, applicants do have something to recommend them, and the referee's task is to give an honest account of their good qualities, not necessarily overlooking any deficiencies but not highlighting them, and to show a degree of positive support. If someone deserves high praise then he or she should receive it.

The following might serve as an example of a general 'character' reference:

> **Confidential**
>
> Dear Sir or Madam,
>
> **Ms Jenny Butley**
>
> I first knew Ms Butley as her teacher at Brookfield School, where I taught for eight years. During her time at the school, she showed herself to be a capable and hard-working pupil at any task she was assigned. She was particularly strong in English and the Humanities, where she displayed both creativity and good organizational skills in her handling of projects. In areas where she was not so strong, she still applied herself conscientiously and with single-mindedness. She was active on the sports side, and represented the school at athletics, swimming and netball. On the social side, she had a calm, even temperament, and was a positive influence on her fellow pupils.
>
> I was also responsible for her work experience placements. She received very positive reports from all the employers to whom she was assigned.
>
> I have kept in contact with her since she left school. She has grown into an articulate and pleasant young woman. She is well aware of the benefits of the course she is applying for as regards her future career prospects.

She has expressed her determination to succeed in it and I am confident that she has the ability to do so.

I would have no hesitation in recommending her. If you have any further queries, please do not hesitate to contact me.

Yours sincerely
Ralph Henderson

Here is an example of the sort of letter, slightly less positive in tone, that an employer might write on behalf of an employee:

Confidential

Dear Mrs Thompson

Darren Anderson

Mr Anderson has been with us for three years first as a cashier then as a trainee manager in one of our supermarkets. There are at present no openings at junior manager level in our company, so he has decided to move on.

He has shown himself to be honest, capable, and hard-working. I believe he knows that he has the skills necessary to take on a more responsible position.

We are sorry to lose him and wish him well in his future career.

Yours sincerely
Dave Kent
Manager

Memos

The function of a memo is usually to deliver a simple message within an organization. It can therefore dispense with the introductory and concluding paraphernalia of an ordinary business letter. Companies frequently used preprinted memo forms so that you have only to fill in the relevant names and the date and write your message in the space provided. If a memo is written on plain paper, it should still contain the name of the addressee (and job title if appropriate), the sender's name (and job title if appropriate), the date, a reference, and a subject heading. It is customary to initial a memo rather than sign it.

A memo might only consist of a single sentence or line. In fact it should be as brief and to the point as possible. The memo seems most at home in a busy office atmosphere where notes are hurriedly glanced at and must make an immediate impression. Consequently long-windedness should be avoided at all costs. An outline plan, if one has been made, can quite easily be transformed into a memo.

Outline: Move to Grey St

1. Get quotes from movers
2. Insurance position
3. Choose staff to help – don't want everybody
4. (?1) Check decorators will be out
5. IT situation – can in-house people manage

Memo:

To: Milly
From: Greg
Date: 6 April 2001
Subject: Move to new offices in Grey St 1/07/01

Please check up on the following and get back to me before the end of the week.

1. Do the decorators know the move-in date and will they be finished in time?
2. Are the quotes in from the movers?
3. Do we need additional insurance for the move? Check with our insurers and eventually with movers.
4. Has Frank notified all the staff who'll be needed to help with the move? (We don't want anyone vital away on holiday.)
5. Recheck with IT manager that they can handle resetting up and don't need outside help.

Thanks GT

A longer memo such as the following could – and in fact should – be cut down.

To: R. T. Briggs
Production Controller

From: L. H. Bassett
Managing Director

Date: 23 February 2001
Subject: Letter from Bryants

I've just had a telephone call from George Black of Bryants this morning telling me that he'd had no reply to an urgent letter he wrote you two weeks ago. I don't know why he didn't ring you direct. Anyway he is not pleased and neither am I. I told him it might have got lost in the post. Has it? Or has it been lost? If it's not lost here or in the post, why haven't you answered it? You'll need to get back to him immediately and grovel a bit. You'd better let me know what happens as well.

LHB

There is too much personal irritation in this. The general point made earlier about putting the main point or conclusion first is even more vital in short pieces of correspondence such as a memo. A more pointed and effective version of the same memo might read like this:

To: R. T. Briggs
Production Controller

From: L. H. Bassett
Managing Director

Date: 23 February 2001
Subject: Letter from Bryants

Please get in contact with George Black of Bryants immediately regarding an urgent letter of two weeks ago to which they have received no reply. If the letter was not received here, explain and ask them to resend it. If the letter was lost or left unanswered here, explain, apologize profusely, give them an answer over the phone and confirm it in writing at once. Make a time to see me about this tomorrow. LHB

That has more chance of making the errant Mr Briggs respond effectively.

E-mails

More and more correspondence in the modern world is being sent electronically, and the trend is only likely to increase. Fax, which at one time seemed to be the solution to cheap, almost instantaneous, long-distance communication, is being largely superseded by e-mail. Almost anything that can be produced by a computer can be sent by e-mail.

For business contacts, e-mail even seems to be taking over from the telephone. You do not have to interact socially, exchange pleasantries, or wait while someone hums and haws when using e-mail.

Everything that has been said so far about other forms of written communication, business letters, personal letters, etc., can apply equally well to e-mail on occasions. Nevertheless, there are a number of useful points, specific to e-mailing, that are as well to remember.

You should generally begin with a greeting, especially to a correspondent you do not know well. You do not have to begin every communication with Hi! (though this is an acceptable way of beginning an informal one). It is also good practice to end with one of the usual signing-off formulae and, where appropriate, a signature. Many e-mail software packages have a facility for storing a 'signature' (usually your name and job title – it should not be too elaborate) and attaching it automatically.

The subject line should be used like the heading to a business letter to focus attention immediately on the matter in hand. Reading the subject line is the only way in which your reader – if he or she receives very many e-mails – can decide whether to read it or not.

E-mail appears in the form of simple, often fairly crude text, and is keyed in immediately by hand. Don't 'shout' by putting your message in CAPITAL LETTERS. Use asterisks *like this* to highlight particular words.

If anything complicated needs to be sent, the best procedure is to copy it over from another file and paste it in or to send it as an attachment. If you send anything as an attachment, make sure that the person receiving it has the necessary software to be able to open it. If in doubt, send a preliminary e-mail to check the position at the other end or use a generic file (such as an RTF file for word-processed material).

Copy the e-mail only to those people who need to see the e-mail.

A typical friendly business e-mail might run as follows (a publisher is writing to a freelance proofreader):

> From: PSmith@hotwellspublishers.co.uk
> To: Mike@Briggs.fiendish.com
> Subject: Next year's schedules
>
> Dear Mike,
>
> I'm attaching a schedule for next year's 'Antidote'. Please let me know if you can't open it and I'll put a copy in the post.
>
> You'll notice that the publication dates – and therefore the dates on which you are due to receive and send back the proofs – are slightly later than the corresponding ones this year. Nothing else has changed, however.
>
> Please confirm that you are able to work to this schedule.
>
> Hope you had a good summer.
>
> Best wishes
>
> Phil

On the general use of information technology in writing, see chapter 12.

10 Reports, presentations, essays, and theses

This chapter deals with the writing of comparatively extended pieces of written work: reports, presentations, essays, and theses. To these are added brief sections on research, on presenting material in lists, and on writing a list of references or a bibliography, tasks which may be relevant to any of these types of writing.

Research

A period of time for research will need to be built into the schedule for most extended pieces of writing. In the case of a doctoral thesis for a university, the collection of data usually takes a number of years. The brief suggestions made here relate more to research for which a shorter time is available.

To plan your research you will need to compile a list of what information you need to obtain and what questions you have to ask to obtain it. From this you can then draw up a list of possible sources: people involved in the activity you are researching, well-informed personal contacts, publications, previous research reports, etc. The various types of research take different amounts of time. Interviewing or surveying a group of people will in most cases demand more time than reading publications or searching the Internet. Allowance for all of these needs to be made in scheduling.

Research involving contact with people

There are two matters that are important when you set out to obtain research data directly from individuals by means of interviews or questionnaires. The first is the principle of 'informed consent'. The people you speak to should be told the purpose of the research and how the data you collect from them will be used. It may be useful to compile a short written statement of your aims that you can send to people or give them to read before the interview. Likewise, it is courteous to offer to send to people whom you interview at length, or who make a major contribution to your project, a brief summary of your findings when the exercise is completed.

The second important matter is that of confidentiality. It is vital to obtain consent, preferably written consent, from people if you intend to use their real names in a published work. In many cases, however, fictional names or lettered or numbered references (Respondent A, Interviewee 2, etc.) are used in place of real names to ensure confidentiality. If you are going to use fictional names, you should explain the procedure you are adopting to your respondents and, again, obtain their consent to it. Remember that organizations may be wary of being referred to by name as well, and that if you do refer to an organization by its real name and then use a job title to denote an individual, that is tantamount to identifying that individual by name.

Research from books and other published sources

Teachers and lecturers frequently provide a book list to assist students in researching an essay topic. It is not usually possible or even necessary to read every word of every book on the list. Use the contents page and the index to locate the sections that relate specifically to the topic you are interested in or skim-read the book, scanning mainly the first lines of paragraphs, to locate the relevant material. If you are pressed for time, it may be counterproductive to get too involved in a book – however intrinsically fascinating and worthwhile – if large sections of it are of no direct use in your project.

Make a careful note of the publication details of every book you consult, when you consult it, so that you do not need to go back to the book again when you are preparing your bibliography (see the section 'References', pp. 291–2).

Research on the Internet

The Internet gives access to a vast amount of information on almost every imaginable subject. To locate material on the Internet, go through your service provider to one of the main search engines. Typing in a keyword (e.g, *Shakespeare, biodiversity, Gettysbury (battle of)*) will then produce a list of sites you can visit, often including sites with links to further related sites. The results are usually valuable, but the process is somewhat hit and miss, as search engines sometimes list sites that are no longer operative. Researching via the Internet is not necessarily quicker than reading books.

The taking of accurate notes, of course, is crucial for all types of research. For advice on that subject, please see the section 'Note-taking', pp. 295–300.

Reports

The size and scope of reports differ widely. They may fill only one or two pages; they may extend to the size of a small book. The term 'report' may suggest something that is entirely factual and objective. This is not always the case, however, as the reporter might be intending to use the opportunity to put forward a particular point of view or to propose a particular course of action. It is vital to distinguish in report-writing between what is objective fact and what is opinion, what was observed or obtained from tests and surveys, and what are conclusions drawn by the reporter or recommendations that he or she wishes to make.

Structure of reports

No two reports will necessarily have or demand the same structure – though if the preparation of reports is a task that you have to undertake frequently, some degree of standardization is advisable. The following is intended as a general outline. Some of these sections can be dispensed with in some reports, especially shorter ones.

List of contents
Summary
Introduction – terms of reference, background
Facts
Analysis and discussion of factual material
Conclusions
Recommendations
Appendices
References

List of contents

Any report of more than a few pages will benefit from having a list of contents. Though it comes first, it should be prepared last, when all the material is complete. A list of contents is of little use, however, unless a consistent system of headings and numbers has been applied to the various sections of the report.

Headings and numbering

Each section of even the shortest report should have a heading. Generally speaking, subsections should be given a heading as well, one that is typographically distinct from the section headings. Section headings might, for example be given all in large capitals:

1. INTRODUCTION or in bold: **1. Introduction**. Subsections could then be headed in italics: 1.1. *Terms of reference* or in italics and underlined: 1.1. *Terms of reference*.

The commonest and most generally useful numbering system for reports and similar pieces of writing is a decimal one. Each section has a number, each subsection has a number within the section, each paragraph has a number within the subsection. For example:

3. RESULTS

3.1. *Results from questionnaires*

3.1.1. The results from the questionnaires were collated . . .

It is important that the numbering and the system of headings should be consistent throughout the report.

Summary

The summary, like the table of contents, is one of the things you write last. (For general advice on writing summaries, see the section 'Summaries, pp. 300–304). Its purpose is to summarize the whole report, including any conclusions and recommendations, in the space of approximately a single page. The reader should be able to gauge from the summary (together with the contents list) what has been discovered and decided and whether he or she need read the whole report.

Introduction

The most important part of the introductory section is a setting out of the terms of reference of the report: a precise definition of the report's scope. In most cases someone else will have decided what is to be looked into, which particular aspects of the subject are to be covered, and how far the reporters are supposed to go in drawing conclusions and making recommendations. If you are compiling a report at your own initiative, then you will need to set your own terms of reference and state them clearly – they determine the scope and shape of the report and it is impossible to produce an effective report without a clear objective. Such a statement might read:

> *To investigate the various means of heating the planned new council premises in Shadow Lane, to assess each in terms of its suitability, cost-effectiveness, and environmental impact, and to make appropriate recommendations to the council.*

In addition to setting out the terms of reference, the introduction should provide any background information the reader might require. This will generally include:

a description of the circumstances that led to the production of the report;

a statement of the existing position;

a history of the events that brought about the present state of affairs;

an account of the methods used to gather information and assess it;

and

a list of the people who conducted the investigation and are presenting the report.

Body of the report

The body of the report contains both the factual material gathered by investigators and their analysis of that material. It will depend on particular circumstances whether fact and analysis are presented in separate sections or whether analysis proceeds alongside the presentation of facts. This part of a report will typically consist of a mixture of ordinary discursive prose and information presented in the form of lists and tables. For advice on the latter, see the section 'Lists', pp. 279–83.

A report should be readable and easy to follow. It should be written in a fairly formal style – as, for example, in the extract from a fund manager's report below – without being too pompous, impersonal, or technical:

> **Outlook and Future Policy**
>
> With UK interest rates at or near their peak, it appears that the Bank of England may have managed to engineer a 'soft landing' for the economy. Having been through its first business cycle since independence from the Treasury, the MPC (Monetary Policy Committee) will be anticipating that the . . . company earnings outlook should enable acceleration in growth instead of a drift back towards recession. In summary, the prudent management of the UK economy seems to be providing an encouraging environment for further growth in equity markets . . .
>
> (Barclays Combined Income Fund, Manager's Interim Report, September 2000, Barclays Fund Limited)

Headings and subheadings break up the page and make it easier on the eye, as well as acting as an outline guide to the progress of the argument. In order to keep the reader's attention on the main thrust of the report, it may be useful to put any particularly detailed pieces of information, research data, or case studies into footnotes or appendices. It should be borne in mind, however, that if readers who are in a hurry omit anything, then notes and appendices are likely not to be read.

For discussion of the use of paragraphs, see pp. 231–5.

Conclusions and recommendations

Even if conclusions and recommendations emerge, or begin to emerge, in the body of the report, they should still be gathered together and presented in two separate sections at the end. Not all reports are required to produce recommendations but when they are asked for they should be given a separate section.

Appendices and references

The purpose of an appendix, as mentioned above, is to take particularly complex data or information from the main text where it might interrupt the reader's progress unnecessarily. References will be necessary when a good deal of the information on which the report is based has been taken from published sources. For advice on the presentation of references, see the section 'References', pp. 291–2.

Presentations

A presentation differs from every other piece of work so far discussed in this book, inasmuch as it is intended for delivery by a speaker to a live audience. A good deal of writing, nevertheless, goes into the preparation of a speech, lecture, talk, or presentation to a group of business people or colleagues.

The audience

Assuming that the writer is preparing a presentation for delivery in person, then he or she is no longer the 'invisible writer' referred to at the beginning of this part of the book (p. 181). It is even more important when directing a presentation to a live audience rather than to 'invisible readers' to know your listeners and to work out in advance their probable knowledge of the subject you are dealing with. As teachers and university lecturers know only too well, students cannot be relied on to have read the books they are supposed to. Some audiences come as much to be entertained as to be informed. Most audiences contain many people who have only a basic knowledge of the subject, but at the same time most audiences contain at least one or two people who know at least as much about the topic as the speaker, if not more. Do not assume too much, but at the same time do not talk down to your audience. If you are making a presentation to an audience of your peers, then as with composing a report or any other piece of writing, you have greater licence to 'talk shop' and use technical vocabulary. If you are addressing a mixed audience, then do not necessarily bring everything down to the lowest common denominator, but, even more importantly, do not aim to impress the world expert who you know is going to be present. It stands to reason that a presenter should know more about the particular subject that he or she is speaking on than the bulk of the audience. Nevertheless, a well-prepared, well-presented talk that gives the speaker's personal slant on a subject and is enlivened by his or her own enthusiasm and interests is a satisfying experience in itself, and usually an enlightening one even for the expert.

A reader proceeds at his or her own pace and can go back and read again anything that he or she has not grasped the first time. Listeners are directly dependent on the speaker. Repetition and recapitulation (preferably not in exactly the same words) need to be built in. The presentation must be paced in such a way that listeners can keep up. Above all, the organization of the material should be plain and the language used by the speaker should be clear and, as far as possible, simple. As has been noted before, ideally the simplicity of the language should increase as the subject becomes more complex. Using clear and simple language should unite a mixed audience: the less well-informed will be able to understand and the better-informed will be able to firm up their understanding.

No two audiences are the same. The size of the audience usually has a bearing on the tone of the presentation. Generally speaking, a more informal and conversational tone is suitable for a small gathering, and, as the size of the audience increases, the tone needs to become more formal. Interaction with the audience – in the form of questions and answers – is easier when numbers are small. There is a difference between a seminar where participants often expect, and are expected, to contribute and a lecture where questions, if allowed at all, are only usually allowed at the end. A less experienced speaker addressing a largish audience is probably best advised to restrict questions to the end. An interruption in the middle can quite easily relate to something you were going to discuss anyway, forcing you to rearrange your material, or divert you on to a relatively minor topic, giving you less time to communicate the more important matters.

Because no two audiences are the same, speakers and presenters need to be both clear about what they want to put across and yet flexible about how precisely they do it. It can often happen that you speak on the same subject on two different occasions and find that the first audience catches on quickly and you have time to spare, while on the second occasion the audience needs a far more thorough explanation of the main points and time runs out fast. Both possibilities need to be taken into account in your preparation.

Time and material

Speakers are usually bound by time in a way that writers are not, so it is wise, first of all, to have a clock or watch positioned where you can see it easily while making the presentation. It is better to finish slightly early than late. But it is not a good thing to run out of things to say well in advance of time so that you have to rely on questions – of which there may be none, or no useful ones – to fill up your allotted span. To guard against the possibility of petering out, you should, ideally, have more to say than you actually intend or need to say.

At the same time, you need to know the relative importance of all the points on your list. When you are collecting material, it should be allocated to one of three categories: things that the audience must be told; things that it would be useful for the audience to know; things that it would be nice to mention but which are not vital. The items in the first category are what the presentation is all about and must be communicated. You would expect to be able to deal with at least some of the items in the second category, subject to fitting them around those in the first. The items in the third category are there mainly to enable you to keep going interestingly if the take-up of the material in categories one and two is swift. You do not necessarily have to structure the whole thing so that the unimportant material is all left to last. A main point might have attached to it some category two or three material that you can insert if things are going well. As long as the main points are identified and put across clearly in the time available, the rest is a matter of judgment.

Structuring

The old adage runs: 'Tell 'em what you're going to say, say it, then tell 'em you've said it.' It works. An introduction – in which you outline the material that you intend to present – a presentation in full of the essential material together with as much of the 'useful' and 'nice' items as time allows, followed by a recapitulation of the main points is the scheme to adopt. The main structural difference between a presentation and, for example, a report is the importance of the ending. Whereas readers of a report might be content to read only the initial summary and might expect to stop before the end, the audience will remain until the end, may remember best what you said last, and may want something which they can applaud. A strong conclusion – some people suggest a final meaningful question (*Can we really allow this situation to continue?*) or a call to action (*We know the problem; we know the solution. Now let's do something about it*) – is necessary. The audience needs to be reminded, finally, what it has all been about and they need to know that you are coming to an end. Don't let the presentation fade out. Even if you keep the less important material for the latter part of your talk, finish by returning to the main theme and restating it powerfully. This usually means devoting a good deal of preparation time to your closing words.

Writing before speaking

How much a speaker should write down is a moot point. All the experts are agreed that it is a bad thing to read a speech or even to write a speech, memorize it, and deliver it from memory. Speakers have to be able to think on their feet, react to the audience, and react to the passing of time. If you are tied to a written or memorized text, you do not have the freedom to adjust. If you are looking at a piece of paper, you cannot look at the audience and establish a rapport with them.

On the other hand, an inexperienced speaker especially may feel that he or she needs the reassurance provided by a full text. The answer is to write down what you have to say as fully as you like – always bearing in mind that you are going to be saying it out loud – but not to be dependent on the text in that form when you deliver it. There are various ways in which this can be done. First, you can write out the text in an easily legible form – double-spaced, clearly printed – with the crucial statements or points highlighted in some way. Your aim is to get from one highlighted point to the next, not necessarily following the exact wording of the original, though if you have taken the trouble to write it out and then read it through a few times, a good deal of the original wording will undoubtedly remain in your mind. Alternatively, having written out a full version, you can condense it into a one- or two-page summary or a set of cards (numbered and perhaps loosely attached at the corners) that you can take into the lecture hall with you.

Visual aids

Visual aids, such as a whiteboard, flip chart, slides, or transparencies projected from an overhead projector, are often extremely useful in making a presentation. The crucial matter is to ensure that they add to, and do not detract from, your efforts as a speaker. Do check that all the equipment you need to use is set up and working properly before you begin, and that any slides or transparencies are in the right order and ready to be inserted the right way up. Make sure that anything you write or hang on a board is clearly visible to the audience, and try to arrange matters so that you spend as little time as possible with your back to them.

The same basic rule applies to text handouts. It is sometimes advised that handouts should be distributed at the end of the session – unless people need to refer to them as you go through your talk. If you hand them out at the beginning, the audience may be more interested in reading them than in listening to you.

Speaking

It is beyond the scope of this book to give more than a few hints for the effective delivery of a spoken text. Look at the audience, and smile occasionally. Humour is a welcome ingredient in any speech, but don't strain to be funny or set too much store by any one joke in case it falls flat. It is helpful to identify one or two friendly faces in the audience that you can rest on periodically to give yourself confidence. But everybody in the room needs to feel that you are speaking to them, so let your gaze go over the whole assembly from time to time. Do not stare at the clock or ceiling or out of the window. If you have notes or cards to hold, it gives you something to do with your hands. Try not to fidget or fiddle, but gestures can help to put points across and to establish contact with the audience. Speak reasonably slowly and do not be afraid to pause occasionally – nerves and inexperience often make speakers talk too hurriedly. Remember the audience has to keep up by listening and understanding as you go along. Since this is a fairly trying occasion, especially if it is your first experience of public speaking, take time not only to prepare, but also to rehearse. Read your written text out loud – if you have prepared one – and rehearse speaking out loud from your notes, cards, or summary. It may help to tape yourself doing this or to find some sympathetic friend or colleague to listen to you. It is usual to feel tense or nervous before you start – even experienced speakers and experienced actors do. If you are well prepared and well rehearsed, however, your confidence will grow as you warm to your subject and you will deserve the applause you receive at the end.

Lists

Lists are a very useful way both of breaking up a solid run of text, thus giving a more interesting look to a page, and of highlighting particular points. A lengthy sentence such as:

> The purpose of this meeting is to discuss the formation of a subcommittee to report on the feasibility of building an extension to the existing village hall, to select the members of the subcommittee, to establish its terms of reference, to agree a budget for its work, and to set a date for the presentation of its report.

could equally well be set out in the form of a list.

> *The purpose of this meeting is:*
>
> *to discuss the formation of a subcommittee to report on the feasibility of building an extension to the existing village hall;*
> *to select the members of the subcommittee;*
> *to establish its terms of reference;*
> *to agree a budget for its work;*
> *to set a date for the presentation of its report.*

The list takes up considerably more space on the page than the original sentence, but it is much more readable.

There are two matters that sometimes cause problems when material such as this is set out in list form. One is grammatical continuity between the opening section of the sentence and the listed items; the other is punctuation within the list. These will now be looked at separately.

Grammatical continuity

It is all too easy to forget that a list of this kind should be subject to the normal rules of grammar – it is, after all, often an ordinary sentence that is being presented in a different format. Consequently, the items in the list should run parallel to each other as far as their grammatical structure is concerned. To put that another way: you should be able to attach the introductory clause or phrase to any item on the list and the result should be a grammatical sentence. You should also be able to attach it to each of the items in turn and come up with roughly the same sort of sentence each time. Consider the following:

After lengthy discussion, the committee agreed that:

the present schedule was unrealistic
a new schedule would have to be drawn up
to ask the project leader to set a new finishing date for the project
to consider hiring more staff and
making new funding available

As a series of rough preliminary jottings such a list might be all right, but it is unsatisfactory as a final product. It would be grammatical nonsense to write: *The committee agreed that to ask the project leader* or *The committee agreed that to consider hiring new staff* or *The committee agreed that making new funding available.* What has happened here is that the introductory clause has been lost sight of as the list goes on. If the introduction had simply read *the committee agreed*: then it would have been in order to continue *to ask the project leader* or *to consider hiring more staff.*

Either the wording of the items on the list or the wording of the introductory clause needs to be changed in order to achieve a satisfactorily parallel structure.

After lengthy discussion, the committee agreed that:

the present schedule was unrealistic
a new schedule would have to be drawn up
the project leader should be asked to set a new finishing date for the project
she should consider hiring more staff and
new funding should be made available

There is not an exact parallelism in that most of the verbs are passive and *she should consider hiring* is an active construction, but that does not affect the grammatical soundness of the whole. An alternative solution might be:

After lengthy discussion, the committee agreed:

that the present schedule was unrealistic
that a new schedule would have to be drawn up
to ask the project leader to set a new finishing date for the project
to consider hiring more staff and
to make new funding available

Since the verb *agree* can be followed either by a *that* clause or by an infinitive with *to*, there are no objections to the above on grammatical grounds, even though the items are not exactly parallel.

Punctuation

The examples in the previous section have been deliberately left unpunctuated. The general conventions for punctuating lists are relatively simple.

The introductory clause should end with a colon. The items in the list – if they are not complete sentences – should begin with a small letter and end with a semicolon. If the final item in the list represents the end of the sentence, then it should end with a full stop.

After lengthy discussion, the committee agreed that:

– *the present schedule was unrealistic;*
– *a new schedule would have to be drawn up;*
– *the project leader should be asked to set a new finishing date for the project;*
– *she should consider hiring more staff; and*
– *new funding should be made available.*

Notice that in the entry before last the semicolon comes before *and*. If for any reason the sentence continues beyond the last item in the list, then that item too ends with a semicolon:

After lengthy discussion, the committee agreed that:

– *the present schedule was unrealistic; and*
– *a new schedule would have to be drawn up;*

and that the project leader should be asked to:

– *set a new finishing date for the project;*

> – *hire more staff; and*
> – *apply for increased funding;*
>
> *subject always to the approval of the board of directors.*

Variations on putting a semicolon at the end of individual items in the list are a comma or even to leave it with no punctuation. The final item in the list, since it represents the end of the sentence, should, however, always end up with a full stop.

Where the items on the list are complete sentences, however, and are not grammatically dependent on the opening statement, they should begin with a capital letter and end with a full stop or a question mark.

> *There are three main objections to the proposal:*
>
> 1. *The proposed site is close to the river and might be subject to flooding.*
> 2. *The existing access road is very narrow and would need to be widened.*
> 3. *Traffic to and from the site will pass the local primary school causing additional road safety problems particularly at the beginning and end of the school day.*

Or:

> *The questions we must ask ourselves are these:*
>
> *Why have standards declined so markedly over the last three years?*
> *Can responsibility for the decline in standards be laid at the door of any particular individuals?*
> *If so, what should be done with those people?*
>
> *and most importantly:*
>
> *How can the situation be remedied?*

Numbering

Generally speaking, short lists do not need to be numbered and the items are best prefaced with a dash (–) or a bullet (•). Longer lists, or lists in which the individual items need to be specifically referred back to, are best numbered with Arabic numerals (with or without full stops) or by bracketed small letters (a), (b), (c) etc. Small Roman numerals (i), (ii), (iii) are best reserved for subdivisions within a list.

The estimate should include the following:

(a) *the cost of renewing the flat roof over the garage:*
  (i) *if the existing boards are sound;*
  (ii) *if the existing boards need replacing;*
(b) *the cost of making good the slate roof at the back of the house . . .*

Essays

It is unlikely that anyone who is not a professional writer or scholar will have to write an essay outside the context of an academic course. While concentrating on essay-writing, this section will also comment on academic writing in general.

English literature is rich in essays – the names Francis Bacon, Charles Lamb, and George Orwell spring immediately to mind. There is a great deal to be learnt from the work of such writers, particularly Orwell as a relatively modern exponent of the genre. For additional and more recent inspiration, however, the aspiring essay-writer is recommended to look at good-quality journalism and good-quality critical writing. An editorial is a small-scale essay; an article in a newspaper or magazine discussing a particular topic is a larger-scale one. There are some differences in the style appropriate to journalism and the style required for academic exercises, but, nevertheless, techniques of discussion and argument can be learnt from journalistic sources. Likewise, when you search for information and ideas in books written by experts, look also at the way the experts have tackled the subject and the style they have used.

Analysing the title

In the vast majority of cases essays are written on a subject set by a tutor or examiner. If you do not understand or interpret the title correctly, you are unlikely to produce work that will satisfy whoever set it and has to mark it. Look carefully at the title and sort out which are the key words in it – not only those that relate to the subject, but also those that relate to the type of treatment of the subject that is expected. If you are asked, for example, to *Analyse the causes of the French Revolution*, nothing will be gained by simply latching on to the words *French Revolution* and giving a potted history of events in France from 1789 to, say, 1794. A straightforward listing of the various historical events, economic factors, etc., that led up to the Revolution is unlikely to fare much better. Some form of analysis – an attempt to rank the various causes in order of their importance or a comparison of what one historian suggests were the major causes with those suggested by another – is necessary to fulfil the requirements of the question.

By and large, examiners and other essay-setters do not play tricks on the people who are writing for them. The nature of the task is indicated in the title – the essay-writer merely has to interpret it correctly. The majority of essays fall into one of five different categories:

1. **Descriptive or narrative essays** (key words: *describe, outline, summarize, give an account of*, etc.). This is probably the easiest type of essay to write as it simply requires you to marshal the factual information you have on a subject in a clear and logical fashion.
2. **Analytical essays** (key words: *analyse, assess, evaluate, examine, investigate, how far . . . , to what extent . . .*). These require more in-depth knowledge of the subject. The writer needs to be able to break down the topic into its major parts and ask, and provide answers to, relevant questions relating to it. He or she also needs to be able to evaluate the relative importance of a number of different factors. A question such as *To what extent is the economy of the eastern central United States dependent on the Mississippi River?* involves not only a knowledge of the contribution that the river makes to trade, but also a weighing up of the importance of other areas of the economy that have nothing to do with the river.
3. **'Compare and contrast' essays**. These demand a mixture of factual knowledge and critical thinking. Generally speaking, the differences between two people or things are more interest-

ing and important than the similarities, and the structure of the essay should reflect this. (A good approach is to devote a single section to the factors that things have in common and a number of separate sections to the factors that distinguish them from each other.)

4. **Discussion essays.** This is the type of essay that usually leaves most freedom to the writer. Typically, the title puts forward a controversial statement of opinion on a topic: *'He who can, does. He who cannot, teaches.' Discuss.* The writer then has the choice of either adopting a neutral stance, giving equal weight to both sides of the question in the body of the essay before coming to a personal conclusion, or embracing one point of view enthusiastically and trying to refute the arguments that might be put by the other side. In both cases, however, it is necessary to know what might be said for and against a particular position.
5. **Explanatory essays** (the key words are usually question words such as *what . . . ?*, *how . . . ?*, *why . . . ?*). Such essays mainly call on factual knowledge. A question such as *What is meant by 'biodiversity'?* is intended to bring out your own understanding of the term and your knowledge of how leading thinkers in the field have interpreted it. You would also need to support your conclusions by references (using this example) to natural environments.

Planning and structure

The importance of planning has been emphasized throughout this book. Essay-writers, including examination candidates, should need no reminding that time spent in planning generally means less time taken in writing and a more satisfactory result overall.

The structure of an essay is to a large extent dictated by convention, though it does not differ radically from the structure of most other pieces of writing. An academic essay must have an introduction, it must have a conclusion, and there should be a sufficient number of sections or paragraphs between these two to accommodate the various ideas and arguments that the writer is putting forward. But, whereas in a great deal of business writing the advice is to start with your conclusion – because you cannot be sure that your reader will stay to the end – the essay-writer can usually count on a reader having to, and hopefully wanting to, read the whole essay. Consequently, you should not express all your arguments at the outset.

When planning an essay, it is probably best to organize the body of the essay first. Sort out the material you have gathered from your reading or other research into sections corresponding to the points you wish to make and arrange these in a clear and logical order. Remember that this progression must be clear and convincing to the reader as well as to yourself. When you have done this, writing the introduction should be comparatively easy because its main function, in addition to providing any essential background information, is to set out the method or approach you propose to adopt in tackling the question. The conclusion should follow logically from and sum up what has gone before. It should not merely repeat what you have said before; if possible, you should save a final telling point or a particularly neat way of expressing your main idea for the conclusion. At the same time, however, and even more importantly, your conclusion should not contradict what you have said before or lead off on a totally different track.

Let us give a specific example of how an essay might be planned. Say, for instance, that you are confronted in English literary studies by the basic question *What is tragedy?* Like many essay topics, it is designed to test your knowledge both of the theory of the subject and of specific instances and of the relationships between the two. It is also an enormous topic – you are unlikely to have read every significant definition of tragedy or every single tragic play ever written. It is worth remembering that you are not being asked to provide a definitive answer to a question that has vexed the sages for centuries. You are being asked to demonstrate that you have absorbed what you have read or have been taught, that you understand the subject, that you can write interestingly and knowledgeably about it, and that you can conform to the usual conventions in terms of length, format, and style. So you need, if you are widely read, to select material to fit within a reasonable essay length (say 1000 or 2000 words) or, if you are less widely read, to use the knowledge that you do possess to best advantage.

The material you have to organize is likely to consist of one or more definitions of tragedy culled from various sources, the writings of literary theorists or reference books, together with what you know of a number of serious plays. You might decide that the best tactic is to compare and contrast a number of different definitions. Author A suggests that tragedy is such and such, a definition which particularly suits plays X, Y, and Z. Author B, on the other hand, highlights this particular aspect of tragedy as he or she was particularly influenced by the plays of . . . , where author C. . . and so on. Alternatively, you might select one particularly significant definition – say Aristotle's definition of tragedy as a work 'arousing pity and fear and leading to a catharsis of these emotions' – and then try to apply it to plays from various periods, Greek tragedies, Shakespearean tragedies, and contemporary tragedies. Having come to a decision on the basis of your knowledge of the subject and your particular interest in it, you can choose your approach and make your plan.

After that, write your introduction. A useful tip, for essays of the type that is being used as an example, is to try to avoid beginning with a bald definition:

> *The New Penguin English Dictionary* defines tragedy as: 'a serious drama in which destructive circumstances result in adversity for, and usu the deaths of, the main characters'. I intend to use . . .

You intend to use the definition, all well and good, but many other essay-writers have used precisely the same formula to get themselves started. If you can vary the formula with the definition from the start, it is much better:

> Like most dictionaries *The New Penguin English Dictionary* defines tragedy in a very general way – 'a serious drama in which destructive circumstances result in adversity for, and usu the deaths of, the main characters'. But far more specific definitions have been given by . . .

Or:

> All definitions of tragedy are written on the basis of the dramas that the definer knows and of the spirit of the age in which he or she happens to be writing. A modern definition such as the one given in *The New Penguin English Dictionary* . . .

It is difficult to illustrate a conclusion because, as has been said, it must necessarily follow from the specific points you have discussed. But let us assume, for the moment, that you have been discussing Aristotle's definition of tragedy and applying it to dramas of various epochs. You might well have come to the conclusion that the ancient Greek notions do not fit entirely with the practice of modern dramatists. But, if you have not discussed it before, you might take Aristotle's notion of 'catharsis' and use it to give a different angle in your conclusion:

> Aristotle's definition, therefore, though vastly influential and productive, is by no means universally valid. Shakespeare and modern playwrights rewrote his rules and still produced tragic effects. But Aristotle's thinking on the subject was not confined to the literary sphere. The idea of 'catharsis', the purging of emotion through watching a play, shows that it had a social dimension as well. Tragedy, like any other literary genre, needs to be defined not only in literary terms but in relation to the wider world. While tragic plays continue to be written, performed, and watched, the vicarious experience of suffering – which is what tragedy finally is – is something that individual human beings and possibly whole societies sometimes need.

Academic style

Academic style ought not to be distinct from good style generally. The overall advice given in this book with regard to clarity, simplicity, economy, etc., applies equally well to writing essays, dissertations, and other academic exercises. However, one or two points need to be given special emphasis.

Informal words and expressions should not be used in academic writing. For example: verb forms should be written out in full (*do not* not *don't*, etc.). Personal constructions (*I am doing this . . . , I intend to do that . . .*) are generally less recommended in academic writing than elsewhere. They may be appropriate in an introduction where you state directly what you intend to do, and there are certain kinds of essay – for example, essays in practical literary criticism – where a subjective response is in order, but generally the tone of the writing in the body of an academic essay should tend towards the impersonal. A great deal of academic writing is also, necessarily, somewhat tentative because the writer is simply not in a position to make authoritative and definitive statements on a subject. A proper impersonality and tentativeness are sometimes difficult to achieve without resorting too much to rather clumsy abstract constructions and passive verbs: *it is sometimes thought that . . . it has often been argued that . . . as has been suggested by many writers on the subject.* Where possible, such phrases should be replaced by, or at least varied with, more direct expressions: *Some people/experts/scholars think . . . X, among others, has argued that . . . as many writers on the subject have suggested.*

Dividing your work up into suitable paragraphs is as important in academic writing as in any other kind. When you are presenting an argument, the linking devices that indicate how a new paragraph relates to the one that preceded it acquire particular importance. Try to make sure that the connection is clear and that you signal to the reader how the gap between the paragraphs is to be bridged:

> . . . and this remained the case throughout the whole of the nineteenth century.
>
> At the beginning of the twentieth century, however, . . .

Or:

> Research carried out in America, Australia, and South Africa points to the same conclusion.
>
> There is, consequently, little point in trying to argue, as some scholars have done, that this is a purely European phenomenon . . .

Quotations

Quotations are a necessary part of most essays. Most essay-setters and markers like you to include quotations because they show, or at least suggest, that you have read up on the subject. But an essay should never become a structure in which quotations carry all the substance and the writer's contribution is simply to link them all together, nor should quotations be included where they are not relevant. Quote, preferably, to support or illustrate a point – not to make a point. And try to quote in such a way as not to interrupt the flow of your own argument.

Shorter quotations should be integrated into the text: *As Shaw says in the preface to* Pygmalion*: 'It is impossible for an Englishman to open his mouth without making some other Englishman despise him.'* Or: *A house,* *according to Le Corbusier, is 'a machine for living in'*. Where what you are quoting is a complete sentence, it should normally follow a colon and begin with a capital letter. A phrase of a few words needs no punctuation apart from inverted commas. On the use of quotation marks, see also pp. 160–64.

When you are quoting a passage of more than, say, thirty words, the usual practice is to mark it off from the body of the text by leaving a space above and below it and by indenting it (leaving a wider than usual margin on both sides):

> The same point has been made in a slightly different way by Keats's biographer Stephen Coote:
>
> > Those who really know the reality of beauty recognise that it can never be truly experienced except in its relationship to suffering, the pain that is never over, 'never done'. In the horror of this recognition, beauty itself becomes drained of life and warmth.
> >
> > (Coote, 1995, p. 167)
>
> Coote highlights in particular . . .

When a quotation is marked off in this way, it does not need to be placed in inverted commas.

If you omit a word, phrase, etc., from the passage then you should indicate the fact by an ellipsis (. . .): *As Winston Churchill said: 'Never . . . was so much owed by so many to so few'*. An ellipsis should also be used if you break a quotation off before reaching the end of the sentence or if you omit the original author's opening words: *According to Lord Acton: '. . . absolute power corrupts absolutely'*. Just as it is sometimes necessary to omit words from a quotation, you may sometimes have to alter the precise wording to fit comfortably within your sentence. Marco Polo is reported as saying 'I have not told half of what I saw'. If you wanted to use that quotation about someone else, you would need to adapt the wording: *Like Marco Polo, he had not 'told half of what [he] saw'*. The *he* in square brackets indicates that it was not the original wording.

In an academic essay all quotations from published sources must be attributed. The exact method you use to attribute quotations in the body of your text will depend on the way in which you present your references.

The system recommended in this book and described fully in the section 'References', below, is known as the 'Harvard system'. If you are providing a proper list of references in accordance with this system – as you should for a formal essay of any length – then a formulation such as: *As Rita Carter (1998, p. 15) says: 'The left brain . . .'* can be used. The author's name and the date of publication of his or her book or article are sufficient for the reader to identify from your references which work you are referring to. The page should also be included to make it easier for the reader to consult the work you are quoting for verification or further information, should he or she so desire.

If you need to refer to the same work more than once in the course of an essay, given the economy of the Harvard system, it is not necessary to use the Latin phrases *ibid.* or *op. cit.* If you do use them, remember that *ibid.* means 'the same' and refers back to the work from which you took the quotation immediately preceding the present one: *Professor Smith says '. . .' (The Small Garden, p. 24), but later qualifies this by saying '. . .' (ibid., p. 37)*. '*Op. cit.*', on the other hand, refers to a work by a particular author that you have quoted from at some point in an earlier part of the essay: *Dr Jones argues that '. . .' (Art and Architecture, p. 125), but Professor Smith refutes the argument by saying '. . .' (op. cit., p. 234).*

When a book has been written by two authors, it is usual to give both names at references in the text (*Smith and Jones, 1999, p. 2*); where three or more authors have collaborated, for example, Smith, Jones, and Brown, the usual style is (*Smith et al. 1998, p. 612*).

References

The reference list or bibliography at the end of your essay, thesis, etc., should consist of a full list of the works you have quoted from or used in preparing your essay, arranged in alphabetical order by the authors' surnames. References should provide the following information:

> the name of the author or authors;
>
> the year of first publication, or, if the edition you are using is a later one, the number of the edition and its publication date;
>
> the full title; and

the place of publication and the name of the publisher.

The information should be presented in that order.

There are slightly different styles of presentation, depending on whether the work in question is a book or an article in a journal. The usual 'Harvard' style for a book is as follows:

Carter, Rita (1998) *Mapping the Mind* London: Weidenfeld and Nicolson

Gregory, R., Harris, J., Heard, P., and Rose, D. eds. (1995) *The Artful Eye* Oxford: Oxford University Press

The title of the book is printed in italic. If your essay is handwritten, then you should underline the title.

The style for articles in journals is slightly different:

Quilley, S. (1999) 'Entrepreneurial Manchester: The Genesis of Elite Consensus' *Antipode* 31:2, pp. 185–211

The title of the article is given in quotation marks and italics are used for the title of the journal or magazine. It is also customary to give the number of the journal and the page numbers of the article.

The style for an article that forms part of a collective work is similar:

Rawson, E. (1986) 'The Expansion of Rome' in Boardman, J., Griffin, J., and Murray, O. eds. (1986) *The Oxford History of the Classical World* Oxford: Oxford University Press

If you are quoting material from the Internet, the following system can be used. Follow the quotation with a numbered reference in brackets (Internet 1), (Internet 2), etc. In the reference list, under a general heading 'Internet', list each Internet address next to its number. For example:

Internet

1. http://www.ipl.org/reading/shakespeare/shakespeare.html
2. http://www.daphne.palomar.edu/shakespeare/

Dissertations and theses

A dissertation or thesis is usually the weightiest and most important piece of work that students have to produce in the course of their education.

Accordingly, educational institutions provide extensive guidance on the conduct of research and on the writing and presentation of such extended pieces of writing. Those guidelines should be your principal guide. The section that follows is a brief introduction to this type of writing rather than a detailed account of it.

Managing length

A thesis or dissertation is in some ways similar to an essay, albeit a very long essay, but in other respects it probably has more in common with a report. As with a report, the main problems tend to be coping with the amount of material likely to be produced by research and marshalling information in a coherent way.

The importance of organization and planning increases proportionately with the length of the work and the volume of material it contains. A work of dissertation length will usually require chapters. The nature of the project will determine what those chapters are and the order that they are to come in but, once the content of each chapter has been decided, then each can be written more or less in the form of an essay. As such, each chapter will generally require its own introduction and its own conclusion. Each chapter is not, however, an essay in its own right, but a part of a whole, so that each introduction should link the new chapter with what has gone before, while the conclusion, besides summing up what has just been discussed, should point ahead to the next section.

As in a report, headings and subheadings will help readers navigate their way through the chapter. Also like a report, a dissertation will benefit from a table of contents and probably from the use of footnotes, chapter notes, or appendices for additional material that does not fit into the running text. Footnotes are useful, if the notes are short, because they do not necessitate the reader searching elsewhere. But if your notes become lengthy, they should be put at the end of the chapter in a separate section, and any note longer than a page should be included in an appendix. You will also need to provide an abstract or summary of your work.

It may be difficult, especially when you are making the first draft of an individual chapter, to keep in mind the overall shape of the work. But a piece of writing of this magnitude will need several redraftings. As you revise your work, try to look at it from the reader's point of view and ensure that the necessary links and pointers are in place to ensure a logical progression and flow.

Style

The style of a dissertation need not differ markedly from that of an essay, except insofar as an essay may allow a more personal approach. The emphasis in a short essay is on the points – perhaps personal and controversial – that the writer wants to make and he or she will provide just sufficient supporting material in the space available. The emphasis in a thesis is on the extended detail of the material collected. The thesis-writer must defend his or her thesis, but argument alone will not suffice if the evidence does not carry conviction. Consequently, a neutral, balanced, impersonal style – taking particular care to avoid rash statements and generalizations – is generally what is called for.

For additional material that could be relevant to dissertations and theses, please see the sections 'Note-taking' and 'Summaries', as well as the sections on 'Research', 'Reports', 'Essays', and 'References' that precede this one.

11 Notes, summaries, agendas, and minutes

The writing tasks discussed in the immediately preceding sections of this manual can be made much easier if the comparatively mundane business of taking notes and making summaries is carried out effectively. This chapter contains advice on both of these, together with a section on preparing agendas and taking the minutes of meetings.

None of these is a compositional task like the writing of a report, essay, or letter. They all are mostly concerned with working with written or spoken words supplied by other people. A common requirement for all of them, therefore, is the ability to understand what other people are trying to communicate and, in particular, to distinguish between what is significant and what is of less importance. This skill can be developed on its own through careful reading and listening. But it can also be usefully linked with the writing skills discussed in the earlier part of this manual. In acquiring the ability to organize your own material and signal your most important points, you become better able to recognize the use that other people make of the same or similar procedures. Similarly, from concentrating on other people's words, and analysing and assessing them, you may be able to extend the range and scope of your own technique.

Note-taking

The ability to take good notes is an invaluable skill for anyone who has to prepare a piece of writing that is not entirely dependent on his or her own inspiration and thinking. People who cannot or do not make good notes have to spend precious time retracing their steps when they come to the actual point of writing, especially if they no longer have to hand the source material they originally used. Moreover, taking proper notes does more than simply save time. The act of writing something down very often helps to fix it in the memory. If you take notes, paradoxically, you may find you do not have to rely on them too heavily when you come to write.

Clarity and speed

Notes are only useful if you can understand what they mean when you come to read them again, days, months, or even years afterwards. Notes, therefore, have to be clear. Unless you are taking notes on behalf of someone else or intending to lend your notes to a friend or colleague, they only have to be clear to you. Even so, you may be making notes at the beginning of the academic year for an exam that takes place at the end of it.

Notes also frequently have to be made at speed – especially if you are making notes on a lecture or presentation rather than on something you are reading. If you happen to know shorthand, you have an immediate advantage. The average person does not, but it is still possible to reduce the amount of ink put down on paper by using abbreviations and symbols and by shortening words. Standard abbreviations (for example *e.g.* and *i.e.*) can live alongside your own abbreviations of names of people or characters in books, or single letters for things or concepts that occur repeatedly in the text. It is common practice to use + for 'and', < for 'less than', > for 'greater than', ∴ for 'therefore', ∵ for 'because', and so on, and you can add to these at will as long as you know what you mean.

The usual way to shorten words is to leave off the endings, for example: *min* (minimum), *max* (maximum), *poss* (possible), or by omitting some or all of the vowels, *fncl* (financial) *dvlpmnt* (development). You can also borrow a technique from simple shorthand by writing words as they sound, especially those that can be represented by a single letter or character *R*, *U*, *Y*, *4*. If you have a mobile phone and send text messages frequently, you may already be well practised at this. It is almost inevitable that, if you have to take notes regularly, you will develop some kind of personal shorthand writing.

The best way to ensure clarity is to go back over the notes you have written while the material is still fresh in your mind. In this way you can check that everything is legible and makes sense. If the notes are to be kept for any length of time, then it will probably be useful to organize them, including headings and underlining or colour-highlighting to mark the particularly important points.

What to note

If you are taking notes for a specific purpose, then as you read or listen, you will be mentally sorting the material into the relevant and irrelevant and only noting down what is relevant. You can, in fact, make a list of headings before you start and allocate your notes to the appropriate headings as you write them. If the purpose is specific and limited, you may discover as you check the notes after the event that you can discard some of them because they appear less relevant with the benefit of hindsight or because the point is covered elsewhere.

Often, however, the purpose is more general. You may, for instance, be listening to a lecture on a topic, several aspects of which could come up in exam questions at a future date. In that case, you will want as full a record as possible. The key, though, is still to recognize and latch on to the essential material.

Taking notes from speakers

A good speaker should make it comparatively easy for members of the audience to take notes. The basic procedure that most speakers adopt – see the section on 'Presentations' pp. 273–8 – is to tell you what they're going to say, to say it, and then to tell you that they've said it. This pattern, if adhered to, gives you three opportunities to make notes. The introduction will probably give you a basic idea of the structure of the talk. Try to jot down the structural outline. You may even be able to make a framework of headings for other notes if you work quickly. Then comes the main body of the talk, leading to the conclusion – which is likely to be at least in part a recapitulation – giving you an opportunity to check that you have covered everything of importance.

You will not want to miss out entirely on the experience of the talk by being preoccupied with taking notes to the exclusion of everything else. Speakers and lecturers usually rely on a sense of contact with the audience and do not want to see their listeners' heads buried in notebooks. Speakers should signal the fact that they are making points that they consider particularly noteworthy. Listen out for the signals, and use them. Otherwise try to divide your attention between the speaker and your notes.

Taking notes from text

One method of making notes from a text is simply to underline or highlight the important sentences or draw a line down the side of the page next to an important passage. This is only workable if the book is your book, you are going to keep it to hand, and you do not mind writing on it. A separate set of notes has the advantage of being independent of the volume in question, and you have the benefit of partly fixing things in your mind by writing them down.

A good written text, like a good speech, has signals and structural elements which the note-taker can use to advantage. Headings in the text provide useful pointers and, in a paragraph, the first sentence is often the one to concentrate on (though remember, there is no rule that states that every paragraph has to begin with a 'topic sentence'). The main idea may be all that you actually need to note down.

Here, as an example, are the opening paragraphs of a piece of literary criticism, together with the kind of notes that might usefully be made on it.

> Any great play will, perhaps, to some degree take on the nature of its protagonist. At least this seems to be the case with *Hamlet*. It is as if the play itself shared the hero's propensity for analysing his own being. Its preoccupation with language, thought, and action, the main constituents of drama, is supplemented by a direct concern with the idea of a play, by discussions of such matters as 'the purpose of playing', the production of stage illusion, the degree of identity between an actor and his role and the response to be expected from an audience, and by the inclusion of a play within the play.
>
> My main concern, however, is not with the paradoxes of the theatre but with language. The play requires a particularly critical sensitivity to language on the part of its audience. Indeed it could be said to generate

such a sensitivity in them. Where there is so much deceit and equivocation in what characters say, one has always to try and ascertain the purpose for which language is being used and what motivates a particular choice of words. These considerations lead ultimately to the question of what language is in relation to thought and action. I am not claiming that *Hamlet* is unique in encouraging a response of this kind, merely that the demand for this kind of response is more urgent than in other plays.

Stephen Curtis, in an essay 'The Cool Web', 1974

Let us assume that we are making notes on this passage for the purpose of writing an essay on *Hamlet* rather than summarizing the writer's whole argument, because it begins and ends with general reflections that are not necessarily relevant to an essay on the play itself. The notes might be set out like this:

Hamlet – nature of play

Like hero, self-concerned, i.e. is a play that deals with nature of theatre

- 'purpose of playing' (Act 3, sc. ii)
- stage illusion
- actor and role
- audience reaction
- play within play

Language – main concern

Play requires 'critical sensitivity to language' on part of audience

characters use language to deceive ∴ analyse their purposes and motives

lead to → general question of relations between language, thought, and action (this also, see ↑, basic concern of theatre)

There is no reason to try and save space when making notes. In fact it is better to leave gaps for additional notes or comments you might want to add later (perhaps in a different-coloured ink) as you read further or other ideas occur to you. Notice also the use of headings to denote the topic of a section or paragraph and the use of underlining to highlight the main points. Inverted commas – or some other form of marking – should also be used to distinguish quotations from your own paraphrases. When you come back to the notes later, and the source is no longer available to be consulted, you need to be able to tell at a glance what are your words and what the author's to avoid accusations of plagiarism.

When taking notes from published texts remember to record the bibliographical details so that you can include the work in your bibliography (see 'References', pp. 291–2).

Summaries

Producing summaries is an activity closely connected with the taking of notes. The simplest way to produce a summary is to try to connect a set of notes within a simple linking framework. If, for example, you wished to summarize the opening paragraphs of the essay on *Hamlet* quoted in the previous section, you could take the notes you made (p. 299):

Hamlet – nature of play

Like hero, self-concerned, i.e. is a play that deals with nature of theatre

- 'purpose of playing' (Act 3, sc. ii)
- stage illusion
- actor and role
- audience reaction
- play within play

Language – main concern

Play requires 'critical sensitivity to language' on part of audience

characters use language to deceive ∴ analyse their purposes and motives

lead to → general question of relations between language, thought, and action (this also, see ↑, basic concern of theatre)

and link them together like this:

> *Hamlet*, the play, examines the nature of theatre, just as Hamlet, the character, examines his own nature. Besides containing a play within the play, it discusses theatrical questions, e.g. how actors relate to their roles and audiences respond. It also examines language critically. The characters use language to deceive, prompting analysis of their motives, and there is a general concern with the relations between thought, language, and action.

Because a summary is a piece of continuous prose it cannot usually contain quite as much information, within the space allowed, as a good set of notes. In addition to connecting the notes, therefore, you may well need to edit and rearrange them.

Length of a summary

If you are asked to produce a summary, you will often be told what length to aim at: 'Make a summary of this in about 200 words.'

If no length is set, then it is recommended that a shorter passage should be reduced to approximately a quarter of its original length and a longer passage to one tenth. But everything depends on the purpose for which the summary is being produced. A summary for a business report should not, if at all possible, exceed one page. As a report might run to a hundred, several hundred, or a thousand or more pages, the proportions need to be much smaller than one to ten.

Summarizing your own work

A summary is often an integral part of a longer piece of work such as a report or a dissertation. You only write the summary, however, when the rest of the work is complete. As it is your own work, you will know it very well – possibly even too well to be able to undertake the drastic downscaling required to fit, say, 200 pages of work onto one page without an effort. You need to ask yourself one question: what does the reader absolutely have to know in order to understand what this exercise was all about, how it was conducted, what the results were, and, where appropriate, what recommendations were made? Your introduction, conclusion, and recommendations are the places where this information is likely to be found. They, consequently, should be less drastically compressed than the body of the report. From that, you omit all but the absolutely essential detail. If the reader wants to understand the exact process by which you arrived at your conclusions, he or she must read the whole report.

When summarizing your own work it can often help to allow an interval of time between the compilation of the main text and your compilation of the summary. In this way you will be able to gain a better perspective on what are the key issues that need to be included in your summary.

Summarizing other texts

The essence of producing an effective summary is recognizing the main points made by the piece of writing that you are summarizing. It is, therefore, firstly an exercise in reading and understanding, because if you cannot understand what the writer is trying to communicate, then you cannot hope to reproduce his or her ideas in a shorter form. This may seem an obvious point, but not all writing is clear and the sense is not always easy to extract. When the main thrust of the piece is clear in your own mind, then go through the text and either underline the key points or make a separate list of them. Here, for example, is a text based on an article in a textbook for learners of business German: C. Conlin, *Unternehmen Deutsch* (London: Chancerel International Publishers Ltd, 1995, p. 131).

> According to a recent study carried out in the USA the manufacture of personal computers is a very environmentally-unfriendly activity.
>
> Until now it was thought that computers had a negative impact on the environment principally when they were in use or when they were discarded or recycled. The new study, however, suggests that, even before a new PC is switched on for the first time, it has already:
>
> > consumed as much electricity as the average household would use in the course of a whole year;
> >
> > used up as much water as it would take to fill the average bath tub every day for six months;

> produced twice its own weight in waste; and
>
> pumped as much carbon dioxide into the atmosphere as a car would in travelling 4000 miles.
>
> What makes matters worse is that, in comparison with other electronic consumer goods such as TVs and hi-fis, PCs have a very short lifespan. Planned obsolescence used to be thought of as a feature of the motor-industry. Nowadays, it is the computer industry that is continually enhancing the specifications of its products and leaving last year's models behind. Some companies are reputed to replace their entire stock of personal computers every year.
>
> The message to the environmentally-conscious consumer is clear. Avoid buying a new PC. Either upgrade your existing model or buy another one second-hand. If you absolutely have to buy a brand new PC, opt for one of the 'green' models now appearing on the market.

This is a text of 251 words and the aim is to produce a summary of about a quarter that length, say 65 words.

The main points might be listed as follows:

1. manufacturing computers is environmentally unfriendly
2. planned obsolescence of computers makes matters worse
3. consumers should avoid buying new PCs

That is the basic skeleton of what the article is saying. To this we can add a few details.

1. manufacturing computers is environmentally unfriendly as a result of

    electricity and water consumption
    waste and CO_2 production

2. planned obsolescence of computers makes matters worse

    replaced more often than other equipment

3. consumers should avoid buying new PCs

    upgrade, buy second-hand, or buy 'green'

There is one other point that needs to be mentioned, namely the article is not based on first-hand knowledge, but reports the results of a study carried out in the USA. That fact needs to be mentioned to put the whole in the correct perspective.

Working on the basis of the second set of notes, we might then come up with a summary such as this:

> According to a US study, computer manufacturing is environmentally unfriendly, because making a PC consumes disproportionate amounts of water and electricity and generates large quantities of waste and carbon dioxide. Through planned obsolescence, PCs are replaced more frequently than other electronic devices. This aggravates the situation. Consumers are recommended to upgrade their existing PCs, buy second-hand or, if they have to buy new, to buy 'green'.

Once the summary is complete it should be checked for length and for accuracy. In particular you should check that in shortening the text you have not altered its stance on the subject. The above article, for instance, is written from a generally 'green' perspective. If the purpose is to render the essentials of an original text, it would be misleading to inject a note of greater scepticism by beginning 'A US study claims *or* alleges . . .'

One final point on summaries. While you may not be called upon very often to make summaries, summarizing is a worthwhile skill in itself, insofar as a great deal of editing work involves pruning and deleting while retaining the general shape and sense of a text. If you can summarize the work produced by someone else, you may find it easier to remove superfluities from your own.

Agendas and minutes

Agendas and minutes provide the written framework that gives shape to the verbal proceedings of a meeting. The tasks of drafting an agenda and writing up the minutes often fall to the same person, though that person is seldom in overall charge of the meeting. If you happen to be given either or both of these jobs, then you will need to collaborate closely with the chairperson – or whoever else is in charge – before, during, and after the meeting. Collaborating with the chair not only ensures that the meeting runs as smoothly as possible, but also makes life easier for yourself.

Different organizations are likely to use different conventions for agendas and minutes. If you are unfamiliar with them, then study the records of previous meetings to find out what the standard procedures are. If, for any reason, you think the existing conventions should be changed, then obtain the agreement of the chairperson and any other interested parties before you begin.

Agendas

An agenda is principally a list of points for discussion at a meeting, but it has other purposes as well. Besides giving advance notice that a meeting is to take place and stating its purpose, it also prepares people for the meeting. It is often accompanied by documents that have to be read by the participants if they want to understand fully what is going on so they can participate effectively. In addition, the agenda helps the chair to keep control of the meeting and provides the framework around which the minute-taker constructs the minutes.

What goes onto an agenda?

There are certain standard items that belong to most agendas. First a title (*Team Meeting, Annual General Meeting of the Broxworth Cricket Club*) or a statement of the nature and purpose of the meeting (*Public Meeting to discuss the threatened closure of Wickhampton Junior School*), followed by the date, time, and venue of the meeting, and a list of the people who will be attending it. Then come the opening of the meeting by the chair, apologies for absence, the reading and/or approval of the minutes of the previous meeting (the minutes do not have to be read if they have been circulated beforehand), and matters arising from the minutes. These are followed by the specific points for discussion, often ending with 'Any other business' and closure by the chair. All the various items on the agenda are numbered and a traditional agenda for a club committee meeting or similar event might look like this:

Meeting of the Wonsley Drama Club Committee

Wednesday November 21st 2001, 7.30 p.m. at 70 Hansford Square

To attend: Rowena Moxon (chair)

Jim Bean (sec.)

Mike Roy

Andrew Hill

Peggy Chandler

Angela Gauntlett (director, *Blithe Spirit*)

1 Apologies for absence
2 Minutes of last meeting
3 Matters arising from minutes
4 Report on progress of current production, *Blithe Spirit* (Angela Gauntlett, director)
5 Approval of additional budget for current production
6 Preparations for Club Christmas party
7 Any other business
8 Date and venue for next meeting (please bring diary)

Jim Bean (Hon. Sec.)

Simple agendas of this sort are a staple of community life throughout the country. It is, however, possible to do more with an agenda and, especially in professional contexts, it is often desirable to do more.

First there is the question of timing. It is generally reckoned that, to be effective, a meeting should not last longer than an hour and a half. If there is more to discuss than can be accommodated within ninety minutes, then a break should be built into the agenda. Within that framework, it may be possible to allocate a specific amount of time to each item – this is a matter for the chairperson to decide on.

Then there is the ordering of the items for discussion. Urgent items should come first and, where all items are roughly equal in terms of urgency, it is probably better to put matters that can be dealt with quickly at the top of the agenda. Items requiring longer discussion can go further down. 'Any other business' can be dispensed with if the agenda has been circulated in draft form before the meeting and all the participants have been given an opportunity to suggest additional items for inclusion.

Finally, the chairperson and secretary will often know in advance who will be speaking to a particular point and this can be specified in the agenda.

Bearing all this in mind, an agenda of the following sort might be drawn up (dispensing with the formal preliminaries such as approving minutes):

Millstone Dictionary Project

Team Meeting

Conference room, December 4th 2001 10–11.30 a.m.

To attend: Steve Huggins (chair)
Bridget Newman (sec.)
Sally Collins
Ralph Hodgson
Kathryn Sneath

1 **Schedule**
Steve to give details of revised schedule (10 mins)

2 **New freelancers**
Sally to update on progress in finding additional freelance compilers (5 mins)

3 **Expert compilers**
Ralph to present system for speeding up compilation by channelling difficult words to designated expert compilers (20 mins)

4 **Motivating freelancers**
Steve to suggest bonus scheme to motivate freelancers and call for additional/alternative suggestions (25 mins)

5 **Date and venue of next meeting**
Please bring diaries!

Preparation and circulation of agenda

When the chairperson and secretary have agreed on the matters to be discussed at the meeting, a draft agenda should be drawn up and circulated to everyone who is to attend. This should take place about a week before the meeting. If there are any comments on the agenda that lead to its being changed, then the revisions should be made as quickly as possible so that the final agenda can be circulated, together with any supporting documents, early enough to allow people time to prepare.

Minutes

Minutes form a permanent record of what took place at a meeting, and may be required for legal as well as professional purposes. They also act as a reminder of decisions taken and action decided upon, besides being an aid to the drafting of the agenda for a subsequent meeting. They should be impartial, giving a fair and true account of what was said, and should be kept brief yet also clear. It should be possible for anyone who did not attend the meeting but who is interested in its outcome to gain an accurate impression of what happened.

Before the meeting

Even if the minute-taker is not involved in drawing up the agenda, his or her work begins before the meeting takes place. The person taking the minutes needs to be familiar not only with the agenda, but also with any supporting documentation. The crucial factor in taking minutes is to grasp what is important and relevant among the many matters said in the course of a meeting. Anything you can find out in advance about the subjects to be discussed, or who is likely to say what, will be valuable.

As with agendas, different conventions concerning format apply in different places. You will need to find out in advance what sort of minutes are required. A simple action plan, setting out what was decided and who has been made responsible for doing what, may be sufficient. More often, the minutes will consist of a general account of what was said without remarks necessarily being attributed to specific individuals. Sometimes minutes need to be written up very formally, with the identity of every contributor duly noted. The usual practice can be discovered from previous minutes or by consulting the chairperson.

In addition, you may need to consult with the chairperson to ensure that you have the right to intervene if you need clarification of any point. It is not always clear, for instance, whether a decision has been reached or who has been assigned a particular task. The chairperson should not allow the meeting to proceed until the point has been cleared up, but you may need to speak up and ask for the matter to be clarified.

During the meeting

It is the minute-taker's job to record who was present at the meeting (except in the case of a very large meeting), who was absent, and who sent apologies for absence. The main work comes when the meeting gets under way.

Some of what has already been said in this book about taking notes (see 'Note-taking', pp. 295–8) will apply to the taking of minutes. But a meeting is far less structured than a talk and there may be very little recapitulation (though a good chairperson will often summarize before passing on to the next item on the agenda). You will need to devise a method of taking notes that does not prevent you from listening carefully so that you can sort out what is important and needs to be noted and what can be safely omitted. You may also need to be able to identify who said what.

A method often adopted is to use a pad with two wide margins. Use the left-hand margin to record the name of the speaker, the central and largest section to jot down the key points in what he or she said, and the right-hand margin to record decisions taken and who is responsible for further action:

4. Club Christmas dinner

Dave F.	Last year's d. poorly supported, not good value, dismal venue – propose cancel this year	
Jane C.	New caterer contacted, sure could do better deal, welcome suggestions for alternative venue, still support for idea of d., approached by club members	
Alice B.	supported Jane – long tradition – suggested Cricket Club premises	
	Several other members supported A & J.	
		Jane C. to contact CC & report back

The minutes should always follow the agenda exactly. Each section of notes should be identified by the number of the item on the agenda or the heading taken from the agenda.

Format

Like any other notes, minutes should be written up as soon as possible after the event. The degree of formality required in the presentation of minutes varies. Verbatim minutes of the Hansard type, in which every word is taken down and attributed to a particular person, can, realistically, only be taken by a professional shorthand recorder or secretary and therefore fall outside the scope of this discussion. You may, however, be required to mention by name everyone who spoke, without actually citing his or her actual words. In such instances, reported (or indirect) speech (see also pp. 19–20) is used:

4. Club Christmas dinner

David Farrer proposed that this year's dinner should be cancelled, on the grounds that last year's had been poorly supported, had not been good value for money and had been held at a venue that he described as 'dismal'. Jane Carpenter replied that there was still support for a Christmas dinner among the membership and that she had contacted a new caterer who

> seemed to offer a better deal. She asked for suggestions for an alternative venue. Alice Bahadur suggested the premises of the local Cricket Club . . .

This, however makes for very long and full minutes. It will usually suffice to concentrate on the background to an issue, the issue itself, the decision that was reached, and any action that was decided on, without necessarily referring to any contributors to the debate by name:

> **4. Club Christmas dinner**
>
> Because of poor attendance at last year's dinner and dissatisfaction with the venue and catering, it was proposed that this year's event should be cancelled. However, several members expressed support for continuing the event. A new caterer, offering better value, has been found and a new venue, the Cricket Club, was suggested. The proposal was consequently not carried. Jane Carpenter has been asked to contact the Cricket Club with a view to using their premises for the dinner and to report back.

There is enough information here to give a non-attender at the meeting a reasonably clear idea of what went on. This style of writing minutes does, however, often lead to a heavy use of passive verbs and impersonal instructions (*it was proposed that . . .*, *it was argued that . . .*, *there was agreement . . .*). A mixture of the two styles with limited personal attribution of remarks may be the best solution:

> Because of poor attendance at last year's dinner and dissatisfaction with the venue and catering, David Farrer proposed that this year's event should be cancelled. However, several members expressed support for continuing the event, . . . etc.

After the meeting

Once the minutes have been written, they should be shown to the chairperson for checking. If approved, they should then be circulated, at the latest with the agenda for the next meeting.

12 Using information technology

Writing aids

The computer's greatest gifts to the writer are probably its most basic ones: the ability to store documents, parts of documents, or much-used words and phrases in its memory, so that they can be retrieved and reproduced by means of a few keystrokes or clicks of the mouse button, and the fact that it allows you to revise, correct, and restructure a document more or less at will without having to rewrite the whole text. The more you can put into the memory, the less work you have to do. In particular, if you have to write standard letters, then the complete letter can be recalled and your only task is to make the adjustments necessary to the particular circumstances.

Modern software can do far more than this. Computers can give assistance with the business of actually composing a piece of writing. A 'letter-writing wizard', for instance, will lay out the framework of a letter for you, offer you a choice of a blocked or semi-blocked format, adjust itself to formal, informal, or business style, and provide you with a list of complimentary closes to select from. It will not, however, write the letter for you. While you are writing, modern programs will automatically signal spelling mistakes and grammatical errors. Spellcheckers check what you have keyed against a word list held in its memory. The grammar checker operates on a similar basis. As aids, they are not at all to be despised and you should check what you have written whenever an error is signalled. But you cannot rely on them entirely, and, by the same token, when a warning appears on the screen you need not always assume that the computer is right and you are wrong.

For discussion of e-mails, see pp. 265–6.

Where a computer can also be of great help is in improving the presentation of the finished product. Many features that used to be the preserve of desktop-publishing programs are now incorporated into word-processors. Since they are available to the ordinary person chiefly through the resources of computer technology, this is the place for brief sections on typefaces and layout.

Fonts

Word-processing programs come loaded with a number, often a large number, of different typefaces or fonts. A number of these (such as ***this*** or *this* or ***this***) are very definitely for special use only, on advertisements or the like. The more workaday faces are generally divided into serif and sans serif varieties.

A serif is a tiny projection to the stems of letters at the top or bottom. A serif *k*, for instance looks like this:

K

The equivalent sans serif letter looks like this:

K

Sans serif characters are very neat and are reckoned to give a modern look to a piece of writing. But they can become somewhat wearing on the eye over large stretches of text and are also said to look less 'serious'.

The default fonts on most word-processing programs are serif ones. It is probably best to use a serif font for the body text of a piece of writing, especially if it is a long one, switching perhaps to sans serif for a section that you wish to mark out from the rest.

Most fonts can be produced not only in their regular form (known as Roman), but also in **bold**, or in *italic*, or with underlining. The availability of bold and italic has made underlining much less common than it was when texts were handwritten or typed. Bold is now generally used for headings – for example at the head of a business letter or in a long document that is broken up into separate sections. Italics are generally used to highlight particular words in the body of the text. It is also possible to use bold in the body of a text, but this should be done sparingly, as it has the effect of laying a very heavy emphasis on a word or phrase, as if you were raising your voice at that point. Compare:

. . . the operative word is *immediately*

with

. . . the operative word is **immediately**.

The size of the letters can also be varied. Type size is measured in points – a point being 0.351 mm (or $^1/_{72}$ of an inch). If you are going to print out a document on A4 paper, then 9 point is reckoned to be the smallest size for legible print. Anything larger than 12 point, on the other hand, looks 'special'. A type size between 9 and 12 points is therefore recommended for general use.

Whatever choices you make of font and font size, it is best to work out a fairly simple system and stick to it. A profusion of different character shapes and sizes should not be used in a serious document.

Layout in word-processing

The art of layout for plain text lies mainly in the management of blank space. It is the spaces that make a page look attractive and professional as much as, if not more than, the actual print. It may be tempting to try to fit as much as possible into a line or onto a page, but it is better to overrun onto a second page than to give the impression that you are counting the cost of every sheet of paper.

So, margins at the top, bottom, and sides of the page should be generous. You should leave a line between paragraphs and, if necessary, adjust the leading (pronounced *ledding* from the strips of lead that printers used to insert between horizontal rows of type) between lines to make sure that the bottoms of the letters on the line above do not impinge on the tops of the letters on the line below.

Lists have already been discussed in an earlier section of this book (pp. 279–83). They add interest to a page by bringing in more white space. It is worth noting here that word-processing programs can help you make lists – or convert existing texts into lists and add bullets or numbers to it – very easily.

Word-processing programs also make it very easy to justify text, that is to make it print out with an even right edge. This paragraph:

> The art of layout for plain text lies mainly in the management of blank space. It is the spaces that make a page look attractive and professional as much as, if not more than, the actual print. It may be tempting to try to fit as much as possible into a line or onto a page, but it is better to overrun onto a second page than to give the impression that you are counting the cost of every sheet of paper.

is unjustified. Justified, the same paragraph looks like this:

> The art of layout for plain text lies mainly in the management of blank space. It is the spaces that make a page look attractive and professional as much as, if not more than, the actual print. It may be tempting to try to fit as much as possible into a line or onto a page, but it is better to overrun onto a second page than to give the impression that you are counting the cost of every sheet of paper.

Books are usually printed with justified text. The disadvantages of justification are that the spaces between words may become stretched and it will often be necessary to break and hyphenate words at the ends of lines. Some people argue that a ragged right edge makes a text less wearing to read. It is certainly not necessary to justify a relatively short text such as an ordinary letter. Also, if you are submitting a typescript to a publisher on disk to be set up by a printer, it is best to leave the text unjustified so that an editor checking through your text can tell at once whether the spacing in each line is correct.

Graphics

It is beyond the scope of this book to illustrate the types of graphics that can be generated by computer programs and inserted into your writing. Three simple points can be made about graphics. First, they should have a caption. One picture may be worth a thousand words, but the reader should not be left unaided to try to work out the meaning of a chart or graph. Second, they should be positioned as close to the relevant section of text as possible. A short piece of writing may look unbalanced if one or more graphics are inserted into it. In that case, it may well be preferable to group the graphics together at the end. Otherwise, the visual should be placed as close to the piece of text it relates to as it can. Word-processing programs do not, as a rule, allow you to make the text 'flow around' a graphic, however. For that you will need a desktop-publishing program. Third, if you use graphics in a long work then they should be numbered, either continuously or chapter by chapter, and a list of them and the pages on which they occur should be placed at the beginning after the contents list.

Glossary of grammatical terms

abbreviation A shortened form of a word, phrase, or title, used for convenience and to save space, e.g. *BBC* for 'British Broadcasting Corporation', *NATO* for 'North Atlantic Treaty Organization', *Dr* for 'doctor'.

abstract noun A noun that refers to something that cannot be seen and touched, e.g. *happiness* and *unity*. Compare **concrete noun**.

acronym A type of abbreviation that is made up of the initial letters of words and is pronounced as one word, e.g. *UNESCO* for 'United Nations Educational, Scientific, and Cultural Organization', and *laser* for 'light amplification by stimulated emission of radiation'.

active Used to describe a verb in which the subject of the sentence carries out the action described by the verb, e.g. *hit* in *He hit me*. Compare **passive**.

adjective A word that describes a person or thing more precisely by indicating a quality that he, she, or it possesses, e.g. *big*, *deep*, and *blue*.

adverb A word that gives more information about an adjective, verb, etc., saying when, where, how, e.g. *immediately*, *there*, *very*.

adverbial The part of the sentence that provides further information, usually about the verb, e.g. *carefully* in *They chose the site carefully*.

adverbial clause A subordinate clause introduced by a word such as *because*, *if*, *when*, *where*, and *while*.

adverbial phrase A phrase based on or around a main adverb, e.g. *as soon as possible*; *strangely enough*.

agent The doer of the action of a verb, e.g. *Hugh* in the passive sentence *The supper was cooked by Hugh.*

agreement (or concord) The correspondence that exists between two or more words or phrases that must have the same number, gender, etc., for the sentence to be grammatical, e.g. *She* and *has* in *She has a friend.*

apposition The relationship between two noun phrases that refer to exactly the same person or thing and define him, her, or it more closely, e.g. *Paris* and the *capital of France* in *Paris, the capital of France.*

appositive clause A clause which is attached to an abstract noun such as *belief, fact, knowledge,* or *suggestion,* and which indicates what is believed, known, suggested, etc., e.g. *the belief that God exists.*

article See **definite article; indefinite article.**

attributive adjective An adjective that comes before the noun it relates to, e.g. *red* in *a red dress.*

auxiliary verb A verb that is used in front of a main verb, e.g. *do, is, have, will, shall: I do sometimes make mistakes.*

back formation The process of forming a new word by removing the ending from another word, e.g. the verb *laze* from the adjective *lazy.*

case The form of a noun or pronoun that changes according to its use in a sentence, e.g. *Colin – Colin's, I – me.* See also **object case; possessive case; subject case.**

clause A group of words containing a subject and a finite verb which forms a whole sentence or part of one, e.g. *They still hope | that she'll come back* is a sentence containing two clauses.

collective noun A noun that refers to a group of people or things, e.g. *committee, crew, government, flock, herd, team.*

comment clause A short clause inserted into a sentence to show the speaker's attitude to what they are saying, e.g. *to be frank,* or *to put it another way.*

common noun A noun that is not a proper noun, e.g. *road, boy, happiness.*

comparative The form of an adjective used when making comparisons, e.g. *lighter, sweeter, more comfortable.* See also **superlative.**

comparative clause A type of subordinate clause that expresses a comparison between two or more things, e.g. *as long as I could* in *I waited as long as I could.*

complement The word or phrase that follows a linking verb (*be, seem, feel,* etc.). In *James is a computer expert,* the complement is *a computer expert.*

complex sentence A sentence consisting of a main clause and one or more subordinate clauses, e.g. *I can't come | because I'll be in London on Tuesday.*

compound sentence A multiple sentence consisting of two or more main clauses, linked together by *and, but,* or *or,* e.g. *Henry is a lorry driver and Jane works part-time in a supermarket.*

concord See **agreement.**

concrete noun A noun that refers to something that can be seen, touched, tasted, etc., e.g. *table* and *lion.* Compare **abstract noun.**

conjunction A word which connects other words, phrases, or clauses together, e.g. *and, or, while.* There are two types of conjunction: **coordinating conjunction** and **subordinating conjunction.**

consonant The sound represented by any of the letters *b, c, d, f, g, h, j, k, l, m, n, p, q, r, s, t, v, w, x, y,* and *z.*

continuous tense A tense of a verb that expresses actions that are going on, were going on, or will be going on at a particular time, constructed using *to be* together with the *-ing* form of the verb, e.g. *I am cooking.*

contraction 1 A word formed by shortening a word and attaching it to the word before it, e.g. *'re* for *are* in *you're.* **2** An abbreviation in which the first and final letters of the full form are retained, e.g. *Mr, Dr.*

coordinating conjunction A conjunction that links words, phrases, or clauses that have equal status, e.g. *and, or,* and *but.*

coordination The grammatical process of linking together elements of a sentence that have equal status, e.g. in the sentences *The day was fine | but rather chilly* and *James likes coffee, | but Henry prefers tea.*

countable noun A noun that can form a plural and can be preceded by *a* or *an*, e.g. *table, equivalent*. Compare **uncountable noun**.

dangling participle A participle that is wrongly or ambiguously placed, e.g. *blown to bits by the blast*, in *Blown to bits by the blast, workers were removing the rubble from the building.*

defining clause See **restrictive or defining clause.**

definite article The word *the.*

demonstrative pronouns The words *this, that, these* and *those*, which point out or demonstrate which of a number of things are being referred to.

determiner A word that comes in front of and relates to a noun. Determiners specify the particular object or person, or the number of objects or persons, in a group that a noun refers to. They include *a, the, this, that, all, each, every, few, more, much, many, some, which, whichever*, and *what.*

diphthong The combination of two vowel sounds, e.g. the *a* sound in *hay* or *rain*, the *o* sound in *note* or *coat.*

directive An order or request to other people to do or to stop doing something, e.g. *Stop!*

direct object The word or phrase – usually a noun or pronoun – that is directly affected by the action of a verb, e.g. in *The car hit a tree*, the direct object is *a tree.*

direct speech The way of referring to the exact words that a person has used, e.g. *'I'm sorry, but I can't help you'* in *'I'm sorry, but I can't help you,' she said.* Compare **reported or indirect speech.**

double negative The use of two negatives in one sentence, e.g. *I don't owe you nothing.*

emphatic pronouns The pronouns which are the same in form as **reflexive pronouns** (*myself, himself*, etc.) and which usually follow immediately after the noun or pronoun they relate to, e.g. *myself* in *I myself have said as much.* Their function is to give emphasis.

exclamation An expression of surprise, approval, or annoyance, e.g. *What fun!*

feminine See **gender.**

finite clause A clause that contains a phrase with a **finite verb**, e.g. *I read the book.*

finite verb A verb that is used with a subject, in one of the tenses (past, present, etc.) and with an inflection that relates it to the subject, in contrast to an infinitive or a participle. E.g. *has* in *She has three children.*

first person Used to describe the pronouns *I* (singular) or *we* (plural) or the form of the verb used with *I* or *we.*

future tense The tense usually formed using the auxiliaries *will* or *shall.*

gender The classification of nouns and pronouns as masculine (e.g. *uncle, he*), feminine (e.g. *aunt, she*), or non-personal (neither masculine nor feminine, e.g. *it*).

genitive case See **possessive case.**

gradable Used to describe an adjective that can stand for a quality which can vary in degree, e.g. *young* in *a young person*. Compare *non-gradable.*

imperative mood The form of a verb that is used for giving orders, e.g. *Listen!*

indefinite article The words *a* and *an.*

indefinite pronouns Pronouns that refer to people or things without stating specifically who or what they are, e.g. *anyone, everybody, nobody, something, all, both, some.*

indicative mood The ordinary form of the verb used for making statements or asking questions. Compare **imperative mood; subjunctive mood.**

indirect object The additional object that occurs with some verbs that involve the action of giving, e.g. *me* in *He gave me a kiss.*

indirect speech See **reported or indirect speech.**

infinitive The base form of a verb, that, in English, is often formed with *to*, e.g. *to come, to go.*

inflection A letter or letters added to the base form of a word to show its number, tense, person, etc. E.g. the inflection *-s* is added to the majority of nouns in English to form their plural; the inflections *-ing* and *-ed* are added to the base forms of most verbs to form their present and past participles respectively.

interjection One of a group of words that have the exclamatory function of expressing an emotion such as surprise, approval, anger, or pain: *ah!*, *oh!*, *ouch!*, *psst!*

interrogative adverbs Words that begin questions, e.g. *how*, *when*, and *where*.

interrogative pronouns Pronouns that begin questions: *who*, *whom*, *whose*, *what*, and *which*.

intonation The variation in pitch of the speaker's voice to show that they are asking a question, expressing surprise, etc. E.g. when asking a question, the pitch of the speaker's voice usually rises towards the end of the sentence.

intransitive verb A verb that does not have a direct object, e.g. *advanced* in *The army advanced*. Compare **transitive verb**.

invariable nouns A noun that is either always singular or always plural, e.g. *scissors*, *cattle*.

irregular Used to describe a word or form of a word that does not conform to a standard pattern. A verb is described as irregular if its past tense and past participle do not follow the standard pattern of adding *-ed* to the base form. Examples are: *come* (past tense *came*, past participle *come*); *drive* (past tense *drove*, past participle *driven*); *eat* (past tense *ate*, past participle *eaten*); *run* (past tense *ran*, past participle *run*); *see* (past tense *saw*, past participle *seen*). Regular nouns form their plural with *-s* or *-es*; the noun *child* is irregular because its plural form is *children*. Compare **regular**.

linking verb A verb such as *be*, *seem*, or *feel* that links the verb's subject with a complement, e.g. *is* in *James is a computer expert*.

main clause A clause that is complete in itself. Every major sentence must have at least one main clause, and a main clause on its own can constitute a sentence.

major sentence A sentence that contains a finite verb, e.g. *We drove to London*.

masculine See gender.

minor sentence A sentence that does not contain a finite verb, e.g. *Impossible!*

modifier A word which provides more information about other words and describes the things or people that they stand for more specifically, e.g. *car* in *car keys.*

mood A form of a verb: see **imperative mood; indicative mood;** and **subjunctive mood.**

multiple sentence A sentence with more than one clause, which may consist of more than one main clause or a main clause together with a number of subordinate clauses e.g. *Hugh writes books but Sandra is a sculptor.*

multi-word verb See **phrasal verb.**

non-defining clause See **non-restrictive clause.**

non-finite verb A form of the verb that is the infinitive (usually preceded by *to*, e.g. *to sing*), the present participle (e.g. *singing*), or the past participle (e.g. *sung*).

non-gradable Used to describe an adjective that cannot be used with such words as *very, slightly*, etc., e.g. *perfect, impossible, unique.* Compare **gradable.**

non-restrictive or non-defining clause A type of clause which contains information that is incidental and could be omitted from the sentence, e.g. *which comes halfway down the page* in *The paragraph, which comes halfway down the page, mentions you by name.* Compare **restrictive or defining clause.**

noun A word that stands for a thing, a person, or a quality, e.g. *instructor, happiness, Australia.*

noun phrase A group of related words, one of which is a noun or pronoun, e.g. *a child, a small child, a child with learning difficulties, a child who is of above average intelligence.*

object The word or phrase – usually a noun or pronoun – that is affected by the action of the verb and often comes after the verb, e.g. *a tree* in *The car hit a tree.* See also **direct object; indirect object.**

object case The form of a pronoun when used as the object of a sentence or when it follows a preposition, e.g. *me, them.*

participle See **past participle; present participle.**

passive Used to describe a verb in which the subject is affected by the action of the verb, e.g. *was cooked* in *The supper was cooked by Hugh*. Compare **active**.

past participle The form of a verb that is used to form the perfect tenses of verbs and the passive; in regular verbs, the *-ed* form of the verb, e.g. *cooked, exhausted*.

perfect tense A past tense of the verb formed with the auxiliary verb *have* together with the *-ed* form of a regular verb or the past participle of an irregular verb, e.g. *I have cooked, I had sung*.

person See **first person**; **second person**; **third person**.

personal pronoun A pronoun such as *I, you, her*, or *them*.

phrasal verb (or multi-word verb) A verb in which the base form is accompanied by an adverb or a preposition or both: *do down, do up, do away with*, usually with a distinct meaning that is not always deducible from its component parts, e.g. *do away with* means 'to get rid of'.

plural The form of a word used when it refers to more than one person or thing. *Cats* and *mice* are the plural forms of *cat* and *mouse* respectively, the former being regular, the latter irregular. Compare **singular**.

possessive case (or genitive case) The case or form of a noun or pronoun that is used to show possession, e.g. *Jill's* in *Jill's car*.

possessive pronoun Any of the personal pronouns *mine, yours, his, hers, its, ours*, and *theirs*.

postpositive adjective An adjective that is placed immediately after a noun or pronoun, e.g. *possible* in *everything possible*.

predicative adjective An adjective that is used after a verb such as *be, become*, or *seem*, e.g. *red* in *The dress is red*.

prefix A component that can be attached to the beginning of an existing word to change that word's meaning, e.g. *un* added to *happy* to give *unhappy*; *anti* added to *aircraft* to give *antiaircraft*.

preposition A word that is placed before other words, especially nouns, phrases, or clauses to link them into the sentence, e.g. *after, at, before, behind, for, in, of, out*.

present participle The form of a verb that is used to make the continuous forms of verbs; the *-ing* form of the verb, e.g. *cooking.*

pronoun A word that can replace a noun, e.g. *she, I, mine, themselves, these, both.* See also **demonstrative pronouns; emphatic pronouns; indefinite pronouns; interrogative pronouns; personal pronoun; possessive pronoun; reflexive pronouns; relative pronoun.**

proper noun A noun that denotes a specific person or thing, e.g. *Sam, Shakespeare, New York, October, Christmas, Marxism.*

question A type of sentence in which the speaker asks for information and usually expects a response, e.g. *How did you know?*

reflexive pronouns The words formed by adding *-self* (singular) or *-selves* (plural) to either the object or the possessive form of the personal pronoun: *myself, yourself, himself, itself, ourselves, yourselves,* and *themselves.* See also **emphatic pronouns.**

regular Used to describe a word or form of a word that conforms to the standard pattern. A verb is described as regular if its past tense and past participle are formed by adding *-ed* to the base form (or *-d* if the base form ends in *-e*): *cook – cooked; walk – walked; remember – remembered; arrive – arrived.* Nouns are described as regular if they form their plural with *-s* or *-es.* Compare **irregular.**

relative adverbs The words *when* and *where* used at the beginning of a relative clause.

relative clause A clause which gives more specific information about the noun that it follows and which begins with a word such as *that, which, who, whose, when,* or *where.* E.g. *that I lent you* in *the book that I lent you.*

relative pronoun The word *that, which, who, whom,* or *whose* when used to begin a relative clause.

reported clause The clause that gives the words that are spoken, e.g. *'I'm sorry, but I can't help you'* in *'I'm sorry, but I can't help you,' he said.*

reported or indirect speech The way of referring to what someone said without using inverted commas. In reported speech, the words that are spoken are integrated into the framework of the sentence, e.g. *She said that she was sorry.* Compare **direct speech.**

reporting clause The clause consisting of a subject and a verb of saying, e.g. *she said* in *'I'm sorry, but I can't help you,' she said.*

restrictive or defining clause A type of clause that contains essential information which identifies a particular person or thing. E.g. the clause *that mentions you by name* is a restrictive clause in the sentence *The paragraph that mentions you by name comes about halfway down the page.* Compare **non-restrictive or non-defining clause.**

second person Used to describe the pronoun *you* or the form of the verb used with *you.*

sentence A meaningful series of words, with a capital letter at the beginning and a full stop, a question mark, or an exclamation mark at the end.

singular The form of a word used when it refers to only one person or thing. Compare **plural.**

split infinitive An infinitive with a word or phrase placed between the *to* and the base form of the verb, e.g. *to sweetly sing.*

statement The commonest type of sentence, which begins with a capital letter, ends with a full stop, and presents the listener or reader with a piece of information without necessarily expecting any response from them, e.g. *My husband took the dog for a walk along the towpath.*

stress The additional force or volume given to a particular part of a word when it is spoken, e.g. the first syllable of *later* or the second syllable of *potato* when speaking these words.

subject The word or phrase – usually a noun or pronoun – that comes before the verb in an ordinary sentence. The subject says what the sentence is about: who or what carries out the action of the verb, e.g. in *The car hit a tree,* the subject is *The car.*

subject case The form of a pronoun used when it is the subject of sentence, e.g. *I, we, he, she, they.*

subjunctive mood The form of a verb that is sometimes used in clauses expressing a wish, demand, or recommendation, e.g. *give* in *I suggest she give it more thought.* Compare **imperative mood; indicative mood.**

subordinate clause A clause that is incomplete in itself and cannot stand by itself, e.g. *because I was afraid of being late* in *I ran all the way because I was afraid of being late.*

subordinating conjunction A conjunction that links parts of a sentence that do not have equal status, e.g. *after* in *I found out after she had left the company.*

suffix A component that is added to the end of a word to change that word's meaning, e.g. *-ly* added to the adjective *brief* to give the adverb *briefly.*

superlative The form of adjective that is used to show that a thing possesses a quality to a greater degree than two or more other things, e.g. *sweetest, most comfortable.* See also **comparative.**

tag question A statement with a little tag tacked on at the end, e.g. *is it?* in *It isn't time to go yet, is it?*

tense The form of a verb that relates to a time frame within which the action of the verb takes place, e.g. the present tense refers to action taking place now: *I cook, we are cooking.*

third person Used to describe the singular pronouns *he, she, it* or the plural *they* or the forms of the verb used with them.

transitive verb A verb that has a direct object, e.g. *bring* in *bring some food to the party.* Compare **intransitive verb.**

uncountable noun A noun that does not normally form a plural and cannot normally be preceded by *a* or *an*, e.g. *mud, rice, happiness.* Compare **countable noun.**

variable noun A noun that changes its form in the plural, e.g. *flower – flowers; mouse – mice.*

verb A word that stands for an action, e.g. *kick, spend, spat, hurt.*

voice See **active; passive.**

vowel The sound represented by any of the letters *a, e, i, o, u,* and sometimes *y.*

zero plural A noun whose form does not change whether it is singular or plural, e.g. *sheep.*

Index

Note: Words and phrases discussed in the text are set in *italic*; subjects are set in roman. Page numbers in **bold** refer to the Glossary.